Theatre for Children in the
United States : A History

(TITLE-PAGE ART AND DRAWINGS BY A SIX-YEAR-OLD ADMIRER OF THEATRE FOR CHILDREN. FOR MORE NOTES ON THE DESIGN OF THIS BOOK, SEE PAGE 320.)

Theatre.
for.
Children.
in the United States

A HISTORY by Nellie McCaslin

Norman   University of Oklahoma Press

By Nellie McCaslin

Legends in Action (Evanston, 1945)
More Legends in Action (Evanston, 1950)
Tall Tales and Tall Men (Philadelphia, 1956)
Pioneers in Petticoats (Evanston, 1962)
Little Snow Girl (Chicago, 1963)
The Rabbit Who Wanted Red Wings (Chicago, 1963)
Creative Dramatics in the Classroom (New York, 1968)
Theatre for Children in the United States: A History (Norman, 1971)

The publication of this volume has been aided by a grant from Region 14 of the Children's Theatre Conference Division of the American Educational Theatre Association.

International Standard Book Number: 0–8061–0970–x

Library of Congress Catalog Card Number: 71–160498

To my good friends and colleagues in Region 14, who have furthered and strengthened the concept of theatre for children in this country through their hard work in its behalf, their dedication to its ideals, and their faith in its future.

Foreword
by Paul Kozelka

Nellie McCaslin has written an impressive and important history of children's theatre in the United States in the twentieth century. Her narrative extends from the Children's Educational Theatre of 1903 to the Association Internationale du Théâtre pour l'Enfance et pour la Jeunesse of today. She records the important work of the Drama League and the Association of Junior Leagues of America. She describes the work of significant producing groups, both amateur and professional, and points out the trends in theme and subject matter of plays from earlier fairy tales to current ethnic dramas. She goes from the Federal Theatre of the thirties to present subsidies from federal, state, and private sources. All the leaders we have heard about for years are given attention. All their dreams, ideals, and hard work are described. Everyone interested in children's theatre owes a debt of gratitude to the author for her painstaking research.

Theatre for Children in the United States: A History will be of value to teachers, community leaders, recreation groups, and drama directors, who will find valuable material here about organization and production.

Children's theatre reaches thousands of young people every year. Parents and educators are becoming increasingly aware of the need for exposure to living theatre as part of the cultural growth of children. No one knows exactly what happens to a child as he watches a good play well acted and beautifully staged. Who knows what he gains in concepts of morality, justice, human relationships, and decision-making? Who knows what he carries away in beauty and pleasure? Who knows what he will remember in years to come? We all do know, as Nellie McCaslin says, that the living theatre can be "a place of enchantment." Her chronicle shows how it has served that purpose over the years.

Teachers College, Columbia University
New York City

Preface

Children's theatre in America has been a dream for many, a reality for some, and a challenge to all who have engaged in it. A twentieth-century movement, its activities have grown and expanded from the original experiment in a New York settlement house in 1903 to more than seven hundred known groups operating throughout the United States today. The belief in the values of children's theatre has been a driving force through the years; in spite of difficulties and discouragement, its proponents and practitioners have succeeded in raising it from a little-known and sporadic form of entertainment to the status of a nationally recognized branch of the living theatre.

In the early years there was no clear-cut distinction between dramatic activities in which children participated and those which were designed for their entertainment. As the movement developed, a clarification was made between children's theatre and creative dramatics. This book is concerned with the former.

Although there is still some difference of opinion as to what constitutes children's theatre, it is here defined as living theatre intended for audiences of children of elementary-school age. It may be performed by adults or children or a combination of both, and it may be either professional or amateur. A history of children's theatre, therefore, embraces work done in social settlements, community centers and civic theatres, schools and colleges, as well as that done in the professional theatre. It does not include classes or training in the dramatic arts, though in some instances teaching may be an integral part of the program and therefore receives mention. Puppetry, music, and dance are not included; they are recognized here only if they are a part of a children's theatre program or performing-arts series, but as separate arts, they do not belong to this chronicle.

During the past seventy years the leadership in children's theatre has shifted from one to another of the institutions mentioned. This has caused the pattern to change and to become more compex; one cannot today point to any one type or organization as typical or even usual. The conclusion reached, after a study of the various ventures and experiments, is that children's theatre is a phenomenon which owes its existence to the hard work, faith, idealism, and, in more than a few cases, even financial support of many persons from widely varied backgrounds.

The purpose of this book has been to trace the history of the children's theatre movement from its beginnings to the present time. It is my hope that an account of these activities will be of interest and value to students and leaders of children's theatre groups. It is further hoped that in reviewing the programs of the past, leaders of today may find guidance.

Although many groups are cited, I should like to acknowledge the probable existence of others whose records are not in the archives. Frequently the opening of a new children's theatre was announced, but no further activities were described nor was the closing mentioned. In some instances I have discovered a later reorganization under a new name; in others, a suspension of public performances without public notice. I must further acknowledge the probability of good or even superior work which has gone unheralded; publicity in itself is no criterion of excellence, but it is proof of existence. An accurate count of all of the children's theatre productions would be impossible to obtain, but a serious effort has been made to locate and describe those ventures which appear to have contributed most significantly to the development of this branch of the performing arts.

Much research has been done on the history of the adult theatre, but the complete story of the children's theatre in the United States has until now remained unwritten. The data are plentiful but they are scattered and fragmentary. I have found newspapers, periodicals, and scrapbook collections to be the most fruitful sources of information on the earlier years. Interviews with producers and sponsors of theatre groups have likewise been illuminating and have led, in a number of cases, to the use of unpublished material from their files. Much more information is available after the 1940's than in all of the preceding decades. There was vastly more activity in all parts of the country after World War II, and most of it is better documented than were the earlier ventures. For both of these reasons I have had to be more selective with inclusions between 1950 and 1970 than I was in the earlier chapters. Obviously, every group could not be described in detail but the more experimental, the longer-lived or the better-known and, therefore, more influential ventures were given recognition. I have purposely not interrupted the flow of the text with many footnotes; those which are included identify special sources and quotations. An extensive bibliography is provided for the reader who is desirous of pursuing a particular period or regional activity. *The Children's Theatre News* and the various regional newsletters published today offer the most accurate and comprehensive information available.

I should like to express my appreciation to the many persons who have co-operated in the collection of material. Particular indebtedness is acknowledged to Winifred Ward, Dorothy McFadden, William Kolodney, Sara Spencer, Paula Silberstein, and Frances Schram for their generosity in making available records and unpublished information; to the Association of Junior Leagues of America and the American National Theatre and Academy for the sharing of data from their files; to the many settlement houses and children's theatre producers for interviews as well as the opportunity to become acquainted with their objectives and work; to the regional governors for their co-operation in gathering information on current activities; to June McCaslin

Plotkin for her care in the preparation of the manuscript; and finally, to Jonathan Tolliver and the members of the executive board of Region 14 of the Children's Theatre Conference. Without their continuing help and encouragement it is doubtful that this book would have been written.

NELLIE MCCASLIN

Mills College of Education
New York City
June, 1971

Contents

Illustrations

xv

Theatre for Children in the
United States : A History

I

An Introduction

The time is the present; the scene, an auditorium; the place, an American city. The hour is approximately two-fifteen on any Saturday afternoon between October and May. Colorful posters on the front door of the building announce the performance within: *Cinderella, Tom Sawyer, Beauty and the Beast, Hansel and Gretel,* or any one of a dozen other well-known and popular children's stories. It may, on the other hand, be a program of dance or the *première* of a new script by a professional children's theatre company. Chartered buses, lined up at the curb, have just discharged their last passengers, boys and girls, often numbering as many as six or seven hundred. Other members of the audience may be seen hurrying from all directions in small groups: by automobile, public transport, on foot; some with adults, some alone.

Inside the lobby the steady stream of boys and girls fills all the available space and the hum of voices grows in intensity. Ushers appear—high-school students or young mothers, who organize the crowd into lines at each door, tickets held high. The lines move rapidly into the auditorium now, for this audience does not risk missing the opening scene for the sake of a conversation in the lounge. Seats are found and the blocks of rows reserved for groups are quickly filled. Bright colors dominate the scene, though the costumes range, even for the same performance, from party frocks to dungarees. As curtain time approaches, the voices shrill with an undercurrent of anticipation, which distinguishes this sound from the noise of the playground or street.

It is two-thirty. Suddenly the auditorium doors swing shut. The house lights begin to dim, imperceptibly to the adult theatre-goer but unmistakably to this audience, which has been awaiting with impatience the arrival of this moment. Abruptly conversations cease, as the room darkens and spotlights focus on the proscenium curtain, made suddenly rich and probably red in their glow. Music, taped from backstage or live from the piano down front, heralds the beginning of the matinee. The music swells, then fades, as the curtains part. A gasp of delight breaks the silence as the setting comes into view. All attention is now focused on the opening lines. The performance has begun.

Such a scene as the one described is not unique nor peculiar to any one community. Indeed, its counterpart may be found in hundreds of cities and towns throughout the United States on any Saturday morning or afternoon of the school year. At a period in history when television claims first place as the nation's popular entertainment and that "fabulous invalid," the legitimate theatre, struggles to survive, children's theatre is experiencing unprecedented growth. Undernourished from its inception, discouraged by those suspicious of the values to be found in any of the performing arts, in constant need of financial support, children's theatre has proved itself to be more than a tenacious offshoot of man's oldest art form. It has shown its power to survive and its will to persist.

It is no wonder that children's theatre is often described as the hardiest of the performing arts. Nurtured by educators, civic-minded laymen, and those artists whose imagination has been captured by its possibilities, the children's theatre movement in this country has led a haphazard existence during the seven decades since its birth. In concerning ourselves with its origin, certain questions arise. Where did it come from? When was the first play for children produced? Who was responsible? Why did he undertake such a project? What has living theatre to offer that cannot be found in some other, more practical medium? How can we account for the fact that children's theatre in this country has not only survived more than half a century but has at the same time grown both in numbers and spread of activity without ever having been a serious concern of the Broadway theatre?

Once proclaimed by Mark Twain to be "one of the very, very great inventions of the twentieth century," children's theatre has been hailed by educators and community leaders alike as having the greatest potential of all the arts for learning and as a means of bringing beauty into the lives of boys and girls. Winifred Ward wrote in 1939 that "The children's theatre in the United States is of very recent origin but no country perhaps, has at the present time more widespread interest in developing such a theatre."[1] While the support has been given and maintained largely through the efforts of amateurs, the contribution of the professional theatre has not been entirely negligible. The interweaving of their respective activities has formed a chronicle as yet unwritten in any complete or scholarly form.

Children's theatre in this country was not an accidental happening. Nor has it ever been a microcosm of the adult theatre, designed and planned to indoctrinate young audiences in an ancient art form. It has remained, in general, outside and independent of the adult professional theatre, though it has occasionally reflected some of the trends and technical skill of the parent art. Operating on a limited budget in virtually every instance, it has demonstrated more toughness than brilliance and more conservatism than experimentation. It would be easy to say that the financial problems which have dogged its steps from the beginning have determined its course; they have affected it, but there have been other factors involved in the growth and development of this hardy newcomer to the family of performing arts. It is true that many programs have ceased operation for lack of funds, but there have been some which have persisted despite poverty, and others which have closed while solvent. It is generally conceded, however, that what has been accomplished has been done through the

[1] *Theatre for Children*, 21.

efforts of those educators and theatre-lovers whose primary concern was, and is, theatre for children rather than an interest in personal or institutional gain. If poverty has been a hallmark, profit has never been an aim.

For this reason we find the earliest evidence of children's theatre in the social and educational centers of our larger cities rather than on the professional stage. Originating in the social settlements at the turn of the century, drama was first introduced to provide wholesome entertainment and a method of learning for the youngest immigrants and most disadvantaged children in our society. Social workers, from their own experience in the arts and their observation of children's play, early discovered that the living theatre offered unique opportunities for teaching literature and language, and to this end they organized classes in creative dramatics and storytelling. Productions were not only popular but were a means of introducing young audiences to children's stories and to the beauty of scenery and costumes. The Junior League, a women's organization dedicated to social service in the community, was, according to all accounts, the first national organization to undertake a large-scale dramatic program. Other organizations followed, but this group of young women has played a significant part in both teaching classes and touring plays to communities which would otherwise have had no living theatre.

Although children's theatre has long since moved out from these community centers, it has not disavowed the relationship; thus we find the social settlements and civic centers still among the most hospitable of environments. By the thirties, schools, colleges, and universities were beginning to play an important role in the development of children's theatre, and it is to the educational institutions that we now look for trends and guidance.

The American Educational Theatre Association was founded in the mid-thirties, giving professional recognition to a growing field of interest and approval of the subject for serious study. Less than a decade later the Children's Theatre Conference was formed as a major division of AETA. Its regional organization soon brought together leaders and teachers from all parts of the United

States; their sharing of work and ideas was a turning point in the development of this area of educational theatre.

Classes, workshops, and graduate courses in children's theatre soon provided training in techniques. Further, productions under the aegis of educational institutions subsidized experimentation and ensured continuing programs, regardless of box-office receipts. In many cases college and university programs have been closely related to the needs of the community, thereby providing a "town and gown" operation with benefits for both.

Recently government funding has made possible some large-scale projects through which students, teachers, and children have all benefited. These projects include workshops in creative dramatics as well as children's plays. The programs vary widely, but under the leadership of educators and educational institutions, children's theatre entered a new phase.

The professional theatre, until recently, has remained aloof from these activities, though there have been a few producing groups and individual artists who have given it financial and artistic support. With the exception of such well-known companies as Clare Tree Major's Company, Junior Programs, Inc., Children's World Theatre, and the Traveling Playhouse, however, few have lasted for any length of time. Faced with the same problems as the adult professional theatre, in a less lucrative field, most of them have been forced sooner or later to suspend operations, to reorganize, or, more recently, to seek government and foundation grants. Broadway, with two or three notable exceptions, has not been involved in theatre for children, leaving the field to the off-Broadway producers or to the small professional touring companies.

Today the professional theatre, particularly on the East Coast, is aiming to achieve what its predecessors failed to accomplish: permanency and economic stability. Improved transportation, communication, and government funding now provide advantages unheard of in the earlier decades of the century. Whether they will be sufficient to meet the needs of companies whose livelihood depends on engagements and fees, is yet to be seen. It is of note, however, that the fifties and sixties brought a proliferation of professional companies unparalleled in any previous period.

Like its adult counterpart, children's theatre is an art form, possessing in its liveness that special dimension which film, radio, television, even the printed page cannot boast, the capacity to bring a well-loved story to life on the stage, with the spectator a necessary participant in the action. No other medium can evoke the same quality of response or satisfy the same human need for identification with characters in conflict. Communication between actor and audience is a special kind of dialogue, found only in living performance, whether classic or popular; it is this quality, perhaps, which has helped children's theatre maintain its tenuous hold on life, despite the attractions of film and television.

The values of children's theatre have been defined and defended by its proponents from the beginning. And these values have changed little, except in the manner of phrasing. Appropriate entertainment for young people, opportunity for learning, appreciation of the theatre arts—these are the three most frequently stated reasons for offering stage plays to children. It is not the purpose of this book to measure the quality of the results achieved by the producers, past or present. It is, on the contrary, an attempt to trace the history of a phenomenon in our culture, which has persisted from the time of its establishment in the early years of the century to the present day. And it reveals, as an integral part of the account, the aspiration and goals of the practitioners and the record of their work.

The shifting sponsorship of children's theatre indicates not only the locations of the major activities but the agents responsible for influencing the quality, purpose, and growth. The nearly seventy years which this history spans fall into a pattern of decades, with the shifts in leadership occurring at almost ten-year intervals. The chapters are therefore divided accordingly, with those activities, organizations, and persons responsible for the significant accomplishments included chronologically. Because of the relatively short period of time involved, many of the leaders are still alive, some still active. Producers who founded companies are, in a number of instances, still involved in them, if not directly, at least in an advisory capacity. Colleges and universities which established courses in children's theatre and creative dramatics have tended to expand rather than curtail their programs; on some campuses children's plays have become permanent departmental offerings, produced and presented on a regular basis.

The literature in the field, until recently scanty, has increased. Plays for children's theatre, textbooks, and a variety of books and pamphlets on creative dramatics and theatre for children are today available. News of productions and workshops appears regularly in periodicals and newsletters published by the professional organizations, the American Educational Theatre Association and the Children's Theatre Conference, as well as in other educational publications. Professional theatre critics have rarely concerned themselves with children's productions; however, listings and accounts of productions do appear in many newspapers throughout the country, generally on the education and society pages. Children's theatre, admittedly still a fledgling, has at last received recognition.

As we look back over what has been accomplished, we are concerned with what is yet to be done. Theatre for children has gone far since the year 1903, yet we hear complaints of its mediocrity as often as we hear statistics of its growth. The time has come for children's theatre in this country to prove more than its resilience. With the rising costs of production and a generation of boys and girls used to the most sophisticated techniques of the mass media, theatre must succeed as an art or relinquish the dream which so many have held for its future. The implications are great for we are concerned with more than theatre for children. The boys and girls of today will be the adult audience of tomorrow and, therefore, the patrons of living theatre in America. Its future is dependent on their support.

How does one describe this theatre of which we are speaking? What are the qualities which distinguish it? Have they remained constant or have they altered with the shifting leadership and the changing times? Is it possible for one, who has not experienced children's theatre at first hand, to imagine what it is like, with all the similarities to and differences from the theatre of the adult? Let us try.

Imagine a theatre, in which every seat for a play performed by an unknown cast has been sold in advance. A theatre, in which a well-known story draws more attention than the *première* of a new script. A theatre, in which involvement is spontaneous and disbelief is willingly suspended. A theatre, for whom there are no critics, except for the audience itself: an audience, both exacting and accepting. A theatre, in which stars have no drawing power and lavish mounting is acclaimed but not required. A theatre more often shoddy than rich yet hailed only for its power to evoke a response. A theatre, which only yesterday may have been the town hall, the school auditorium, or an off-Broadway playhouse but which is now, by common consent, a place of enchantment. This is children's theatre.

II

Beginnings of Children's Theatre
in the United States

1900-10

Children's theatre, as it is conceived of today, in school, community, and professional stage, is a twentieth-century movement. The prejudice against the theatre in America which lingered as late as the turn of the century and the general prevalence of the traditional school curriculum which placed its emphasis on academic subjects contributed to the cultural climate in which theatre for children was not yet an established part. The concept of entertainment planned, organized, and executed for the express purpose of giving children wholesome pleasure was shared by few. According to all accounts, children's theatre in the United States is of very recent origin; the first to recognize the need for it were the social settlements in the late nineteenth century, but the first significant children's theatre was not founded in this country until 1903.

As for the schools, there were apparently only a few oriented toward a new philosophy which embraced the performing arts and play as a definite part of the curriculum. The Dewey School of the University of Chicago, for example, in outlining plans carried on during its first years (1896–1903), mentioned dramatic play in the study of literature and social sciences. According to the description of this experiment in education, "the idea involved a radical departure from the notion that school is just a place in which to learn lessons and acquire certain forms of skills."[1]

Helen Parkhurst made a similar observation, in speaking of denial of the creative impulse in the traditional curriculum: "Until the educational world wakes up to the fact that curriculum is not the chief problem of society, we shall, I fear, continue to handicap our youth."[2] The Ethical Culture Schools of New York, likewise experimental in philosophy, had included since the late nineteenth century pageants and festivals in which many children participated.

Dramatics in the elementary-school program apparently held little interest for schools in general, if the contents of professional journals of the period may be used as a guide to both curricular offerings and practices. A number of articles on the teaching of music and art were published in issues of *Child Study* and *Education* prior to 1910, but there is infrequent reference to the use that could be made of dramatics and storytelling, and this did not include either by statement or implication the finished play. One article by Margaret Love Porter in 1910 described what she believed to be a new method of teaching literature through the acting out of stories. In a footnote she expressed her indebtedness to Emma Sheridan Fry, dramatic director of the Children's Educational Theatre in New York, an institution to be discussed later in this chapter. From Emma Fry she conceived the idea of dramatizing stories in her reading class of elementary-school pupils. The values of this experiment were stated to have been the social development of the children, the better understanding of the material, skill in oral communication, and flexibility of body. Since this was such an effective teaching method, the author regretted the fact that educators in general had neglected its possibilities.

Such experiments as Margaret Porter's were unusual, however, and it can be safely said that with few exceptions the elementary-school curriculum did not include or emphasize the dramatic arts.

On the college level there was likewise very little being accomplished under the auspices and with the encouragement of aca-

---

1 Katherine Camp Mayhew and Anna Camp Edwards, *The Dewey School*, 466.
2 *Education on the Dalton Plan*, 27.

demic institutions. There were references to the formation of college dramatic clubs and the giving of "high class plays" by college students. When drama was included in the curriculum, it did not always bear the name but was smuggled in under the titles of elocution or public speaking. Teachers of foreign languages, recognizing the value of acting plays in a foreign tongue, had made use of dramatic techniques, but drama in English was represented in only a few colleges and universities. Among those which did recognize theatre were the University of Pennsylvania, Yale, Harvard, Radcliffe, Columbia, Barnard, Vassar, Bryn Mawr, Smith, and the Women's College of Baltimore, all located in the East. In each instance it was the classic drama which was presented, with very little accompanying course work in either the literature or history of the theatre.

Western institutions which had given public performances of Shakespearean and other classic dramas were the University of Chicago, the Universities of Michigan, Ohio, Illinois, Nebraska, Kansas, and California, and Stanford University. In many instances the plays were given with neither interest nor guidance on the part of the faculty. Modern plays were rarely presented, and plays for children were not mentioned.

A major reason for the neglect of the drama in the curricula of American colleges was the fact that the theatre in this country had always lacked generous, widespread public regard. America was not accustomed to giving the art of drama and acting much respect. A revolution in public sentiment was necessary before it could be accorded the rank of music and painting in institutions of higher learning. This was to come but not until the social settlements had initiated the first programs.

Community Theatre for Children

It was in the communities of America rather than in the schools that the first steps toward children's theatre seem to have been taken. According to Constance D'Arcy Mackay, early patroness of community theatre, particularly theatre for children, there had been some effort in this direction as early as 1850. Since it was not an organized movement, it can hardly be considered the beginning of children's theatre, but it does indicate an awareness on the part of some adults of the need for appropriate dramatic material for the nation's youngest citizens.

There are records of productions for children as early as 1810, and during the next few decades such plays as Joseph Jefferson's *Rip Van Winkle, Little Lord Fauntleroy,* and Mark Twain's own version of *Tom Sawyer* were performed.

In the mid-nineteenth century an operetta appeared in the form of incidents from *Mother Goose,* strung together in scenes and containing such well-known characters as Little Boy Blue, Miss Muffet, the Old Woman in the Shoe, and Mother Goose herself. The author's name was lost, but the work was given a number of community productions in both England and America and was apparently acted by the children themselves.

Another interesting enterprise, which likewise does not fit the definition of children's theatre in the sense in which it is here used, was, nevertheless, so unusual that it seems worthy of mention. The Grand Duke's Theatre or the Grand Duke's Opera House was a remarkably popular, if short-lived, venture of a group of adolescent boys in Baxter Street, downtown Manhattan. Among them they apparently combined a number of talents, for they got up an amateur variety show which appealed to adults in the community. (In this instance, it was the child player for the adult audience.) It was their good fortune to have the Grand Duke Alexis of Russia in their audience one night in 1872, and his delight in their spontaneity and youthful vitality caused him to patronize a performance. The boys took his name and were known from that night on as the Grand Duke's Players. There are no further records of their activity; at any rate, they made no effort to entertain the young nor did they start a tradition of child-actors.

During the last decade of the nineteenth century there was another stir of activity, similar to the one which had recognized the value of the operetta *Mother Goose.* In New York, Chicago, and Boston settlement houses there were simple dramatizations of favorite fairy tales done by and for their youngest groups. *The Sleeping Beauty, Cinderella,* and *The Three Bears* were enacted. While these particular stirrings did not develop into children's theatre in America, it was a settlement house, the Educational Alliance in New York, which established the first regular children's theatre program.

THE CHILDREN'S EDUCATIONAL THEATRE

Acknowledged by all authorities to be the first significant theatre for children, the date of the founding of the Children's Educational Theatre therefore became the birth date of the movement. The date was 1903 and Alice Minnie Herts was the director. The Children's Educational Theatre had a definite educational policy governing production, it established a budget, and it maintained high standards in the selection of plays, acting, and staging. While it lasted only six years, it was, from all reports, an excellent and influential undertaking.

Alice Minnie Herts came to the Educational Alliance, located at Jefferson Street and East Broadway, to assume charge of the recreational program. Wisely, she at first observed the interests and activities of the neighborhood people who frequented it, and then reached conclusions of her own as to how she might contribute to their needs. Drama was obviously a favorite activity with young and old, but it was being carried on largely without direction, and the selection of plays seemed to her mediocre. The existing dramatic club was made up of older people, but Alice Minnie Herts undertook to establish a children's theatre as a regular part of the program. The Educational Alliance was operated for the purpose of teaching better communication in a new language and American ways to the Russian and Polish immigrants who inhabited that section of the city. Miss Herts also wanted to demonstrate that there was better literature than that offered by either the existing program or the local professional entertainment. The Children's Educational Theatre was primarily a social enterprise developed to meet a pressing need of the lower East Side of New York.

While it has been stated that there was no entertainment for children at this time, there were adult vaudeville shows and the nickelodeon, both of which attracted large numbers of children between the ages of ten and fourteen. Prices were low and programs were frequently vicious, a situation which disturbed the settlement house workers, who had made a survey of juvenile attendance at such places of amusement.

Thus, the Children's Educational Theatre was established to meet an adult demand, not to demonstrate an educational theory. Alice Minnie Herts herself stated that she "saw the great opportunity not to impose upon people from without, but to help people create an ideal from within."[3] In order for her audiences to learn discernment, they would have to be more than mere recipients of entertainment. Obviously, it would take more than one play to accomplish this purpose, and so a series of plays was established.

October, 1903, marked the opening with *The Tempest*. To assist in classwork preparatory to the production, she hired Emma Sheridan Fry, who had previously taught in Franklin Sargent's American Academy of Dramatic Art and had had several years of experience on the stage. Miss Herts speaks in her book, *The Children's Educational Theatre*, of the widespread neighborhood interest in this production; it was probably the first stage play, and undoubtedly the first Shakespearean one, that most of the audience had ever seen. The excitement of the children spread to their parents, with the result that one thousand copies of the script were reported to have been sold in the neighborhood of the Alliance prior to the opening date.

The Tempest was followed by *Ingomar, As You Like It,* and *The Forest Ring*, all of which were greeted with the same enthusiasm from large audiences of young and old. Prices were low: tickets were originally five cents and were later raised to ten. The policy of Sunday matinees enabled families to attend together; while there were evening performances, it was the Sunday matinee that held the greatest popularity.

[3] *The Children's Educational Theatre*, 5.

The series of matinees in 1904 opened with Frances Hodgson Burnett's *The Little Princess*, a play which was to become a favorite. In July of that year Jacob Heniger joined the staff and remained with the theatre until its closing in 1909. Not only the neighborhood but many important personages in theatrical and educational circles knew of the work and occasionally even attended performances.

Among the most popular of the plays which were given was *The Prince and the Pauper*, dramatized by Abby Sage Richardson, and made possible by Daniel Frohman. It was said that the "exceptional" audiences of educated, interested citizens might not have reached the theatre, had it not been for the deep interest of Samuel Clemens. Samuel Clemens became a member of the board of the Children's Educational Theatre and was an outspoken supporter of its work.

For the next few years this enterprise flourished. Financially, it was not a success, for the low price of admission failed to cover the production costs; however, the capacity audiences and widening sphere of interest it was attracting throughout the city satisfied the directors and board that the work was successful. The first published accounts of its accomplishment attracted further attention and led to correspondence with community leaders in many other parts of the country who were seeking to establish a similar type of activity.

In June, 1908, at the end of the Educational Alliance's fiscal year, the work, which had outgrown its present quarters, was incorporated as a separate organization under the title of the Educational Theatre for Children and Young People. The new board of directors included Samuel Clemens, the Reverend Percy Stickney Grant, Robert Collier, Otto Kahn, and Miss Herts. Rehearsals were held at the home of Robert Collier and on the stage of the Lyceum Theatre. By early September, *The Little Princess* was ready to be presented. Many performances were given around the city using different casts; in all of the Educational Theatre productions, there was always a second and often a third cast prepared to go on. To further the movement, the Children's

Educational Theatre responded to the request of the Women's Education Association of Boston to give a demonstration in that city. Cast members, together with an orchestra, were taken to Boston on Sunday, February 21, 1909. There were eighty in all.

Meanwhile, although the general consensus among educators and leaders in social service was highly favorable to its work, there was some controversy as to whether the Children's Educational Theatre was abandoning its original purpose and thereby exploiting the child actors. Some accused Miss Herts of trying to make actors of children before they knew what was happening to them and of encouraging showing off and dressing up.

It was during the same year that the New York Sunday closing law for places of entertainment was put into effect, with the result that the Sunday matinees, which had been so popular, were abolished. This blow, added to lack of funds and inadequate rehearsal facilities, finally brought about a complete closing of the theatre in 1909.

A financial report of the first five years of its existence was published, disclosing the following facts:

165 Matinees	800 Average attendance
75 Evening performances	532 Average attendance
177,060 Total attendance	

$28,033.63	Total disbursements
6,958.18	Total receipts
$21,065.45	Deficit paid by board members[4]

A short interval passed between the closing of the Children's Educational Theatre in 1909 and its rebirth two years later as the Education Players. While it was under different management, it held to the principles laid down by Miss Herts, Jacob Heniger, and Emma Sheridan Fry. According to Constance D'Arcy Mackay, who was at that time closely following children's dramatic activities, a significant thing had happened which, she be-

[4] Anon., "The Theatre as an Educative Agent," *Current Literature*, Vol. XLV (October, 1908), 441–44.

lieved, was a result of their work. For the first time plays for the public schools were being written and published. In 1911 the Education Players began to work in connection with the public schools; the players were adults with children as spectators rather than as their co-players.

The influence of the original Children's Educational Theatre could hardly be overestimated. Beyond such tangible outcomes as the one mentioned above were statements made in its behalf. Among them were endorsements by Charles W. Eliot, then president of Harvard College, and Percival Chubb, director of festivals and plays at the Ethical Culture Schools. Garfield W. Moses' enthusiastic comment in *Charities and the Commons* stands as a prediction that has been fulfilled:

> This Children's Theatre will grow from more to more. In its very nature it is not a local institution or a mere adjunct of settlement work. It should reach children of all classes and all conditions. Through it the future educational drama may be shaped, and this drama, of course, is not to be confined to one section or one class.[5]

Moses went on to say that America needed a real theatre for children which should be housed in a building of its own, equipped for the purpose. To this end there must be developed authors who would write children's plays just as certain men and women have concentrated on the specialized field of children's books.

No other children's theatre group had attracted so much attention nor had so much written about it by those most closely connected with its functioning. Its importance would seem to lie in two factors: that it was the first organized children's theatre in the United States and that it adhered to a definite policy of educating its members and its audience, through an insistence on the best in both dramatic literature and standard of public performance.

[5] "The Children's Theatre," *Charities and the Commons*, Vol. XVIII (April 6, 1907), 32.

HULL HOUSE IN CHICAGO

Meanwhile, the children's theatre idea had spread to other settlement houses in the United States. A number of them were establishing programs which, if not as ambitious as that of the Educational Alliance, were directed to the same goals. Since they grew over a period of years from simple, individual performances, no specific founding dates can be determined. Hull House in Chicago and Christadora and Neighborhood Houses in New York were among the social settlements to have significant achievements to their credit.

Hull House, under the guidance of Jane Addams, faced problems similar to those of the Educational Alliance in the fostering of better citizenship for the mixture of nationalities that crowded the west side of Chicago. The arts were always an important aspect of its program even before adequate facilities had been acquired. The first art exhibit was held in 1891, the first music school began to function in 1893, and dramatic activities were carried on informally in the larger rooms and gymnasium long before an actual stage was built. The theatre held great fascination for the neighborhood people for it was apparently the one agency which released both young and old from the drudgery and poverty of their existence. While the dramatic arts program developed slowly during this early period, no celebration was so popular as the traditional Thanksgiving and Christmas pageants held each year in the big living room of the settlement house.

Specific plays which were done during these first years were *Snow White* and *Puss in Boots* for the youngest children and *Mat Tyler* for the older boys.

By 1930 there was a history of six dramatic clubs at Hull House, all of which had started with small children and preserved their continuity through the years. Meanwhile, a well-equipped little playhouse seating five hundred persons had been built, and national recognition of its contribution to children's theatre had been given. Edith D. Nancrede, the director during this time, produced such classic plays as *The Tempest, A Midsummer*

Night's Dream, some of the comedies of Molière, and *Alice in Wonderland*.

HENRY STREET SETTLEMENT IN NEW YORK

The Henry Street Settlement House on the lower East Side of New York has been described as one of the outstanding examples of successful pioneering in the field of children's theatre. Before 1910 activities were carried on informally at the settlement, with both dance and drama receiving particular emphasis. As Lillian Wald, director of Henry Street, explained, the dramatic instinct was strong in the Jewish children who made up the community, and these young people were encouraged to interpret the rich inheritance of their parents and neighbors in pageants and festivals. These programs, held in the spring, were in the folk traditions of the neighborhood people and were the beginnings of the later well-known and highly praised Henry Street Festivals. Like Jane Addams, Lillian Wald believed strongly in the values of theatre. Special mention must be made of Alice and Irene Lewisohn, who constructed a five-hundred-seat theatre on Grand Street between Pitt and Willett, which became known as the Neighborhood Playhouse. It was not opened until 1915 but the plans for its operation were laid in the preceding years. These plans included the presentation of what the directors believed to be suitable moving pictures and plays for children in the afternoon, and plays for adults in the evening.

While the Neighborhood Playhouse as an institution does not belong to this early period, the spirit and activities which led to its founding do. Likewise, although it was never a children's theatre exclusively, it played an important part in the evolution of children's theatre and its two founders, Alice and Irene Lewisohn, were devoted workers toward this end.

NETTIE GREENLEAF'S CHILDREN'S THEATRE IN BOSTON

Another early children's theatre was founded in Boston in

1903 by Mrs. Nettie Greenleaf. Less ambitious in its program than the Children's Educational Theatre, it gave short plays similar to the ones put on by the settlement houses. From all accounts, it was well patronized. It was located on Huntington Avenue near the library and drew its actors from the Dorothy Dix Home for Stage Children. They gave only matinees and might have lasted for a much longer time, had it not been for the new fire laws which were enacted at this time. After the disastrous Iroquois Fire in Chicago, fire laws all over the United States were strengthened, and the little theatre where Mrs. Greenleaf's players performed was condemned as unsafe.

PEABODY HOUSE

There was some early activity in children's drama in Boston's Peabody House. A production of *Cinderella* was held there, and it was apparently very appealing to the boys and girls who attended. During the year 1913 a production of *The Snow Queen*, written and directed by Lucile Loveman, was given. A member of the Harvard 47 Workshop in Playwriting, Lucile Loveman was apparently so eager to try out her work with and for children that she assumed all the expenses involved in the production.

THE BROOKLYN PAGEANT

Another type of program was put on by the settlements of Brooklyn in 1911. It was a large city pageant to which many community houses contributed scenes. While this kind of project has been carried out frequently since under the auspices of civic or local organizations, it was unique at the time as a means of drawing together community efforts. The ten settlements of Brooklyn, New York, united in 1911 in giving in Prospect Park the *Pageant of Patriots*, the first children's historical pageant ever given in America.

Reports and references to dramatic activities for children in the first decade of the twentieth century give evidence of growing interest on the part of settlements and communities in this form of recreation. While it was far from a general practice, there is indication that more was being done by such groups as the ones described than by educational or professional institutions.

The Professional Theatre

During these early years there was little consideration given by the commercial theatre to appropriate children's fare. The activity was chiefly in the amateur field, with the professional theatre contributing little to the cause. Henry A. Clapp, drama critic for the *Boston Daily Advertiser*, raised a voice in protest of this situation at the turn of the century. He recalled his own two experiences in the adult theatre as a child in Boston, experiences which had remained with him as thrilling memories throughout his life; but he deplored the fact that for the majority of children in 1900, there was little being produced that was planned especially for them: "But today, in this land—is it not curious?—adults are so greedy of the theatre that they have practically crowded children out of places of theatrical amusement."[6]

Looking back at the period, one observes that the commercial stage provided vaudeville, musicals, stock companies, Broadway, and the road show but no plays planned with young people in mind. While the theatre was a popular institution in America after the turn of the century, its appeal was to adults, and little of what they were being offered was appropriate for boys and girls.

SARGENT'S CHILDREN'S THEATRE

Franklin Sargent's Children's Theatre did not develop as its founder had hoped, but it was nevertheless a concrete step in the direction of good entertainment for children and young people. Sargent, who was director of the American Academy of Dramatic Art in New York, undertook the project at the suggestion of Edward E. Rose, the playwright, who believed there were in the

[6] *Reminiscenses of a Dramatic Critic*, 7.

city large numbers of children who would like to see plays performed. The adult content and high prices of admission prevented
their having this experience. Sargent concurred in this belief and
accordingly established in 1899 a children's theatre in the Carnegie Lyceum Auditorium. With a group of child actors he prepared such plays as *Jack the Giant Killer*, *Alice in Wonderland*,
and *Humpty Dumpty*. The children's audiences which he antici-
pated did not attend in large numbers, however, and according to
a 1902 account in *Theatre*, the children seemed only mildly interested in the project. Instead of closing, Sargent began to offer
plays that would be interesting to adults as well as children, but
in which the child element would predominate. *Oliver Twist* and
semihistorical one-acts were among the offerings. Apparently the
programs continued, for the theatre operated for a third season.
Since the group did not adhere to its original purpose of presenting children's entertainment exclusively, it is significant only in
its recognition of a need and its founding for the purpose of
answering that need.

MR. BLUEBEARD

There was the production of *Mr. Bluebeard* in Chicago in 1903;
not a children's play, it was, in the absence of more appropriate
entertainment, advertised as a play to which children might be
taken. There were, as a result of this advertising, many children's
matinees. The play itself, unfortunately, is remembered only for
the tragic fire which destroyed the Iroquois Theatre and many
young members of the audience.

BROADWAY PLAYS FOR CHILDREN

There were on Broadway two plays during this first decade of
the twentieth century which were popular with audiences of
children, although neither of them was produced with this consideration in mind. The first of these, Maude Adams' *Peter Pan*,
opened in New York on November 6, 1905, to ecstatic audiences.
Although the original production ran for only 123 performances,

it was revived frequently during succeeding years, becoming the best-loved fantasy in America and a national tradition in England.

The other play, *The Blue Bird*, which opened on October 1, 1910, was intended for adults but was ideal for the children who were fortunate enough to attend. While these two productions must have been singularly beautiful and certainly appropriate, they were beyond the means of the majority of children.

THE STOCK COMPANIES

The stock companies, which lingered on in a number of American cities until the depression years, occasionally advertised plays for the family, some of which were children's classics. Titles like *Rebecca of Sunnybrook Farm, Mrs. Wiggs of the Cabbage Patch,* and *Little Women* were reported in local newspapers as early as the first decade of the century and as late as the thirties. Romantic plays like *Daddy Longlegs* and *The Little Minister* were also advertised as suitable entertainment for the young, although they could not be construed as children's theatre. Such plays as the above were given only occasionally, however, with no thought to a continuing program or a special series planned for boys and girls. When the stock companies finally disappeared, their function of providing popular entertainment was taken over by the movies, television, and university and community theatres in towns where such theatres existed.

The social settlements, almost exclusively, contributed toward the growth of theatre for children during the first ten years of the twentieth century. Some of the more progressive schools and imaginative teachers had already introduced dramatic play and pageantry into their curricula, but the practice was not yet generally accepted.

While the movement was to be carried on by other more privileged groups in the future, the settlements continued to support as well as to pioneer in the field of theatre for children. It would be difficult to evaluate the results according to present theatrical standards, but there is little doubt that they laid the groundwork for the educational theatre and provided the first criteria for criticism in this branch of the theatre.

III

The Interest Grows

1910-20

The decade between 1910 and 1920 was important in the growth of children's theatre. Nonprofessional groups were beginning to recognize this area of dramatic activity, although the commercial stage was still concentrating its efforts largely on adult entertainment. A new national organization, which was to contribute much to its development in subsequent years, took its first pioneering steps during this period. While the educational institutions were to manifest considerably more interest later on, there is evidence of more than a little activity on both elementary and college levels. It was in the communities of America, however, that entertainment for children received its greatest encouragement. Since their endeavors were supported from the beginning by the Drama League of America, perhaps the best place to begin a survey of the period is with this national organization.

The Drama League of America

An important date in the history of children's theatre was 1910, the year in which the Drama League of America was founded in Evanston, Illinois. While the Drama League was not primarily concerned with this phase of theatre, it did emphasize the best in literature on all levels, and established within its organization a Junior Department, under the direction of Cora Mel Patten. With her help, children's leagues were established in many large cities, and pageants and plays were produced for child audiences.

The League itself was founded by a group of citizens, including both idealistic representatives of the professional theatre and enthusiastic laymen who had become increasingly dissatisfied with contemporary Broadway offerings. A particularly outspoken critic of the commercial theatre was Percy Mackaye, playwright and well-known exponent of the pageant drama, which he was both advocating and producing in various communities in this country. He castigated the commercial theatre, which he accused of recognizing art but debasing it for private profit. At the same time he criticized the churches and schools, which he said ignored art entirely while attempting to uplift the public. It is not surprising, therefore, that Percy Mackaye should have been one of the founders of a new national organization which was dedicated to improving this situation.

The League's aim was to establish a chapter in every town and city in the country and thereby launch a nationwide campaign to support so-called "good" drama and discourage by nonsupport that which was "bad." The spread of membership is best illustrated by the first officers. They were Mrs. A. Starr Best, a clubwoman of Evanston, president; and Dr. Richard Burton of the University of Minnesota, Louis K. Anspacher (playwright), Mrs. Otis Skinner, and Percy Mackaye, as the other officers.

The League apparently was influential in encouraging the appreciation of dramatic literature and in establishing, through its chapters, a number of community playhouses. In 1912, just two years after the founding of the League, there was general optimism regarding its future. In addition to Chicago, there were strong branches in Boston, New York, and Philadelphia.

With the failure of the road show to provide sufficient entertainment for the cities and towns of the United States, the League established a second purpose. At their 1913 convention in Detroit they undertook to promote the interest in little theatres, and for many years ran a placement bureau and acted as clearinghouse for directors of these groups. A magazine, *Drama*, was sponsored by the League and for twenty years (1911 to 1931) it carried articles, both informative and critical, on all phases of the theatre. Such leading figures as Percy Mackaye, Walter Prichard Eaton, Barrett Clark, and George Pierce Baker were among the contributors. *Drama* began as a quarterly in February, 1911, and became a monthly in October, 1919.

An important contribution made by the Drama League was the compilation and distribution of lists of plays suitable for children's use, together with suggestions as to how they might be presented. These lists and aids were made available to interested persons, in addition to the reviews of many of the plays which appeared regularly in *Drama*. The League also published collections of children's plays, thus stimulating an interest in dramatic writing on this level. In 1915 it brought out a play index, *Plays for Children*, edited by Kate Oglebay, the first volume of this sort to be published in America. It was designed primarily as an index to be used by libraries and amateur theatrical groups and included summaries of fifty-three full-length plays, numerous reference books, and an introduction by Kate Oglebay on the "Selection of Plays."

Meanwhile, believing the needs of schools and social centers to be still unsatisfied, the Educational Drama League was organized in January, 1913. Its object was the promotion of amateur dramatics in the public schools, social settlements, and civic centers. According to Constance D'Arcy Mackay, after only one year there were twenty-five clubs and three classes in story-playing. As the Drama League of America helped by making available books, scripts, and materials to community theatres, so the Educational Drama League performed the same service for clubs and schools, where the ages ranged from seven to twenty.

According to a 1914 report in *The Nation*, the Boston League at that time was the largest of the branches. During its three years of life it had acquired a membership of 2,300 staunch supporters, with Professor George Pierce Baker of Harvard as president. *The Nation* describes the educational influence of the Boston League. Advice and assistance were sought by clubs, schools, and individuals both in matters of production and in suggested play lists.

Educators joined in large numbers, and at least two departments were organized to look into the interests of children of elementary-school age.

Winifred Ward, looking back at the work of the League in 1939, paid it high tribute when she stated that the history of children's theatre in America began with this organization: "In the awakening of general interest and dissemination of knowledge concerning children's plays, the Drama League of America deserves highest credit.[1]

An early project of the Drama League was the introduction of dramatics into the playgrounds of America in 1912. Although much of the activity which ensued was unorganized, so far as permanent annual programs were concerned, there are numerous accounts of individual pageants and plays in *The Playground* and *Recreation* magazines. Individually, few can be classified as significant; taken together, they comprise an important aspect of the League's work in stimulating the interest of recreational leaders toward a new type of summer program. One of the most successful and lasting of these ventures was the Municipal Pier Theatre of Chicago. Begun informally several years earlier, it officially launched in the summer of 1917 an extensive program of dramatic activities for children. Long-range planning was done with the conviction that a comprehensive and carefully organized program would be of real value to the metropolitan area of Chicago. The details of this enterprise will be discussed later. In the meantime, several other activities were already under way.

Community Theatres for Children

Survey Magazine in 1915 reported a children's theatre in San Francisco, organized by Mrs. D. E. F. Easton and Garnet Holme, under the auspices of the Recreation League. Its objective was to present bright and amusing plays which would both interest children and awaken their imaginations; to accustom the future audiences of San Francisco to the enjoyment of theatre; to form a center

[1] *Theatre for Children*, 23.

of high dramatic work which would encourage young people to study and act good literature. It was operated on a budget which made the lowest priced seats possible: ten cents for seats in half of the auditorium, twenty-five cents for the other half, with a fifty-cent charge for adults, who had to sit in the rear.

The first season of plays included *Shock Headed Peter, Alice in Wonderland,* and *Aladdin and His Wonderful Lamp.* This theatre was opened formally in the fall of 1915 and by April, 2,500 children had attended. That this group was successful is attested by reports in 1927 that it had increased its offerings to six productions a year, by that time its established standard.

DULUTH, MINNESOTA

A little theatre far from Broadway, which early incorporated activities for children, was the Community Theatre of Duluth. It was founded in 1911 and by 1914 had acquired its own playhouse. While it was not until the twenties that the children's branch was definitely organized, the Duluth Playhouse was one of the first of the community theatres to recognize this need. Since organized children's theatre, as a regular branch of its program, belonged to the next decade, a more detailed account will be postponed until a later chapter.

THE HOUSE OF PLAY

In Washington, D.C., more than one center for children's entertainment was operating. Neighborhood House, a settlement, frequently gave festivals and plays. More formally organized, however, was the House of Play, a regular little theatre for boys and girls. It was opened in 1915 and run under the auspices of the Drama League of the city. Its program of plays was directed exclusively to children and young people. Conducted as a recreation center, the House of Play was open on Saturday with trained leaders directing activities. Since its primary objective was social, development of the participants was emphasized rather than excellence of performance.

KARAMU HOUSE IN CLEVELAND

Another scene of early activity, which was later to become one of America's most famous community centers, was Karamu House in Cleveland. The first steps toward a children's theatre were taken in 1918, three years after Russell and Rowena Jelliffe arrived from Chicago to take over the directorship of the small Negro settlement. Established primarily as a Negro Arts center, Karamu House encouraged expression in music, drama, dance, and the visual arts. From the beginning drama was one of the more popular activities with both children and adults. Whereas in most of the community centers described in this book the children's work came along as an outgrowth of adult theatre, at Karamu House the drama program was begun with children and subsequently expanded to take in adults.

The Jelliffes' philosophy, emphasizing purpose rather than product, did not aim immediately at public performance; however, the children's need for a goal soon made this desirable. Plays, for which an admission of eight cents was charged, were attended by scores of neighborhood children. According to Rowena Jelliffe, who directed the work, the stories they used were taken from the rich background of folklore which many of the children had brought with them from the South. *How Come Br'er Rabbit Do No Work?*, *Saturday Evening* (an animal story), and *Shoes for the Feet* were three of the earliest titles.

With the great migration of Negroes from the South to northern industrial cities such as Cleveland, the twenties were a period of expansion for all of the Karamu groups. The children's plays and adult theatre grew steadily, becoming within a few years not only an important social institution but the most distinguished Negro art theatre in the world. Karamu deliberately utilized the arts to promote interracial co-operation and good will. Human dignity was highly respected in this center where everyone could develop his creative talent and feel that he belonged.

The reputation of the work of this settlement theatre group spread in the Cleveland area, until by the thirties it became nec-

Maude Adams at *Peter Pan* in 1905. Courtesy Theatre Collection, The New York Public Library, Astor, Lenox, and Tilden Foundation.

The full cast of *Aucassin and Nicolette*, a King-Coit production of the 1920's. Courtesy Dorothy Coit.

View of the Heckscher Theatre in New York City showing the Willy Pogany murals, 1922. It was called "the most beautiful children's theatre in the world." Courtesy Theatre Collection, The New York Public Library, Astor, Lenox, and Tilden Foundation.

A Junior Programs, Inc., production of *Jack and the Beanstalk*, 1939. Courtesy Dorothy McFadden.

A Junior Programs, Inc., production of *The Bumble Bee Prince*, 1939. Courtesy Dorothy McFadden.

Little Women, produced by Clare Tree Major in the thirties. Courtesy Children's Theatre of New York.

The Revolt of the Beavers, presented by New York City's Federal Theatre for Children in 1937. Courtesy Theatre Collection of The New York Public Library, Astor, Lenox, and Tilden Foundation.

The Pied Piper of Hamelin at the Children's World Theatre, New York City, 1949. Courtesy Bette Butterworth.

essary to expand into a new building which offered more space for both backstage operation and audience.

ROXBURY HOUSE

At Roxbury House in Boston there was great interest in story-acting and creative dramatics during this period. Plays for children, in which lines were learned and audience was a major consideration, were not a part of the program at the settlement at this time. The educational values of the informal type of program were stressed.

THE NEIGHBORHOOD PLAYHOUSE IN NEW YORK

The Neighborhood Playhouse in New York has been referred to in the preceding chapter as the outcome of the dramatic activities at the Henry Street Settlement. A concrete expression of appreciation for the work done in drama and dance, it was erected by Irene and Alice Lewisohn and opened in 1915. In addition to the teaching of play-acting under skillful adult leadership, the playhouse offered training in the various theatre arts. Nearly all of the costumes, properties, and scenery were made in these classes and workshops.

Jephtha's Daughter, a festival, opened the playhouse on February 12, 1915. Seventy-eight young people were in the cast and many others worked on some phase or another of the production. Even the youngest children shared the excitement of the occasion by pulling threads for fringe on the costumes. The philosophy behind this enterprise was expressed by Lillian Wald in her book, *The House on Henry Street:*

> It is our hope that the playhouse, identified with the neighborhood, may recapture and hold something of the poetry and idealism that belong to its people and open the door of opportunity for messages in drama and picture and song and story.[2]

This was the philosophy which permeated the settlement, and it

2 Page 187.

was Miss Wald's hope that the theatre, in establishing a reputation of its own, should not become a thing apart. Eight years later it was referred to as a "unique theatre," appealing to a public of diverse tastes, interests, and ages. Saturday and Sunday evenings were reserved for the dramas, while the afternoons of those days were given over to ballet, pantomime, and fairy-tale plays. It functioned for the neighborhood but at the same time was attracting nationwide attention for the program it had developed. While the Neighborhood Playhouse organization moved uptown several years later to establish an identity of its own, the original theatre building is still used by the settlement and is known as the Henry Street Playhouse.

THE ASSOCIATION OF JUNIOR LEAGUES OF AMERICA

In connection with settlement houses, mention must be made of another organization, of which much more will be said later on. This is the Association of Junior Leagues of America, whose contribution to the field of theatre for children is unquestioned but whose formally planned activities belong to the period following 1920. As early as 1912, however, Junior League members were gathering in groups for the purpose of entertaining boys and girls. In both Chicago and Boston in that year they were giving simple plays for underprivileged youth.

In Boston seventeen performances of *Aladdin* were presented by the drama branch of the League, to audiences totaling 3,750 persons. Like the plays of the Children's Educational Theatre in New York, this type of entertainment was an effort to counteract the cheap vaudeville shows which were available to minors. Since the Junior League was working in connection with settlement houses, it early assumed a role in the effort to acquaint young people with better literature and children's classics, and to help the foreign born to become assimilated through participation in neighborhood activities.

In New York the Junior League provided an opportunity for children to act in the plays. Through the organization of dramatic clubs and classes, children took part in an activity led by League members.

"BY SCHOOL CHILDREN FOR SCHOOL CHILDREN"[3]

An example of a type of organization which was founded to meet a need, rather than high artistic standards, was the children's theatre of Columbus, Ohio. Charles Weller described it as having great recreational value and being worthy of emulation by other communities. It was a group enterprise, established by the Drama League, the Public Recreation Commission of Columbus, the Board of Education, and the Chamber of Commerce, thus having at the outset the support of the leading civic agencies. A newspaperman, J. Clarence Sullivan, became the director of this new organization. According to Weller's account, Sullivan wrote some of the plays himself, planned and helped build the scenery, directed the productions, and, because of his newspaper background, was aware of the need for local publicity to stimulate interest. The playhouse was the Chamber of Commerce auditorium which seated eight hundred. Since the program was subsidized, it was possible to give the plays free; nevertheless, the budget was quite modest and figures disclosed that forty dollars a week covered all costs of production, including the young actors' carfare to and from the theatre. Performances were given every Saturday afternoon and were repeated many times by the three or four different casts which Sullivan trained simultaneously. Tickets were issued to each of the city schools so that all of the children of Columbus were able at some time to attend. Weller concluded his article with a plea that many more community projects be established as one of the most effective means of vital education.

STUART WALKER AND THE PORTMANTEAU THEATRE

One of the most unusual ventures of this period, so far as or-

[3] Charles Weller, "A Children's Playhouse," *Survey*, Vol. XXXV (February 19, 1916), 615.

ganization and production were concerned, was Stuart Walker's Portmanteau Theatre. An article entitled "The Play of Imagination in the Tiniest Theatre in the World"[4] gives two important clues to its unique character. Stuart Walker was an enterprising young man who for several years had been teaching the dramatic arts at Christadora Settlement House in New York. Despite the interest of the settlement in his work, lack of funds made impossible the building of a playhouse in which it could be carried on. Walker's previous six years of experience in the professional theatre had given him a background in modern stagecraft which was to be invaluable to him in the solution of the problem. He was aware of the new trend in scenic design which emphasized simplicity and discarded the traditional heavy scenery and backdrops. With this principle of simplicity in mind, he ingeniously devised a portable stage which, unencumbered by the usual equipment, could be packed up in ten lightweight boxes. Those boxes then became the personal baggage of the ten players, who either carried them or assumed the responsibility of having them shipped along with them on tour. The little stage, complete with lights and such scenery as it contained, could be made ready in two hours' time and taken apart in even less.

The first public performance of the Portmanteau Theatre was given at Christadora House on July 14, 1915. The bill included three one-act plays: *The Trimplet* by Stuart Walker, *A Pen and Two Candlesticks* by Mary Macmillan, and *Six Who Pass While the Lentils Boil* by Stuart Walker. Walker's hope was that eventually the young people of the settlement would write their own plays, and design and build their own scenery within the framework of the tiny portmanteau stage. His educational philosophy, that all who contributed would learn, included the following objectives: improvement in speech, facility in writing in the English language, good craftsmanship (through building and painting scenery and sewing costumes), self-control as members of a working group, and development of the imagination.

While the Portmanteau Theatre was not organized primarily

---

[4] *Survey*, Vol. XXXIV (September 8, 1915), 551.

as a children's theatre, it included in its repertoire plays suitable for children and emphasized fantasy rather than realistic adult drama. It traveled for several seasons to churches, settlements, schools, private homes, and outdoor locations, both in the New York area and far beyond. Designed for young folks, buoyant with the spirit of youth, but with an underlying philosophy relevant to every age, the Portmanteau Theatre initiated a unique touring program.

THE CHILDREN'S CIVIC THEATRE OF CHICAGO

The Children's Civic Theatre of Chicago or the Municipal Pier Theatre burst into being in 1917. Since the Drama League held particular influence in the Chicago area because of its founding in a near-by suburb, it is not surprising that this enterprise got off to so successful a start. The three founding agencies, the Drama League of Chicago, the Civic Music Association, and the Mothers' Drama Club of the Municipal Pier, organized it originally for the promotion of a civic spirit that spoke for "right living, self-expression of right ideals, individual opportunity and culture." Appropriations were set aside by the City Council and extensive plans, under the guidance of Mrs. Lyman Walton, Chicago president, were laid. It was not until the second season, the summer of 1918, however, that specific activities for children were added. The careful planning of these activities made for a stable and ambitious program, which included choral classes, story-telling, pantomime, play rehearsals, and folk and interpretive dancing. Children's Hour programs, free to the public, were held on Mondays, Wednesdays, and Fridays from one to five, and each Wednesday at two o'clock special programs were presented. Cora Mel Patten organized the work, with Bertha Iles as manager. At the end of three years Miss Patten withdrew and Miss Iles continued what had become by that time a large and popular civic project.

The purpose of the children's work was stated to be:

1. To give inspirational direction through dramatic play, music and dance.

2. To stimulate the imagination and to open avenues more beautiful than are to be found in the city streets.[5]

Children of all classes, including many from the large immigrant population, participated. It was estimated that several hundred attended the classes and from three to six thousand, the weekly programs. Because the auditorium on the pier was so huge, it was possible for enormous classes and folk-dance groups to appear on the stage. In 1922 the junior work at the Pier was incorporated in the following form: The Children's Civic Theatre of Chicago, Incorporated; Bertha L. Iles, director; and it was given credit as being the only children's civic theatre in the world.

Educational Theatre for Children

Interest in children's theatre was not confined to community centers, however, for as early as 1911 some activity on the part of a teachers' college had been reported. Later on in the decade two other experiments, in which drama for young people was a part, were described in the professional journals.

SAN FRANCISCO STATE TEACHERS COLLEGE

The West Coast was the scene of early activity. Mrs. John J. Cuddy, instructor in Oral Expression in San Francisco State Teachers College, was teaching her students how dramatics might be utilized in the classroom. Her belief that drama could be used as an outlet for children's energy and as an effective educative force resulted in the founding of a practical workshop. Dissatisfied with the paucity and mediocrity of available material, she began writing her own plays, and her students, as well as the children in the community, performed them. The plays were given in the Guild Theatre of San Francisco with support from the college. Among their productions was *Jack the Giant Killer*, which was apparently highly successful since they were asked to repeat it in the huge auditorium of the International Exposition held in 1915.

[5] Anon., "Children's Civic Theatre of Chicago," *Drama*, Vol. XVII (October, 1926), 30.

Later on, Mrs. Cuddy's interest in Greek myths led her to dramatize six of them, all of which were given production in a downtown theatre under the auspices of the Stage Guild of San Francisco under the direction of Samuel Hume. Musical scores composed for these Greek plays were prepared by the music department of the State Teachers College faculty.

PLAY SERVICE IN UTAH AND NORTH DAKOTA

Activity was not restricted to the metropolitan centers, however; in the rural areas of the Northwest another type of educational program was being initiated. This was said to have resulted from the needs of rural teachers who wanted to utilize the dramatic arts in their classrooms and communities. Two colleges in Utah and North Dakota, far from the centers of theatrical activity, made a pioneering effort to incorporate material relating to these needs in their extension programs. The experiment in Utah was described by Frank R. Arnold in 1918:

> The state colleges of North Dakota and Utah have established play service bureaus as part of their expansion activities. These offer to the country school teacher a valuable source of practical information which will give her an opportunity to render important service to the community.[6]

Arnold began his report with mention of a previous article which had appeared in the *Boston Transcript* in the spring of 1916, describing play service at the Agricultural College of North Dakota. The idea had appealed to him as equally practical for the area in which his institution was located, with the result that his project was set up at the Agricultural College of Utah. The principal object in both instances was to introduce a better quality of play into the schools and communities of the state. Arnold discussed the peculiar structure of his own state, which was made up of well-organized little Mormon towns. These towns had since pioneer days had meetinghouses with halls or stages, on which various kinds of entertainments had been presented. The interest

---

[6] "Play Service in Utah," *Education*, Vol. XXXIX (December, 1918), 244.

in drama was already there; the only lack, in his opinion, was the play. Therefore, a Community Service Bureau could give immediate aid by suggesting appropriate plays and offering help in the details of production. To Frank Arnold's knowledge, the idea of a college-extension program as agent for this service was a new one, not yet adopted in the East.

OTHER CHILDREN'S THEATRE GROUPS

During these years a number of other groups found their way into production and subsequently into the records of the children's theatre movement. While many of them did not continue their activities or extend the scope of their programs to the degree of the projects described above, they contributed to the growing interest in this aspect of theatre in various parts of the country. There were, for example, the School of Expression in Cincinnati, which conducted a children's theatre giving special performances each year, and an association in Boston called the Children's Players. The latter was established under the auspices of the Boston Women's Educational and Industrial Union. The members were a group of amateurs from college and private dramatic clubs, acting under the union's management. Each year they presented a play for children during the Christmas holiday season.

Professional Theatre for Children

In the professional theatre two Broadway productions were attended by children. Although neither professed to be more than a single elaborate production, appealing to both children and adults, they received excellent notices and stand among the few enterprises of this sort.

SNOW WHITE AND THE SEVEN DWARFS

Snow White and the Seven Dwarfs, dramatized from the Grimm fairy tale by Jessie Graham White, was presented for the first time on November 7, 1912, by Winthrop Ames. It was an attractive production with six different settings, music composed especially for the occasion, and an experienced actress, Marguerite Clark, in the leading role. Reviews commented upon the beauty and charm of the presentation, which was said to have had a special appeal to children. The *New York Dramatic Mirror* stated further: "One must be past the age of enjoyment not to share the thrills which this very charming production engenders."[7]

TREASURE ISLAND

The season of 1915 saw a production of *Treasure Island*, presented by Charles Hopkins at the Punch and Judy Theatre in New York. One of the most attractively pictorial productions that was ever produced, it was well acted and exceedingly well received. While mention was made of the enjoyment it gave to young people, it was not specifically advertised as children's entertainment.

THE CENTURY THEATRE, NEW YORK

At approximately the same time a controversial if short-lived project in children's theatre was being launched. The money for this enterprise was given by William K. Vanderbilt and George Tyler as a present to the children of New York. A playhouse seating eight hundred was built on the roof of the Century Theatre, and from reports written at the time, it was a tasteful and practical auditorium:

> The theatre patron goes by elevator to the roof and lands in a hall directing him toward the children's theatre seating 800. There are no galleries or boxes by the stage or at the side, but half a dozen boxes are at the rear of the theatre. The walls are a warm gray color without decoration. The only decorations are plastic figures at the side and above the stage.[8]

[7] Anon., "Snow White," *New York Dramatic Mirror*, Vol. LXVII (November 13, 1912), 6.
[8] Anon., "Racketty-Packetty House," *Outlook*, Vol. CIII (January 11, 1913), 58.

The opening on December 21, 1912, was attended with much publicity which resulted in numerous published reviews and accounts. The first play was Frances Hodgson Burnett's *Racketty-Packetty House* and the actors, for the most part, were children. While the consensus seemed to be favorable, there was some dissension over the purpose and educational value of theatre for children. *Outlook*, reviewing the opening in January, 1913, said at the outset that it disapproved of children's attending the theatre. It went on to add, however, that if they were to be taken at all, no better place of entertainment could be found than the roof of the Century.

Mrs. Jacob Heniger (formerly Alice Minnie Herts) was more critical of the performance, even though she was completely sympathetic to the idea of theatre devoted to children. She stated the view of some that the project had been hurried into existence on the theory that the "psychological moment" had come for such a commercial venture. This rush, it was thought, prevented careful consideration of the policies and problems involved. For example, Tyler had spent $60,000 on an elaborate production, and to ensure (in his opinion) a good performance of a leading role, he had hired a midget to play the part. While subsequent performances were given, the Century enterprise was not a success, and at the end of a year its doors were permanently closed.

THE TOY THEATRE, NEW YORK

After the failure of the Century, another new project, The Toy Theatre, was announced. Peter Newton, founder, explained that property had been purchased on 47th Street near Broadway and that a wealthy anonymous person had already consented to finance the enterprise. Plans had been drawn up for a theatre which would not be educational but which would present in the afternoons, fairy and folklore plays for the little children, and in the evenings, regular plays and dramas for older children. The $200,000 cost for the building had been almost subscribed, and a stock company was to be installed. Among those interested were

Mrs. Vincent Astor, Mrs. Louis Brandeis, and Mrs. Gifford Pinchot. It was to be managed by Peter Newton and Grace Griswold.

The Toy Theatre was to be designed with the ideals, aspirations, and point of view of children in mind. The street front was to suggest an Old World building in a medieval town. While elaborate plans were drawn up, there is no record to indicate that this highly imaginative enterprise ever materialized.

Publication for Children's Theatre

The need for more and better plays was being expressed on all sides. In an effort to meet this need community leaders and teachers were endeavoring to write plays or adapt well-known children's classics to the stage. Stuart Walker in New York, Mrs. John J. Cuddy in San Francisco, Clarence Sullivan in Columbus, and Constance D'Arcy Mackay and Percy Mackaye through the Drama League were among those whose dramatizations had been given successful public performance.

A PLAY INDEX

While much of the writing of the period was intended for the adult theatre, some of it was directed to the classroom and young people. It was several years before a substantial number of children's plays found their way into print, but in 1918 there appeared tangible evidence of these literary efforts. It was a compilation in the form of *A Play Index*, published in the August, 1918, issue of the *St. Louis Public Library Monthly Bulletin*.

The *Play Index* featured an annotated list of plays for children, edited by Alice I. Hazeltine, containing over 1,200 references. In her Foreword, Miss Hazeltine explained that she had not attempted to differentiate the various plays on the basis of quality. She had simply listed those which were available. Kenneth Graham commented further regarding this point in his study of children's plays: "The vast majority were written for the prime pur-

43

pose of instruction to the exclusion of art and other purposes."[9] Nevertheless, the *Play Index* revealed by the fact of its publication an awareness of the need for children's plays and indicated the number of available scripts.

From the inception of the Drama League of America in 1910, to the various movements described, it is apparent that the activity was largely on the community level. At the same time schools were making use of dramatics, and some teachers' colleges were including in their curricula training which would further this work. A changing attitude toward the theatre on the part of educational institutions could be detected.

Educational and recreational values were held of primary importance, as nearly every published description of a children's theatre activity points out. The influence of the Drama League of America, with its high ideals, its community interest, its publications for school and community use, and its sponsorship of innumerable clubs and groups, could have accounted for these particular emphases. Though still a fledgling, children's theatre was now very much alive and beginning to grow through the support of progressive schools and community centers.

[9] "An Introductory Study of the Evaluation of Plays for Children's Theatres in the United States," 90.

IV

The Community Takes a Hand

1920-30

The years 1920 to 1930 were a period of expansion in children's theatre. The idea of plays for the child audience had been accepted by many educational and recreational leaders during the previous decade, and on community, educational, and professional levels there was resultant activity. The Drama League of America, functioning since 1910, had passed the pioneering stage and had become a strong force in the establishment of community theatres throughout the country. Such books as Constance D'Arcy Mackay's *Children's Theatre and Plays* (1927) and Montrose J. Moses' *A Treasury of Plays for Children* (1921) were published, giving accounts of those experiments which the authors believed to have made a significant contribution in the field of theatre for children. *The Periodical Index* during these years shows a greater number of articles on the subject carried by various types of magazines, while *Drama*, a monthly since 1919, had increased its coverage of news and dissemination of information for the amateur producer.

New dramatic groups and different types of organizations appeared in the early twenties. Many of these were so solidly established that they lasted not only the decade but the difficult depression and war years that followed. One outstanding example is the Association of Junior Leagues of America, which today ranks as one of the strongest contributors to the children's theatre movement. While many of the groups which sprang up during this period were of short duration, the fact of their having been founded at all points to the widening sphere of interest in children's theatre work. Constance D'Arcy Mackay in 1925 distinguished between the two types of programs that were being carried on:

> Plays for children are rapidly becoming divided into two types: those for children's theatres, such as The Threshold Players, under the direction of Clare Tree Major; the children of the Actors' Theatre who act under the direction of the Misses King and Coit; and the Children's Theatre in Copley Square, Boston, which is run under the direction of Emerson College. . . . On the other hand there is also a need for school plays though perhaps too much emphasis has recently been put on drama in education.[1]

Since her first category includes both professional and non-professional theatre, it can perhaps be subdivided into those groups which were professional in their organization and those which were under the direction of educational and community institutions. A survey of all the types of offerings during the twenties, however, seems to suggest these major categories: national organizations interested in the furthering of children's theatre work; children's theatre under the auspices of educational institutions; children's theatre in community and recreational centers; and professional theatre for children.

National Organizations

There were during the twenties two national organizations which contributed to the children's theatre movement. One of these was the Drama League of America, which continued its support of this phase of theatre as one of a number of interests. The other was the Association of Junior Leagues of America, which during the twenties embarked upon an ambitious program

[1] "Drama in Which Young People Can Participate," *Drama*, Vol. XVI (October, 1925), 32.

directed wholly toward the presentation of children's plays. In-asmuch as the Drama League's activities were in full progress at the beginning of this period, a consideration of its contribution comes logically first.

THE DRAMA LEAGUE OF AMERICA

The Drama League of America was frequently referred to in the literature of the twenties with regard to the support and encouragement which it proffered to neophyte groups. An important survey of its mid-twenties activity appeared in *The Playground*[2] in a report of the 1926 League Convention. Several reports were of particular interest: A Pittsburgh representative told of a successful play contest conducted in the schools; he also told of the school drama work in Pittsburgh, for which one thousand bulletins a week were issued under the aegis of the Drama League. Bertha Iles reported on the progress of the Chicago Municipal Pier Program, one of the country's most successful community projects. It was stated that the schools of the West were far ahead of the schools of the East in the matter of equipping their buildings with splendid new auditoriums. The field of amateur drama was reported to have spread by this time through schools, colleges, social settlements, and churches; it had also stimulated the organization of several thousand individual clubs throughout the country. Children's Theatre was considered sufficiently important to be included along with other areas of theatre activity among the round-table conferences.

Announced in another issue of *The Playground* during the same year was "Drama Week," to be observed February 14–20, 1926. Under the sponsorship of the Drama League, it was devoted to the co-ordination of the work of all associations and individuals interested in educating the public to appreciate and demand good drama and in awakening the public to the importance of the theatre as a social force and a great educational movement. It is apparent that the Drama League was an important

[2] Anon., "Report of the Seventeenth Annual Convention of the Drama League of America," *The Playground*, Vol. XX (July, 1926), 237-41.

agent in promoting theatrical activity during the twenties and in raising and maintaining standards.

Despite the ramifications of its program and the good reports of its work, the Drama League as an organization terminated activities in 1931. After twenty-one years of continuous service it was dissolved and the publication of *Drama* magazine was suspended. Mrs. A. Starr Best, one of the founders and first president of the organization, in reviewing its work for the May, 1931, issue of *Drama*, cited certain accomplishments for which she believed the League could be given credit. In her opinion, it had awakened the public to the need for better plays than the commercial theatre was offering; it had educated and organized audiences to demand what they wanted; it had helped little theatres and children's theatres to get started; and it had published plays and lists of plays in *Drama*. Its task was finished and there was no further need for its existence. Thus, the Drama League of America, a force for over two decades in both amateur and professional circles, disappeared from the scene. Many of its members remained active through their affiliation with educational and community organizations; however, new names and new sponsoring agents were to appear in the thirties as the amateur theatre movement for adults and children continued.

THE ASSOCIATION OF JUNIOR LEAGUES OF AMERICA

The Association of Junior Leagues of America is a large organization of women whose work in children's theatre, as well as in other community-welfare enterprises, has always been of a philanthropic character.

As early as 1912, Junior League girls were gathering in New York, Chicago, and Boston to present plays for children. Subsequent work in connection with settlement houses, public playgrounds, and hospitals established the Junior League contribution as an important one in the cultural life of many communities in America. It was not until 1921, however, that it began a program which was to become one of the most important contributions to

48

the children's theatre movement. The year 1921 marked the beginning of formal children's theatre activities among the Leagues, independent of settlements and institutions.

It was in this year that the Junior League of Chicago gave *Alice in Wonderland*, a lavish production in a downtown theatre. Prior to this, Alice Gerstenberg, known in America for her writing of one-act plays, was appointed chairman of a committee which was to study ways in which Junior Leaguers could best utilize their talents. Because the commercial theatre, by and large, dared not risk the financial hazards involved in children's entertainment, this seemed to her a vast and unexplored area in which the Junior League might make a contribution. The 1921 president of the League, Annette Washburn, agreed, and insisted upon the *Alice in Wonderland* production as an opening venture. While the players were amateurs, the staff was professional and newspaper publicity was exceptionally good. The success of the performance was measured by its enthusiastic reception and excellent financial returns. Encouraged to further work, the Chicago League followed up with elaborate productions of *The Little Princess* (in the same year), *Little Women*, *The Land of Don't Want To*, *The Wizard of Oz*, and *Racketty-Packetty House*.

The success of the Chicago venture stimulated activity among various other chapters; by 1926, Leagues in fourteen different cities were producing children's plays. Within another year these efforts were receiving a new kind of support. Samuel French had agreed to publish adaptations of *The Wizard of Oz* and *Raggedy Ann* with music by Ira S. Holden, thus making available printed scripts of these popular children's plays. *The Junior League Magazine* added a new department called "The Play Box" in which articles, questions, and answers pertaining to children's entertainment appeared. With this added support from the national headquarters, the activity swelled, and by March, 1928, fifty-two Leagues were offering children's plays.

The purpose guiding its work was stated to be the entertainment of boys and girls and the building of adult audiences by introducing the young to theatre production. While this basic objective has been held through the years, the organization, scale of production, and implementation of the program have undergone major changes. During the twenties, the Junior League plays were characterized by lavish scenery and costumes and by appeal to certain types of audiences. To cover the costs it was necessary to charge high prices for tickets, although other blocks of seats were reserved for underprivileged children from settlement houses and orphanages, a practice which was in line with the social-service policy of the League. This procedure obviously excluded from attendance the large middle class of children who during this period were being served by the civic theatres and recreational programs which the Drama League had promoted.

Unlike the majority of community theatres, which utilized children in their performances, the Junior League plays were acted by adults. Since the number of good full-length plays was still scarce, the policy of writing their own scripts was established; this practice exists to the present day. From the first, successful manuscripts were filed for future use, thus forming the nucleus of a play bureau which was to expand and become an important part of the program.

A recent publication of the Junior League, in which the history of this enterprise is recounted, states that "Theatre meets a fundamental need of human beings. It allows them to enter worlds larger than their own, to encounter people different from themselves, and to share experiences that may never exist in everyday living."[3] While the program has been expanded and altered, this idea of the *raison d'être* of theatre has remained a guiding principle. Much more will be said in later chapters concerning the work of the Junior League.

Educational Theatres for Children

While the greatest contribution of the educational institution was to come later on, a number of notable children's theatres under the auspices of schools and colleges were formed at this

[3] Mary Eleanor Ciaccio, *Prologue to Production*, 5.

time. The majority of the better publicized are still in existence and have served as models for those which came after them. A study of the administration and programs of these groups will be made in an effort to discover prevailing methods of operation and objectives.

EMERSON COLLEGE IN BOSTON

One of the earliest programs under the direction of an educational institution was the Children's Theatre of Emerson College, frequently mentioned in periodicals of the period. Imogene Hogle, a senior in 1919, began as an undergraduate to put on plays for children. The results of her efforts were said to have been so popular that after her graduation she was asked to continue the work as a regular part of the college program. She became, accordingly, the first director of the children's theatre, with the official founding date given as 1920. There was subsequent growth through curricular offerings and community co-operation, but even in these early years of its existence, the Emerson Children's Theatre established itself as an interesting and stable experiment.

Most of the plays given were well-known classics, but occasional new scripts by faculty members and students enrolled in playwriting classes were accepted for production. The program consisted of a monthly play with performances on Saturday afternoons. Five plays constituted a season but popular demand often made repeat performances necessary. Some of the plays given during this early period were *The Lantern* by Abbie Farwell Brown, *Master Skylark* by John Bennett, *Fra Angelo* by Daniel O. Brewster, *The Royal Drudge* by John Kearns, and *Damon and Pythias* by Ethel V. Bailey. The fantasy plays included such well-known scripts as *Aladdin*, *The Blue Prince*, and *Alice Through the Looking Glass*. A dramatic workshop in which rehearsals were held offered courses in all phases of play production, including children's theatre. By the end of the decade it had a national advisory board on which served such well-known persons as Walter Hampden, Constance D'Arcy Mackay, and

Walter Prichard Eaton. Thus Imogene Hogle's idea of a children's theatre grew from an extracurricular venture into a well-established part of the Emerson program.

NATIONAL COLLEGE OF EDUCATION

Another type of organization established by an educational institution was the children's play series of the National College of Education, then located in Chicago. Unlike Emerson College, where the students were being trained for theatre work, National College prepared only teachers for kindergarten and the elementary grades. There were no drama majors but students and alumnae had a background in childhood education, and it was from this that the program developed. In 1920 the first of the series began. The plays were planned for young children from four to eight years of age and were given a first performance in the Studebaker Theatre in Chicago, since at that time there was no auditorium in the college.

The Alumnae Association assumed the responsibility for ticket distribution and sales and on many occasions provided transportation into the city for groups from suburban areas. Only one production was prepared during the school year, but popular demand made several performances necessary. These developed into touring engagements on five or six successive Saturday afternoons in Evanston, Oak Park, La Grange, Gary, Hammond, and other near-by communities. Etta Mount was director of drama and dance, with Margaret Farrar of the art department as designer of scenery and costumes. Since Etta Mount's major interest was dance, there was great emphasis on movement; beauty and humor, rather than excitement and fright, characterized the performances.

The stories were dramatized by Clara Belle Baker, director of the Children's School of the college, and included *Briar Rose, Cap o'Rushes, The Nuremberg Stove, Penny Lad, The Magic Fishbone,* and *The Five Little Peppers.* Mimeographed synopses of the stories were sent in advance to the schools where performances were to be given, a practice which was later to be adopted by other producing groups. The purpose of the program was twofold: to provide good entertainment for small children in a large city; and to secure funds, through some benefit perform-ances, for a new building which would contain facilities for en-larging the teacher-training program. The following statement from a benefit program (April 21, 1923) was typical of the atti-tude of the period: *"On Fairies' Wings*, presented today by the student players of the National Kindergarten and Elementary College, under the sponsorship of children, in addition to pro-viding delight by a trip to Fairyland, is a step toward the achieve-ment of an inspiring plan."

In 1926 this plan, the acquisition of a new and much larger building, became a reality and the college moved to Evanston. With a well-equipped auditorium of its own, plays were no longer presented in a downtown theatre but the touring program continued. Now, also, there was an annual production during the summer prepared by summer-school students and given out of doors in the garden of Mrs. Andrew MacLeish's estate in Glen-coe. Children attending these performances came from the Dem-onstration School of the college and from playground centers. Students, alumnae, and trustees all contributed to the National College of Education's plays for young children, which were an important offering of the college during the twenties.

THE KING-COIT SCHOOL OF ACTING AND DESIGN

Quite a different type of program in an altogether different type of school was that begun by Edith King and Dorothy Coit in New York in 1923. Not a college but a children's school of acting and design, it carried on its program in the afternoons fol-lowing regular school hours. The pupils ranged in age from five to twelve or thirteen. Its plan of giving only one production a year was apparently most successful, for it was highly praised by leaders in both adult and children's theatre from the time of its founding to its closing in the late fifties. The procedure fol-lowed at the King-Coit School was to acquaint the children first with the story to be dramatized, which, incidentally, was always one of high literary quality. There followed a comprehensive study of the period in which the story was laid, with particular emphasis on the visual arts. Periods spent in drawing, painting, and designing under the guidance of Edith King resulted in ideas for scenery and costumes which were frequently used in the final production of the play. While creativity was a primary objective, technical excellence was apparently achieved as well, for no account of the King-Coit School failed to mention this aspect of its work. Indeed, all reports were in agreement that no professional production of the classics surpassed the King-Coit plays in total effect.

Some of the unusual plays given over the years were *Kai Khrosu, Aucassin and Nicolette, The Tempest, The Story of Theseus, The Rose and the Ring, The Image of Artemis*, and *The Golden Cage* (from the poems of William Blake). With these plays as the culmination of the years' activities, the King-Coit School adhered to a basic philosophy which guided its work for more than three decades. Sheila Moyne in an article written after seeing a production of the Persian play *Kai Khrosu*, stated that "much praise is due to the inspiring work and to the infinite patience and understanding of Miss Edith King and Miss Dorothy Coit."[4] It is interesting that these two women were mentioned earlier in connection with the Peabody House–Buckingham School production of *Aucassin and Nicolette*. Their pioneering efforts in Boston led to the establishment of their unique school in New York. There was some controversy over the methods they used, but at the same time they received high praise for the beauty of their results.

THE CHILDREN'S THEATRE OF EVANSTON

One of the oldest and best-known children's theatres which exists in the country today was founded in 1925 in Evanston, Illinois. Under the supervision of Winifred Ward, professor of dramatic arts in the School of Speech in Northwestern Univer-

---

4 "The Never-Never Land to Iran," *Arts and Decoration*, Vol. XXIV (December, 1925), 36.

sity, the Children's Theatre of Evanston was established to provide worth-while drama for the boys and girls of the North Shore. As in the Emerson College Theatre, the technical staff and many of the actors received valuable experience through participation in these plays. Unlike the Emerson Theatre, however, children of Evanston were also cast in the parts of children or younger characters, thus making for a close co-operation between the university and the public schools. So successful was the result that in 1927 the Board of Education and the public schools joined in sponsorship. While the enterprise has remained an outstanding example of educational theatre, it may be considered at the same time a community institution.

Four plays a year constituted the original program and were given on both Saturday mornings and afternoons. These plays were presented in two of the public-school auditoriums rather than in the university theatre, in order to make them as accessible as possible to the boys and girls of Evanston and the North Shore suburbs. Winifred Ward has been one of the distinguished leaders of the children's theatre movement, not only in the Chicago area but throughout the United States, and the Evanston Theatre has served as a model for university-community co-operation. Through her writing, her direction, her lectures and workshops, which have taken her to all parts of the country, and her later leadership in the national conference of children's theatre groups, Winifred Ward has made one of the most significant contributions in the field.

THE GOODMAN THEATRE FOR CHILDREN

There was established in the Chicago area during these years still another children's theatre which has not only lasted to the present time but is known throughout the United States for its high standards and excellent work. This is the Goodman Children's Theatre of the Art Institute of Chicago, founded in 1925. The founder, Muriel Brown, was a graduate of Carnegie Institute of Technology in Pittsburgh, where she studied theatre with a view toward working with or for children. Attempts in her home town of Indianapolis and later in New York did not materialize into the dream of a children's theatre which she envisioned; but in 1924 in Chicago, Thomas Wood Stevens put her in charge of the children's work at the Goodman Memorial Theatre, a post which she filled for several years. The opening play in the autumn of 1925 was Lady Gregory's *The Golden Apple*; it was followed by *The Captive Princess* and *Wappin Wharf*. So successful was this season that the following year the announcement was made that the children's plays were to be a permanent adjunct of the Goodman Theatre.

The 1926 season included, in addition to *The Blue Bird*, two plays written by the director: *Robin Hood* and *Six Cherry Tarts*. The actors and technical staff were adult students at the Goodman, and the support came from the Art Institute, tuition, and box-office receipts. As time went on it became necessary to add a second performance on Saturday; both performances have been attended from the beginning by capacity audiences of children of all ages.

THE CHILDREN'S THEATRE OF TULSA

One of the largest and most progressive art theatres for children in America was the children's theatre directed by Josephine Layman Story at the University of Tulsa. Established in 1926 as a gift from the university, this unique children's theatre set forth its aims as acquainting the younger generation with the inspiration as well as the fun that drama offers, and showing, through production, that worth-while plays bring beauty into all people's lives.

The children's theatre was correlated with the university in that college students worked directly with the children who enrolled for the Saturday-morning laboratory. In this way, both adults and children were learning together the values and techniques of play production. Performances were given in the early evening rather than during the day. Christmas and Easter plays were prepared in addition and taken to various churches in the community.

During the first season four hundred boys and girls were enrolled; in succeeding semesters this number increased. The confidence of the university in the project was indicated by the larger appropriations given to it. An article describing the Tulsa enterprise called it a step toward state-wide artistic development of drama by amateur groups. It predicted that the time was coming when every public school would be a community theatre. This point of view was echoed by an article in *The Playground*, which named Tulsa as a pioneer in the spreading of good community drama.[5]

OTHER EDUCATIONAL THEATRES

While the activities described above have been among the best-publicized children's theatres, there were others established during these years which made a substantial contribution to their communities. Cora Mel Patten, in an article published in 1927, identified some of the others:

> The Minneapolis Children's Players instituted and directed by Louise Holt, a group of high school students who rehearsed and toured plays to public schools, churches and clubs;
> The Richmond, Virginia High School Players, founded in 1929, which likewise presented plays for younger boys and girls, and
> The Children's Theatre of Illinois Wesleyan at Bloomington, Illinois, under the direction of Ethel Gunn. Its aim was to acquaint children with the best in child literature and instruct them in platform art, pantomime, and plays. Some of their productions during this period were *Racketty Packetty House, Garden at the Zoo, The Stolen Prince* and *The Clown Doll.*[6]

The Union High School of Bakersfield, California, presented plays for children rather than the usual more sophisticated type of highschool entertainment. With Ethel Robinson as director,

[5] Anon., "Children's Theatre at the University of Tulsa," *The Playground*, Vol. XXII (March, 1928), 697–98.
[6] "The Children's Theatre Movement," *Drama*, Vol. XVIII (November, 1927), 51.

they gave such ambitious plays as *Little Women* and *Alice in Wonderland*. At Vassar, Goucher, and Radcliffe interest was also indicated by the occasional production of plays suitable for child audiences.

A survey made by the American National Theatre and Academy in 1951 disclosed that among currently existing children's theatres, the Durfee Dramatic Club of the High School of Fall River, Massachusetts, had since 1925 been offering good plays for child audiences. Likewise Drake University, which today has a well-established series, started its program in that year. Syracuse University began work in 1927, and the Texas State College for Women in Denton laid the groundwork in 1929 for a department of dramatic arts which would include children's plays. Since the 1951 survey was made through questionnaires to currently operating groups, only those which were still in existence were identified. It is interesting, however, that the schools and colleges, which during the preceding decade had evidenced an enthusiasm for the inclusion of drama in education, were beginning to take concrete steps toward the establishment of well-organized programs of plays.

THE JACK AND JILL PLAYERS OF CHICAGO

The Jack and Jill Players Group of Chicago, a private children's theatre school, was founded in 1925 and has survived depression, war, and postwar periods. Directed by Marie Agnes Foley, this group became self-supporting in 1927 and has maintained a steady program of expansion in its touring engagements in the Chicago area. The little theatre was planned for a wide range of ages, from small children of three to high-school students of eighteen. A tuition fee of five dollars a month provided for instruction in the dramatic arts and participation in the regular season's productions. A six-week rehearsal schedule with two rehearsal periods a week was established. Performances were (and are) first given in the small Jack and Jill Playhouse seating one hundred; after this, touring engagements were accepted. Both the number of yearly productions and the number of performances increased as the company became known in the area. Since the local touring performance was emphasized, scenery and costumes were designed to facilitate the technical preparation. While the Jack and Jill Players were a small group as compared with the dramatic branches of community centers and civic theatres, the fact that they have maintained an uninterrupted program for more than forty years points to stability and good organization as a private theatre school.

It is apparent from the reports in periodicals of the twenties and the results obtained from surveys that children's drama in educational institutions was taking root. In universities, colleges, private schools, and even some high schools, programs had been set up with a view toward permanency. In addition to these experiments, however, there were other types of programs in the communities of America, where recreational and social objectives were paramount. While instruction was mentioned in some instances, the aim of community service took precedence. The concept of theatre as an art with positive social values was firmly planted in the communities of America.

Community Theatre for Children

Enthusiasm for community drama persisted throughout the twenties, with the result that both individual productions and ambitious organized programs were established. One illustration of this type of activity was a historical pageant entitled *Children of Old Carolina*, written and produced by Ethel Theodora Rockwell of the University of North Carolina. The theme of the pageant was the part played by children in the history of the state. With sixteen schools participating, the various episodes were rehearsed separately, then put together in what was apparently a beautiful and unified effect. According to all reports this was the first time in America that children had acted a pageant representing their part in the building of a state.

As for dramatic activities set up with a view toward the future, contemporary periodicals indicate that many communities were engaged in the creation of organized children's programs. In some instances they were the outgrowth of adult community theatres, which had been running long enough to be able to add this new branch of entertainment to their regular schedule of plays. In other instances they were sponsored by recreation departments, distinct from any other existing organization. In either case, it was theatre for children and young people, nonprofessional in nature, and directed toward the demand for better or more appropriate entertainment than was locally offered.

GREENWICH HOUSE IN NEW YORK

A children's drama program which started in the mid-twenties and has continued to the present time with very little attendant publicity was that begun at Greenwich House in New York. According to Helen Murphey, who was its founder and its director for more than thirty years, the aim was never to publicize the work but rather to contribute to the cultural development of the youngsters. To that end classes for children were set up, and no more than three or four public productions a year were developed or scheduled. While there have been occasional outside performances from time to time, this practice has been discouraged as incompatible with the philosophy on which the program was based.

Helen Murphey believed that each community must build its own program according to its interests and the abilities of those leading it. Since the children in the settlement were a mixture of nationalities, religions, and widely varying cultural backgrounds, the dramatic productions did not follow any particular pattern. They came as an expression of interest and with the exception of *Alice in Wonderland* were all dramatizations of stories, legends, and myths.

While authenticity has been stressed in the matter of scenery and costumes, production has been simple and handled by children of junior-high-school age. An adult theatre composer was appointed and has been maintained, since music was considered a base on which to build pantomime and movement. One hundred children a week, from ages six to fourteen, have constituted the average enrollment, though this number has varied from year to year. Many of the students have gone on into the adult group of players and some have pursued theatrical careers, although training for the professional stage has not been an aim of the settlement. The most significant thing about the Greenwich program has been the direct continuity it has maintained for over forty years, a record which has been achieved by few, if any, other groups.

PEABODY HOUSE

Aucassin and Nicolette was produced by Peabody House in Boston in 1921 with a combined cast of children from the settlement and the Buckingham School. The performance was given under the direction of Edith King and Dorothy Coit, members of the private school faculty, on May 11, 1921, at Jordan Hall. While there is no further mention of work of this sort being done at Peabody, it is particularly interesting in light of the future activity of these two young women, who shortly afterward established and directed the distinguished King-Coit School of Acting and Design in New York.

CHILDREN'S DRAMA IN THE LITTLE THEATRES

In the little theatres the following children's groups were interesting or successful. Though they differ somewhat in organization and offerings, they share a common origin as the junior branch of an adult community playhouse or club.

THE SCALAWAGS OF COLUMBIA, SOUTH CAROLINA

An early example of children's theatre as a division of a civic playhouse was the Scalawags of the Town Theatre of Columbia, South Carolina. This group, founded in 1920 and directed by Daniel A. Reed, has often been cited as a successful and unique experiment. Two regular productions a year were given for and by the children of the town. *The Piper, A Christmas Carol, Jack and the Beanstalk*, and *Snow White* were among the early plays. In addition to these public performances, the group met every Saturday morning for improvisation, pantomime, and even the writing of original scripts. The children, aged six to fifteen, often produced their own plays which were followed by criticism from their peers. A 1931 description called the group one of the oldest then being conducted by a community theatre, and stated that two of the earliest members were on the professional stage, several others were in dramatic schools, and some were already directing plays in South Carolina high schools.[7] While the object was not to train actors, the stimulation of the group was apparently so great that a pleasant avocation led to careers in the performing and teaching of drama.

THE CHILDREN'S THEATRE GUILD OF NEW ORLEANS

The Children's Theatre Guild of New Orleans opened in 1924. The Guild originated in the Little Theatre of the Women's Club of New Orleans with a membership of two hundred, and within a short time that number had tripled. A four-dollar subscription included tickets to six performances of such children's classics as *The Birds' Christmas Carol*, *The Little Princess*, *Ali Baba and the Forty Thieves*, *Robin Hood*, and *Snow White*. Self-supporting from the start, the Guild maintained a program of good entertainment for young people and at the same time trained grade-school and high-school pupils in the art of play production. It embraced a plan which apparently combined the good qualities of the professional theatre, student training for the stage, and the school program. Ruth Voss directed the staff of professional adults but the actors were children.

THE JUNIOR REPERTORY THEATRE OF MINNEAPOLIS

A successful community group was formed in 1929 in Minneapolis. This was the Junior Repertory Theatre established by Elizabeth Hartzell. The first venture of its kind in the area, it met with an enthusiastic response from both children and adults.

[7] Anon., "Children's Theatre," *Drama*, Vol. XXI (February, 1931), 29.

Some of the productions during the first season were *The Ivory Door, Master Skylark, The Taming of the Shrew, Daddy Long Legs, If I Were King,* and *Peter Pan.*

THE ST. PAUL'S CHILDREN'S THEATRE

During this period the city of St. Paul saw the founding of a children's theatre, likewise a community enterprise. This group, under the sponsorship of the St. Paul Players, was organized as an experiment, to compensate for the poor entertainment offered by local movies. According to the director, Alyne Sholes, the theatre was conducted not only for children but by them, so far as possible. Good children's plays as well as original plays written by the children themselves were presented. Apparently the opportunity to produce their own work was a stimulation to an active participation, for the experiment prospered.

INDIANAPOLIS CHILDREN'S THEATRE

The Civic Theatre of Indianapolis, one of the oldest of the adult community theatres, began its children's work in 1929. Instead of employing a single director for all of the plays in the series, a chairman managed them, with individual directors for each. While the organization is reported to have changed from time to time, the children's work has remained an important activity of the theatre and has contributed to the cultural life of Indianapolis. An average of four plays during a season, presented on Saturday morning and afternoon, has constituted the major part of the program.

THE OMAHA CHILDREN'S THEATRE

Children assumed an important part in the total production of the Children's Theatre of the Omaha Community Playhouse in Omaha, Nebraska. Under the supervision of Bernard Szold, children not only acted but designed and constructed their own sets. The Children's Theatre was founded in 1929 with the King-Coit School of Acting and Design as its model. While this was a community, rather than a private, school of design, it promoted, through participation, an interest in the visual arts. Monthly design competitions, open to boys and girls between the ages of five and fourteen, resulted in regular children's exhibitions. In addition to this aspect of its work, the Community Playhouse reported enthusiastic acceptance of such colorful productions as *Robin Hood*, *The Wizard of Oz*, *Treasure Island*, and *The Blue Bird*.

THE HECKSCHER CHILDREN'S THEATRE IN NEW YORK

Not as a branch of a little theatre but as a part of a foundation, what was described as "the most beautiful children's theatre in the world"[8] was opened in 1922, in New York City. This reaction was echoed by nearly everyone who described the Heckscher Theatre for Children, located at the corner of Fifth Avenue and 104th Street across from Central Park. Founded by August Heckscher in 1921, the foundation was sufficiently well endowed to open as a completely equipped and beautiful institution. The auditorium was decorated in blue, cream, and gold with Willy Pogany's fairy-tale murals on the walls. A well-furnished stage and twelve little dressing rooms upstairs made this theatre as practical as it was charming. The building included, in addition to the theatre area, an indoor playground, gymnasium, pool, clubrooms, and manual-training workshop—indeed everything which the founders thought was required to make life happy, healthy, and progressive for the children of New York. The Heckscher Theatre functioned for several years as an important institution and model community children's theatre center.

The opening production was announced for November 10, 1922, under the direction of Mrs. G. W. Hoffman. She presented an arrangement of scenes taken from the Pogany murals: *The Pied Piper*, *The Sleeping Beauty*, and *Cinderella*. Actors from the Professional Children's School took part, with the ages ranging from seven to seventeen. The second production was *The Snow Queen* as Christmas entertainment in December.

Bertram Hauser, director of the theatre in the mid-twenties,

8 Constance D'Arcy Mackay, "The Most Beautiful Children's Theatre in the World," *Drama*, Vol. XIV (February, 1924), 167.

expressed his philosophy about the purpose of the Heckscher Theatre. He described with enthusiasm the work that was being carried on, saying that both actors and audience were learning what was worth while in the theatre, while at the same time they were having a wonderful experience. The administration and directorship changed, and in 1929 a regular stock company of children under the leadership of Ashley Miller was established. Matinees on Saturday afternoons were financially successful.

CHILDREN'S THEATRE IN RECREATION CENTERS

On the West Coast children's drama was being established under the auspices of community recreation centers and playgrounds. Some of these early experiments have since been commended for their original or effective work.

THE PASADENA PROGRAM

In California, where early activity has already been noted, new organizations were being set up by various community agencies. The Pasadena Recreation Department initiated a drama program in 1927, wherein a committee selected what it considered worthwhile plays. Teachers from six different schools directed the plays, children from the community were cast in the parts, and a committee of mothers assumed responsibility for making the costumes.

CHILDREN'S THEATRE IN LOS ANGELES

In Los Angeles, meanwhile, much effort was being spent in an attempt to establish a permanent children's theatre, which in the beginning seemed doomed to failure. Cora Mel Patten, chairman of the Junior Department of the Drama League of America, whose pioneer work at the Chicago Municipal Pier had met with such extraordinary success, had gone to the California coast in 1924. During her second season there she organized a children's theatre which was sponsored by the Parent-Teacher Association. A program of eight plays was presented. While it was said to have been well attended, financially it was a failure. A second attempt met with the same result. Neither Cora Mel Patten nor the community was discouraged, however, for they believed in the ultimate success of the project.

In 1929 a different type of program was organized, this time one which was largely educational. The plays were staged in the Barker Auditorium, an attractive little theatre seating five hundred. As an offer of concrete support to the community, the auditorium was contributed by the Barker Brothers' Furniture Store, which also loaned properties and decorations. This attempt proved to be the turning point, for a report of its work in 1931 stated that it was in its third successful season. Four plays, presented in the months of November, January, April, and June, constituted the public series, with children from seven to sixteen eligible for participation. To all of these enterprises the Drama League offered its assistance and support.

DRAMATIC ACTIVITY IN BENNINGTON, VERMONT

While activity was spreading through the West, a New England town had instigated an unusual activity which sprang from its own individual interests: the five-year recreational program of Bennington, Vermont, in which dramatic activities for children formed a major part. A year-round program, it was set up to provide the maximum of variety and was conducted both indoors and out. For example, children might participate in a Christmas pageant one year and an out-of-door sleigh parade the next. The Fourth of July was a playground festival sufficiently elastic in organization to permit a different program every year. For Labor Day there were folk dances and for Hallowe'en a parade, in which the children of Bennington took a lively part. While the over-all objective was obviously the recreational value it held, the results were of good enough quality to warrant its inclusion among the more interesting children's dramatic experiments of the twenties.

OTHER CHILDREN'S THEATRE GROUPS

Among community groups organized and functioning similarly during this period was the San Francisco Children's Theatre

Guild. By this time it was regularly presenting six plays a season, thus establishing itself as an important institution in the life of the city. The Tacoma, Washington, Drama League, likewise ambitious in its planning, was offering to the children of the community weekly programs of music, drama, and dance. In Baltimore, Florence Bradley was conducting a children's theatre in which children and puppets performed the plays. A similar combination was being utilized by Gladys Wheat in her own small theatre in Columbia, Missouri. In Niagara Falls, New York, a children's theatre directed by Georgiana Montgomery was sustained by the Federated Mothers' Club and a civic committee of the city. Its program consisted of six plays a year for the younger children, all of which were put on by students from local high schools.

Other groups were known to have existed, though detailed accounts of their work were not published. The Drama League of America, cognizant of their existence and ever helpful to their efforts, made a survey of the situation and compiled their results. The number of groups questioned was not given in the report, but 50 per cent of those who responded stated that they produced plays for children. In most cases this was an annual production, though some put on two, three, or four plays a year. One group reported that it produced a monthly children's program and another that it produced a play every two weeks. Eighty-five per cent stated that they produced with children, 5 per cent with adults, and 10 per cent with casts of children and adults combined.[9]

After studying this survey, the Drama League concluded that the movement was growing and that, in the main, the children's groups were providing dramatic recreation rather than maintaining a junior art theatre.

DRAMA ON THE PLAYGROUNDS OF AMERICA

During the twenties *The Playground* published a number of

[9] Cora Mel Patten, "The Children's Theatre Movement," *Drama*, Vol. XVIII (November, 1927), 51.

items pertaining to dramatic activities which were being carried on in this area of community service. From east to west successful summer experiments were being reported. For example, in New York City in 1928 the playgrounds of Van Cortlandt Park and Port Chester began serious programs for children. A 1928 issue of *The Playground* announced a similar activity instigated by the Arts Festival Committee of the United Neighborhood Houses of New York. The Committee laid the groundwork in the spring by establishing production dates and sites, and then turned the implementation of the program over to the summer play schools, which worked it out under the guidance of the Child Study Association of America.

The Recreation Department of Oakland, California, reported in the same year the work of the Educational Dramatic Section for Young People among its most successful summer experiments. It was reported that 50 plays were given, 566 children participated, and over 14,000 boys and girls made up the total audience. The popularity of the project was so great that a "vagabond" or trailer theatre was sent around from playground to playground at the end of the season as an added feature.

Mabel Foote Hobbs, in an article on the value of this form of recreation to both community and individual child, documented her remarks with several outstanding examples.[10] Among them were the playgrounds of Oak Park, Illinois; Asheville, North Carolina; Hollywood, California; and East Orange, New Jersey, with which she herself had been associated. She reported that, as a part of the comprehensive program in Memphis, Tennessee, a drama tourney had been conducted, in which one thousand children from sixteen different playgrounds took part. Reported in other issues of *The Playground* during these years was work done in York and Wilkes Barre, Pennsylvania; Detroit, Michigan; Rock Island, Illinois; Salisbury, Connecticut; and San Francisco, California. These geographically separated examples indicate that the movement was of nationwide scope.

10 "The Children's Playground Theatre," *The Playground*, Vol. XXI (March, 1928), 662–70.

One other playground program which deserves mention was the Los Angeles project, which belongs to this period by virtue of the date of its founding and its recreational objectives. Beginning as a summer-vacation program, it eventually developed into a year-round activity. In the first years it had one outdoor playhouse in which programs of plays, folk dances, tumbling, and music were put on twice a month. It apparently met with immediate and enthusiastic response. Boys and girls were actors, ushers, stage crew, and audience, thus fulfilling its purpose as a children's community project. This organization has been cited as a forerunner of the new movement toward outdoor entertainment. Certainly the next decades saw the development of arena stages, outdoor festivals, and straw-hat theatre.

Under the auspices of little theatres, community centers, and playgrounds, children's drama became a trend in American recreation. Many of the projects were just being organized in this decade, but the number of citations in periodicals of the period is indicative of the growing emphasis being placed on this form of activity.

Professional Theatre for Children

While the majority of plays for children were the offerings of nonprofessional groups, there was some activity on the professional level. Probably the best-known and certainly the most-publicized figure connected with the promotion of this phase of theatre was Clare Tree Major, whose name has gone down in the history of the children's theatre movement as one of its most indefatigable pioneers.

CLARE TREE MAJOR

Clare Tree Major, unlike the other leaders thus far mentioned, approached what was to become her career from a professional theatre background. Born in England and trained in the Royal Academy, she was associated for a time with the Sir Herbert Tree and Benson Companies there. In 1916 she came to New

York City, where she soon took up an active participation in the
Washington Square Players, now the Theatre Guild. From this
she turned to direction and entertainment for young people. In
1921 she established her own company, composed of young professionals, situated on the second floor of what was later Loew's
Lexington Theatre. There followed a season at the Heckscher
Theatre, and six years later she directed at the Princess Theatre.
By this time her reputation as a producer of professional plays for
children was established. It was in 1922, however, that Clare Tree
Major first realized a new possibility in connection with her
work. One afternoon, following a performance, the dramatic
editor of one of the high-school newspapers of the city came
backstage. He expressed the wish that in addition to the fairy
plays for young children, some of the plays he was reading in
his English classes might be dramatized. Mrs. Major went to the
Association of Teachers of English to see if his suggestion were
a practical possibility. With the encouragement and co-operation
of this group, artistic productions of plays were furnished for
high-school students at prices they could afford. She continued
the fairy-tale plays but was also successful in her new presentation
of classics. In 1923, 50,000 high-school boys and girls saw the
Threshold Players, Clare Tree Major's company, performing the
plays selected for them by Mrs. Major and the New York Association of Teachers of English. This was reported to be the first
time that school work was formally correlated with professional
theatre production in this country.

Handicapped by having to present her plays only on Saturday
mornings at the Princess, Clare Tree Major made still another
move, this time to a basement on Madison Avenue. There, with
the assistance of Marian Depew and a technical staff, she was able
to expand her activities. This venture, run on a subscription basis
with the majority of seats selling for twenty-five cents, was
successful.

Clare Tree Major's belief in professional theatre for children
is shared by many in the field today. She distinguished between
the creativity fostered by the school and the well-dramatized

productions which a professional company offered. She often stated that the school theatre, valuable as it may be, is not all that children should have of the theatre. That is where the other type of theatre comes in, the adult professional theatre playing well-written, properly dramatized plays for child audiences. Her emphasis upon international literature was an intentional one, for she believed that through drama children can develop an appreciation of other lands and other people. As she explained, the child loses himself in vicarious experience and develops his imagination while at the same time learning principles of character.

Clare Tree Major's efforts to publicize her work through lecture and writing, to promote a touring company (which met with subsequent success), and to co-operate with the public schools bore results. Where other commercial ventures had failed, hers succeeded, and was to become an important institution in the lives of American children for the next twenty-five years.

ENTERTAINMENT IN A DEPARTMENT STORE

In addition to Clare Tree Major's Threshold Players, there was other professional entertainment offered to child audiences during these years. While no other entertainment was of comparable scope or duration, there was a conscious effort to present living theatre to boys and girls. One unusual example was the program initiated by Filene's Department Store in Boston. Myra Dunham, a graduate of Emerson College, was in charge of this program which began in 1925. Entertainment for children, consisting of four or five numbers, was furnished at tea time on Saturdays. For the stage, a platform twenty-five by twenty feet was set up in the middle of the dining room. Because of the difficulties of staging—a temporary platform, inadequate lighting, and accoustical problems—the staff wrote scripts which could be adapted to these special conditions. Casts were assembled from colleges, dancing schools, and lyceums in the area. The dining room was decorated in the spirit of the play, thus making for a colorful and festive atmosphere. While not professional theatre, the fact that it was sponsored by a store for the purpose of attracting trade would seem to place it in this, rather than in the educational or community theatre, category.

THE NATIONAL JUNIOR THEATRE IN WASHINGTON, D.C.

Instead of producing the usual children's plays, the National Junior Theatre in Washington, D.C., presented appropriate Broadway plays of good literary quality. Among them were Barrie's *A Kiss for Cinderella, Quality Street, The Tempest, The Prince and the Pauper*, and *A Midsummer Night's Dream*. By the 1930 season, three years after its beginning, it had presented twenty-seven successful productions. The idea of selecting this type of drama, which young people would not otherwise have the opportunity of seeing, was novel, for it was not reported as a policy by any other existing organization.

THE NEW YORK STAGE

The twenties brought two revivals of *Peter Pan*, one by Eva Le Gallienne's Civic Repertory group and the other by a Broadway cast which starred Marilyn Miller. Both were referred to as beautiful and whimsical; however, reviewers of the period, recalling the earlier Maude Adams production, were only mildly enthusiastic. Neither was presented in the interest of children's theatre, yet they were among the few appropriate children's plays offered by the New York stage.

Publication for Children's Theatre

With the spread of children's theatre groups throughout the country, there was an increase in the number of published scripts. As early as 1921 there appeared a collection called *A Treasury of Plays for Children* by Montrose J. Moses. Moses, an American editor and critic, wrote extensively for and about children's drama and was particularly interested in improving the quality of such material. In a 1924 article for *Theatre Arts Monthly*, he expressed the opinion that plays for young people should have beauty of line, color, and imagination.[11] He believed that many writers wrote down to the juvenile audience, failing to give it credit for an understanding of spiritual and instinctive experience. He favored the play which was not easy but which, since it was worth doing, was worth doing well. In 1926 a second volume entitled *Another Treasury of Plays for Children* came out under his editorship; both this and the earlier collection have remained standard in school and community libraries to the present day.

In Peekskill, New York, Moritz Jagendorf, writer and editor of children's plays, was operating a children's theatre in which new scripts were tried out. A workshop which functioned as a playwriting laboratory, it presented an opportunity for the evolution of plays and pantomimes. In Jagendorf's opinion, actually working with children was an excellent means of developing a dramatic literature on their level.

The large publishing houses, meanwhile, had contributed little in this area. An exception was Samuel French, Inc., in New York, which had for some time included a few appropriate plays among its published works. The oldest extant catalogue (1882) of the French company listed twelve children's plays and a few classified as "Fairy and Home Plays." The catalogues from 1910 to 1924 listed twenty-eight "Fairy and Home Plays," twenty-one other children's plays, and five scripts with music. From that year on there was a steady though slow increase, although the number of published scripts, as compared with adult drama, has always been slight.

Whereas in the decade from 1910 to 1920 children's theatre was characterized by its spread among community organizations, in the twenties it underwent a broader type of expansion. The trend toward community sponsorship of children's dramatic work continued but formed two separate movements. One of these was the effort of the little or civic theatres to expand their activities by including plays for young people as well as adults.

[11] "Children's Plays," *Theatre Arts Monthly*, Vol. VIII (December, 1924), 831–35.

The other movement was that inaugurated by the playgrounds and community centers, which was somewhat different in regard to objectives, organization, program, and public appeal.

In the first movement the children's theatre, no matter how successful, was a branch of the adult organization and, as such, was of secondary importance to the sponsoring agent. According to the report of the Drama League, from one to four productions a year were presented, for the purpose of providing good entertainment for child audiences. While the major objective was community service, the descriptions of colorful, beautiful presentations of well-known children's plays would indicate that artistry was an important concern. Since relatively few children in the community could participate in this type of play, with its small cast (as opposed to the pageant, with masses involved), some selectivity was necessarily practiced. In many instances classes in acting, stagecraft, and even playwriting supplemented the program; in this way instruction and participation could be offered to those children who were not in the casts for the public performances.

The other type of community effort, the program sponsored by playgrounds and recreational centers, was typified by its primary concern for masses of neighborhood children. While dramatics had been preceded by other kinds of recreational activity, it was neither subservient to nor in competition with the existing programs. Since it was often a part of the summer playground plans, it functioned to a greater extent during the summer than in the winter months. It was frequently held out of doors with the idea of maximum participation; thus, pageants, parades, and plays with large casts of boys and girls took precedence over the literary play with few characters, which could be staged and heard to better advantage indoors. In many cases music and dance were included in the productions, but there was an over-all emphasis on the recreational and social values to children, rather than on spectacle and artistry.

Both forms of children's theatre could, therefore, develop independently, each fulfilling its own purpose and each organized in accordance with its own ends. The interest of the Association of Junior Leagues of America in furthering the movement through its various chapters was another step, which, by 1929, may be interpreted as a trend in community service. While its program was to undergo considerable change within the next decade, children's theatre was during these years an important phase of Junior League work.

Meanwhile, as the community drama was flourishing indoors and on the playground, the educational program was also expanding. The interest in school plays, which had spread during the preceding decade, continued to grow. There was a significant change in attitude toward educational drama, however, during the twenties. Drama was now in many quarters acknowledged to be one of the most important features of a modern child's education. Perhaps the best summary of activity at the end of the decade was made by Kenneth Macgowan in 1929. In the first systematic attempt to tabulate groups, he pointed out the existence of approximately one thousand college and community producing organizations in the United States. He noted that at least seven thousand high schools had introduced courses in dramatics; there were, as a result, thousands of young people producing plays and pageants.[12] The absence of any strong national organization, dedicated to the raising of standards, was a serious lack, but it would not be long before educators were to assume a leadership role and unite in the interest of the best in school and college theatre.

The appearance of Clare Tree Major's professional plays for children was significant for two reasons: it was the first commercial venture to meet with financial success, and it was to become the first touring company devoted exclusively to children's entertainment. Viewed in retrospect, however, probably the most significant achievement of the postwar years was the stimulation of a love for the theatre. Upon this base were to grow institutions of far-reaching influence and lasting importance to this branch of the living theatre.

[12] Macgowan, *Footlights Across America*.

V

Expansion in Depression

1930-40

The years 1930 to 1940 were unhappy years in American theatre history. The financial depression which struck the country dealt Broadway a savage blow at the beginning of the decade and continued to plague it until 1939. Empty theatres, bankrupt producers, unemployed actors, and the collapse of the road show were obvious signs of the nation's economic plight. As a desperate measure, designed to alleviate the situation, there appeared for the first time in America government-subsidized theatre. The Federal Theatre, short-lived as it was destined to be, made its impact on the cultural life of the nation.

While Broadway was suffering the crippling effects of the depression, theatre for children continued to thrive. Since the commercial theatre had never played a major role in its development in this country, drama for children did not suffer from the bankruptcy of producers or from severely curtailed commercial production. The advent of the Federal Theatre, however, did affect juvenile entertainment and became within the span of its three-year existence one of the most vigorous enterprises in children's theatre history. This relief measure, which appeared in the 1935–36 season, had a singularly stimulating effect upon children's theatre, which had until then been largely in the hands of amateurs and educators.

The relatively low budget used by amateur dramatic groups

and the fact that the amateur theatre was established to meet certain recreational, social, and educational objectives were factors in the ability of the amateurs to survive. Many amateur groups did fail during the depression years but, according to Glenn Hughes, there were 105 well-established community theatres in 1939 as compared to the 69 of ten years before.[1] *Recreation Magazine* (formerly *The Playground*) likewise indicated an expanding and well-organized program of activities in this area as compared with the preceding decade. Drama had become a more acceptable inclusion in the elementary-school curriculum, although informal and creative dramatics took precedence over a formally organized program of plays. On the college and university level, more programs for child audiences were reported in the professional journals during the thirties than in any period to date.

Despite the difficulties being encountered by the professional theatre, several important groups, whose work was directed to children, were launched. Some of these survived the decade and only one was terminated by the advent of World War II. The year 1931 saw the demise of the Drama League, but the Association of Junior Leagues of America, by changing the direction of its activities, emerged as a stronger and more vital force. Finally, the American National Theatre and Academy was chartered, although it did not begin to function for another ten years. Since each of the categories thus far mentioned—community, educational, professional, and national theatres—included plays for child audiences, it can be stated that the children's theatre movement during the thirties, unlike the adult professional theatre, was receiving wide and continued support.

National Organizations

Two national organizations, the Association of Junior Leagues of America and the Federal Theatre, placed particular emphasis

[1] *A History of the American Theatre*, 419.

upon children's entertainment. Since the Drama League ceased to function in 1931, its contribution during this decade was negligible.

THE ASSOCIATION OF JUNIOR LEAGUES OF AMERICA

The Association of Junior Leagues of America, which had attracted attention during the twenties for its lavish productions of plays for child audiences, continued its work. According to Mary Ciaccio, 1930 to 1932 were "peak years,"[2] so far as the large centralized performances were concerned. The first Junior League Children's Theatre Conference held in Chicago in 1930 marked, in a sense, an epoch in organized amateur dramatics. Young women from fifty-five different cities throughout the country gathered to discuss procedures and problems. It was apparent that the Junior League had an opportunity to build up an original and entirely American type of theatre for children. Because of its national organization and the leisure time of its members, it could afford to seek and try out new plays as well as to help educate young audiences for the appreciation of good living theatre.

Although the work being done at this time was attracting attention among Leagues and persons interested in children's entertainment, it underwent a major change in 1932. This was the result of the Junior League Conference on children's theatre held in Cleveland, Ohio, which was to change the direction of the League work in regard to both policy and organization. The big centralized productions had been available only to children whose families could afford to buy expensive tickets and to groups of children from institutions who were recipients of free admission. The conference suggested that only by studying the communities in which plays were given could larger and broader audiences be reached. Accordingly the Association sent a field representative to the individual Leagues to help each discover

[2] *Prologue to Production*, 6.

its own best channel of production. This action led to co-operation with various community organizations, including the public schools. The new policy of local performances on a small and much less expensive scale made touring possible; thus, an entirely new method of production evolved. The touring program was successful and has continued to the present day. The national headquarters continued to give help, though individual Leagues have always been autonomous within their communities.

"Grand Rapids and Cincinnati were the first Junior Leagues to undertake an in-school trouping program."[3] According to an ANTA survey in 1950, the Junior League of Milwaukee Children's Theatre was approved by the public-school system in 1933 but was not granted permission to give plays in school time until 1944. The service of taking plays to the schools has grown, and in many instances, in addition to giving the time and space for plays, the teachers have co-operated by preparing the children in advance through materials supplied by the League.

San Francisco in 1934 was the first city to establish a co-operative community effort, the Junior League and the Children's Theatre Association. Since then dozens of community children's theatres, bureaus, and councils, for both planning and production, have been formed under League leadership with the total community's participation and support. During the mid-thirties, as some professional productions became available, the Junior League was able to supplement its own programs by acting as sponsor.

Despite some fluctuations in total number of productions from year to year, the Junior League's program has continued to expand since 1936. Training courses and workshops were developed throughout the country, and under the children's theatre department of the Association of Junior Leagues of America standards of organization, management, and productions were checked systematically.

The Junior League of Lynchburg, Virginia, and the Lynch-

[3] Wyatt Jones, "The Junior League Story," *Town and Country*, Vol. CX (August, 1956), 53.

burg Little Theatre, which combined in 1938, has been cited for its outstanding success. The schools, Parent-Teacher Association, merchants, newspapers, and radio station promised support, with the result that the whole town became aware of the venture. Tickets which sold for ten cents paid for only about half the cost of the production; the deficit was made up by the Lynchburg treasury. Since the auditorium of the Little Theatre held only three hundred, eight or ten performances had to be given in order to take care of the thousand or more children who wanted to see the plays. Local bus companies co-operated by taking children to the theatre and back to school at the low school children's fare. Two boards directed the project: one was an advisory board made up of representatives of the Little Theatre, Parent-Teacher Association, art supervisors of the schools, and the League; the other was composed of the president of the League and the production managers who did the actual work of putting on the show. World War II halted the progress of the Lynchburg enterprise, but by the 1946–47 season activities had been resumed.

Regarding national activity, the following report was made for the 1939–40 season: The Junior Leagues of twenty-five different cities presented Junior Programs, Inc. In some cities they sponsored Clare Tree Major's Children's Theatre. In others they continued a close affiliation with little theatres, putting on plays and occasionally using children in them. Sixty Leagues trouped plays to the public schools. The children's theatre group of the Los Angeles Junior League, as an example, traveled over five hundred miles to give nineteen performances of *Cinderella* in outlying public schools.[4]

The outstanding nonprofit organization sponsoring and producing children's plays was unquestionably the Association of Junior Leagues of America. Virginia Lee Comer was children's theatre advisor during this time and has been given credit for much of the success of the program. Hundreds of volunteer

[4] Susan Welty, "In the Children's Theatres," *Players Magazine*, Vol. XVII (November, 1940), 19.

workers throughout the country, however, were needed to carry out the details of so ambitious an enterprise.

THE AMERICAN NATIONAL THEATRE AND ACADEMY

The American National Theatre and Academy (ANTA) came into being in the thirties but did not function until ten years after its founding. The idea of a national organization, financed by federal funds and dedicated to the furthering of both professional and nonprofessional theatres in this country, was first presented to President Franklin D. Roosevelt in 1933. He was cordial to the idea and suggested that specific aims and plans for implementation be worked out. The following year such plans were completed and presented for his approval. On July 5, 1935, a bill was passed by Congress and signed by the President, giving the American National Theatre and Academy official recognition. According to publications from the national headquarters in New York, ANTA was a national organization of theatre services, information, and activities, Congressionally chartered and independently financed by its members and interested donors. It was dedicated to the purpose of extending the living theatre by bringing the best in the theatre to every state in the nation.

The depression was responsible for the inactivity of the American National Theatre and Academy for the first few years. The Federal Theatre project, an emergency measure financed by federal funds, took precedence over it and functioned actively for a three-year period. World War II followed, and during that time it seemed inadvisable to begin an important national art program. Thus ANTA lay dormant until 1945. Inasmuch as its work belongs to a later period, a discussion of administration, organization, and activities will be reserved for the time in which they were actually put into practice. The groundwork for this important organization, however, was laid in the early thirties, and children's theatre was one of the areas included in its plans. One major point of difference between ANTA and the Federal Theatre was that while the former was federally chartered, it was to be privately financed; the latter, established as a relief measure, received immediate government funds.

THE FEDERAL THEATRE

From one point of view the Federal Theatre could be considered professional theatre. The actors were paid and, in most instances, had been professional until the effects of the depression had put them out of work. On the other hand, since the Federal Theatre was established and administered by the government and financed by federal funds, it differed from the commercial theatre in that it was not dependent upon box-office receipts for its existence. Perhaps it can best be described as a national theatre composed, in the main, of professional actors but not commercial in respect to the relationship between investment and profit. Finally, since it could be (and was) terminated by an act of Congress, it differed completely from the commercial theatre which is financed and directed as private business and continued only so long as it is deemed profitable.

The Federal Theatre, an emergency relief measure offering entertainment to the public and employment to actors, was established on April 8, 1935, by Congress, under the direction of Hallie Flanagan of Vassar College. Three important points were made at the time of its founding: persons employed were to be taken from the relief roles of the states; to those employed, work was to be offered within their own skills and trades; those who could not do the work were to be returned to the care of their states.[5]

Theatre leaders who attended the first meeting of regional and state directors in October, 1935, represented many kinds of background and achievement. From the professional theatre came Eddie Dowling, Elmer Rice, Charles Coburn, and Hiram Motherwell; from the universities came E. C. Mabie, Frederick Koch, and Glenn Hughes; from the community theatres came Thomas Wood Stevens, Jasper Deeter, Frederic McConnell, and Gilmor Brown; and from *Theatre Arts Monthly* came Rosamond Gilder. The aim of these leaders was to set up theatres which could grow

[5] Hallie Flanagan, *Arena*, 16.

into social institutions in the communities in which they were located, thus providing possible future employment for at least some of the persons connected with them. It was further hoped that a new and truly creative theatre in the United States might be established. The plan called for the organization of regional producing centers which would recognize the different geographic areas, their traditions and interests, customs, language patterns, and occupations.

The Federal Theatre, in accordance with this aim, was established in many cities throughout the country. Since our concern is with children's theatre, only the work done in that area will be discussed, although it constituted but one aspect of the offerings of the Federal Theatre during the years 1936 to 1939. Statistics compiled from the files of the National Service Bureau in Washington revealed that drama for children was presented in the following cities throughout the country during those years: New York, New York; Gary, Indiana; Los Angeles, California; Seattle, Washington; New Haven, Connecticut; Portland, Oregon; Cleveland, Ohio; Denver, Colorado; and Tampa, Florida.

One of the cities in which this activity was most extensive was New York. On June 2, 1936, the Federal Children's Theatre opened at the Adelphi Theatre with *The Emperor's New Clothes*. Reviews were good and after its original run, it was taken on tour and played on portable stages in parks. Over 100,000 persons, mostly children, were said to have seen it in the following six weeks.

Encouraged by the success of this opening production, the local administration wanted to establish a program which would continue to meet the theatre needs and interests of the children who made up its audience. In order to gauge these interests, questionnaires were sent out from the office of the New York Children's Theatre Division to the heads of a large number of settlement houses. The results, based upon past experiences of the directors, indicated that the age group from four to seven preferred fairy and historical plays; the age group from eight to eleven preferred adventure and historical fantasy; and the age group from twelve to sixteen preferred operettas and more serious works. In addition to this survey, a group of educators headed by Lois Hayden Meek, director of the Child Development Institute of Teachers College, Columbia University, was studying audience response. The stated policy of the Federal Children's Theatre was that no plays would be given which provided entertainment only. The plan of organization was to include a circuit of theatres for children which would be set up in theatres, schools, settlements, and parks. The first run was to take place in a centrally located theatre building, after which the play would travel to these neighborhood centers.

The second year in New York brought a production of *The Revolt of the Beavers* for younger children and *Flight*, an aviation chronicle, for children somewhat older. The former aroused some controversy as to its entertainment value and as to possible Communist propaganda behind it. Since the Federal Theatre project was frequently under attack, these criticisms neither frightened the administration nor changed its policy. It is perhaps pertinent to include at this point a statement by Hallie Flanagan, regarding the selection of plays: "Washington did not dictate individual plays, leaving such choice to the various directors, with, however, the suggestion of emphasis on new American plays, classical plays, children's plays and a special program for Negro companies."[6]

One highly successful Federal Children's Theatre project was established in Cleveland, Ohio. It began operation inauspiciously in March, 1937, in a radio-station garage. From its unpublicized opening before an audience of only sixty-seven children, it developed into an important institution of the city, playing to thousands of boys and girls every week. Performances were toured to the public schools and given during school time. Some of Cleveland's most prominent musicians, designers, and dancers contributed to its effects. Cleveland's theatre for youth, directed by Elbert P. Sargent, was a unique enterprise. It was the only one

6 *Ibid.*, 200.

whose primary object was theatre for children. In less than two years it grew to a theatre of impressive size. Staffed by professional adults, it was a theatre such as many communities had often dreamed of.

Another effective Federal Children's Theatre group, according to reports written during the period of its operation, was the one in Gary, Indiana. In this city children were the actors under Federal Theatre supervision. The six hundred interested children were divided into fourteen different units. These units were both musical and dramatic and often combined in offering programs to child audiences. The opening production of this theatre was *Expedition to the North Pole*, a dramatization from A. A. Milne's *Winnie the Pooh*.

Traveling across the country during those years, one could see various regional groups at work. In New Orleans children and young people were deeply involved in playmaking as a result of the new national organization. In Chicago the children's play series, which had built up a following with *Rip Van Winkle* and *A Letter to Santa Claus*, opened a new production of *The Emperor's New Clothes* in June, 1939. *Little Black Sambo* and *The Bandbox Review* were advertised for a summer's touring through the city's parks.

In Cincinnati a fine project was built from a discouraging start. The theatre was housed in its own building and was offering opera, adult drama, and plays for children throughout the state. On the West Coast there was unusual activity reported in Pasadena. Two new productions of *Hansel and Gretel* and *Pinocchio* were praised for their extraordinary beauty and imaginative production.

In Portland, Oregon, there were difficulties encountered in trying to present *Night Beat*, an original Christmas play by George Wilhelm, assistant director of the project, who set Roark Bradford's *Christmas Sermon* against a background of Negro spirituals and carols. Questions were raised because it had no manger and no Wise Men; but after a public-school committee had seen it at a private showing, all opposition vanished. The play was booked by schools, churches, and settlements; at the municipal auditorium it played before three thousand children.

In Seattle the group reported difficulty at first because most of the people had to be sold on theatre itself. A children's revue, *Mother Goose Goes to Town*, began to attract the public. But it was not until a Negro company took the leadership in a program entitled *Br'er Rabbit and Tar Baby* and *An Evening with Dunbar* that Seattle really responded.

Besides the actual producing of plays for child audiences, the Federal Children's Theatre was concerned with the following: research—to determine the best times for performances and the most suitable admission charges; promotional problems—to get the co-operation of school principals in taking children to the plays; repertory problems—to find appropriate plays for presentation; audience analysis—to determine the reactions of children to the plays; caravan theatre—to take plays out to the parks during the summer; festivals—to present Christmas festivals during Christmas week; dance-project production—to introduce dance as entertainment to audiences of children; theatre for youth—to attempt to set up theatre for high-school students; and community-drama division—to send dramatic directors to settlements and neighborhood centers.

Despite Hallie Flanagan's satisfaction with the results of the project and the enthusiastic reception which it received in many quarters throughout the country, the Federal Theatre, including the Federal Children's Theatre, was ended by an Act of Congress on June 30, 1939. Ostensibly, it was ended for economic reasons, although the three years of its existence had been fraught with criticism regarding the subsidizing of art, the establishment of a theatre as a relief measure, and suspicion of Communist influence.

Whatever the shortcomings of the Federal Theatre may have been, it was a far-reaching experiment which brought living drama to many communities in the United States which might otherwise never have had it. Because it was not dependent upon the box office for its existence, it could afford to try out new techniques and new scripts. Many young actors and writers were given their start by the Federal Theatre. The children's branch was conceded to be one of its most successful activities, introducing thousands of boys and girls to this form of entertainment. While it did not last long enough to see the development of an art in which each region and eventually each state would have its unique, indigenous dramatic expression, the record shows a new school of playwriting and new production techniques which were made possible by a government-subsidized organization. At its best the Federal Theatre was a bold experiment which, in addition to its other contributions, gave an unexpected and vigorous boost to the children's theatre movement. How much it affected the future development of children's theatre can only be surmised, but there is no doubt about its having introduced thousands of children to this branch of the performing arts.

The Educational Theatre

The educational theatre, according to articles in contemporary periodicals and to questionnaires later sent out by ANTA, continued to spread. On elementary, secondary, and college levels, classes, clubs, and dramatic activities were being established. During the twenties some educators and parents were endorsing the idea of drama as a worth-while curricular inclusion. By the thirties articles on the subject, written for professional journals, voiced criticism of existing practices or suggestions for improvement, rather than defensive arguments for its acceptance.

There was early objection to drama's being admitted into the curriculum until it had proved itself. But by this decade the strong appeal of the work and gratifying results had resulted in an almost universal welcome of the dramatic arts in the curricula of progressive schools throughout the country. The distinction between creative dramatics and children's theatre was being recognized in more and more instances, with a greater use of the former in elementary-school classes, particularly in the more progressive schools. The organized dramatic club or school theatre, however, existed in the majority of high schools, and educators raised serious questions regarding objectives. There was growing feeling that a program which tended to place the emphasis upon the result rather than upon the educational and social values of the literature was undesirable. Drama, because of its wide scope of appeal and usage, was becoming recognized as one of the greatest unifying agents in the curriculum.

During this period there was also concern for various aspects of children's dramatics. Some teachers described their use of children's classics, ballads, and other worth-while stories, which they dramatized rather than using mediocre material which was available in printed form. There was further recognition of the values to be gained from studying and organizing literary material. Drama was accepted not only as an aid to the study of English literature; it was also acknowledged as a means of teaching composition.

With so much interest in the content and purpose of educational drama, it is not surprising to discover that a number of enduring dramatic departments on the university level were established during this time. On the elementary level much of the activity was carried on within the school program and without publicity. One notable exception to this, however, was the Little Theatre for Children in Stoneham, Massachusetts.

THE LITTLE THEATRE FOR CHILDREN

The Stoneham children's theatre was originated by Beverley Freitag, a fourth-grade teacher.[7] While it was established in a school, it received publicity as an effective community contribution. Beverley Freitag envisioned a theatre for and by children, and with the help of Everett Getschell of Boston University and Clayton Gilbert of the New England Conservatory of Music, she formulated plans for its establishment in 1933. Beverley Freitag was well acquainted with both children's literature and play production and was an experienced teacher of boys and girls. Her

---

[7] Lillian Foster Collins, "The Little Theatre in School," *Drama*, Vol. XX (November, 1929), 52.

objectives were to provide children with wholesome entertainment at their own interest level and to give them an opportunity to express themselves in drama under proper guidance.

Children from the first through the ninth grades were eligible for participation. Plays were given every five weeks, with tickets priced at twenty-five cents for children and fifty cents for adults. The art supervisor was in charge of scenery and costumes, and a list of patrons expressed community approval of the project. The greatest significance of the enterprise was in terms of community interest and enthusiasm. As much a community project as it was a school theatre, it has been included in the latter category because it was established by a teacher in a school with definite educational aims. At the time of its founding it represented a most unusual venture.

MILLS COLLEGE CHILDREN'S THEATRE

On the college level, meanwhile, considerable activity was taking place. Mills College in California began a program of children's plays in 1931. This program, although it subsequently developed into an important offering, was begun as a means to an end. The end was the experience of young adults in working with and for children. In the beginning, volunteer teaching of dramatics to children, directing of plays for child audiences, and dramatization of juvenile stories were the skills that the college deemed of greatest importance. When the value of this work was recognized, course credit was given; but when the response of the children in the community to the work of the college was manifested, the objectives were broadened to include the audience. The "means" thus became another end. Since the arts were an important aspect of the Mills College curriculum, it was natural that music and dance should be correlated with the drama. The program, which began with two dramatic productions given at Christmas time and in the spring, developed over the years into a season of seven plays, in which music, dance, and drama were carefully integrated.

SYRACUSE UNIVERSITY CENTER

Syracuse University, mentioned in the preceding chapter, embarked on a full-scale program in 1930 under the direction of Sawyer Falk. Children's Theatre was an example of the belief in theatre as a true community activity which should be a part of the people's everyday life and not something connected only with Broadway.

While the organization of the children's theatre has varied from time to time, the supervision has always rested with the university. Rehearsals were held at different places in the city, with classes on Saturday mornings on the campus. Thus, Syracuse University, a semipublic institution, became an integral part of the community by contributing to its recreational and educational program.

TERRE HAUTE CHILDREN'S THEATRE

Among educational theatres on the college level which included plays for children was the Terre Haute Children's Theatre, connected with the State Teachers College. Similar to the Children's Theatres at Tulsa and Syracuse, it was developed as a combination college and community project. Rollo Farmer, the first director, began the program in 1931 with *Ali Baba*, which was enthusiastically received by the youthful audience. Its activity has continued to the present day and still retains the college-community emphasis.

THE ADELPHI COLLEGE CHILDREN'S THEATRE

From the beginning the Adelphi College Children's Theatre was different from the other theatres thus far described in its focus on an integrated arts experience for the education of both child and adult. Its goals were set in 1937 and they have remained constant, though the program has grown and the name has since been changed to the Children's Center for the Creative Arts. There has always been recognition of new ideas and new techniques at Adelphi, but these have been used to enhance the program, not to change it. In brief, the Adelphi concept of a children's theatre was a meeting place, which would serve the child by providing workshops in the arts and, at the same time, serve the college student as a laboratory for experience with children. It should further serve the community through providing speakers, conferences, information, and touring productions by adults for children.

While these services did not all take place in the beginning, they have been developed over the years. Weekly classes in dramatic arts at the college and in a public school in Cedarhurst, an extension of the Adelphi Children's Theatre sponsored by the Five Towns Music and Art Foundation, have served the interests of many children. The needs of the college students preparing for teaching were likewise recognized, and an opportunity to participate in the program as well as to take courses in the education and arts departments correlated theatre experience with the students' major interests. Performances have always been the result of class activity and are shared within the educational program rather than in public. According to Grace Stanistreet, director of the Adelphi Children's Theatre:

> It provides children with the opportunity for pleasure, experience, and study in the arts. It is called a theatre because the arts are integrated and meaningful in this, which is a natural medium of expression for children and which offers keen enjoyment to them from either side of the proscenium.[8]

UNIVERSITY OF IOWA CHILDREN'S THEATRE

A children's theatre located at the University of Iowa was carrying on an extensive program in 1932. It was known to have assumed a position of leadership, attaining a high degree of excellence.

THE GOODMAN CHILDREN'S THEATRE

The Goodman Children's Theatre of the Art Institute of Chi-

[8] "What is Adelphi Children's Theatre?"

cago, founded in 1925, had become by the thirties an established cultural institution in the Chicago area. While it could be described as a community theatre, since it emphasized the presentation of worth-while plays for local audiences of children, the fact that it was maintained by a school of the theatre rather than a community playhouse places it more appropriately in the category of educational theatre. The Art Institute, the tuition of the students, and the box-office receipts continued its support, while third-year students acted in the plays.

The late Charlotte Chorpenning, whose name has been linked with the Goodman Theatre since 1931, accepted the position of director of children's plays in the spring of that year. Prior to her appointment she had taught at the Winona State Teachers College, Hull House, and Northwestern University. Despite her long and distinguished association with the Goodman Children's Theatre, she is probably best known throughout the country for her playwriting and dramatization of children's stories. Her contribution to the field of juvenile dramatic literature was outstanding, both as to quantity and quality of work. As a theatre director, she was able to study audience reactions; and as a writer, she was able to put these observations to literary use.

During her first years at the Goodman six plays a season were presented. This number was later cut down to four but additional weekend performances were given. Despite the increased number of performances, the theatre was sold out six weeks in advance. The popularity of the Goodman plays has persisted through the years even though there have been a number of other excellent groups presenting theatre for children in the Chicago area.

Charlotte Chorpenning's own major purpose, as she defined it midway in her career, was to give the children in the audience useful experience through their identification with the characters in the dramas. She believed that the moral or philosophic meaning of a play belonged in the story and not in the dialogue alone. Her observations on what interested children of each age level are still a valuable guide to the playwright, and the list of her published scripts constitutes a large portion of the bibliographies of children's theatre plays. Charlotte Chorpenning's death in 1955 was a loss not only to the Goodman Theatre but to the children's theatre movement in the United States.

OTHER CHILDREN'S THEATRES IN EDUCATIONAL INSTITUTIONS

Other schools and colleges whose children's theatres were founded in the thirties were the Idaho State College and the Wilmington, Delaware, High School, in 1930; the Champaign, Illinois, High School and the Superior State College in Michigan, in 1935; and the University of Michigan and Wayne University in Detroit, in 1939.[9]

Also mentioned in periodicals during this period were the Children's Theatre of the State Teachers College of St. Cloud, Minnesota, and the Children's Theatre of the University of Nebraska in 1937; and the summer program of children's plays at Coe College in Iowa in 1938.

Among the private studios producing children's plays, the following began operation during these years: the Randall Junior Playhouse in Hartford, Connecticut, and the Sharp School of Speech in Seaford, Delaware, in 1930; the Children's Studios of Speech and Dramatic Arts in Washington, D.C., the Children's Studio of Speech and Dramatic Arts in Chevy Chase, Maryland, and the Armand School of Dance and Drama in Detroit, in 1932; the Tucson Children's Theatre in Tucson, Arizona, in 1933; the Perry Mansfield Summer Studio and the Children's Theatre of Wilkes Barre, Pennsylvania, in 1935; and the Children's Players of Hazel Aamodt in Minneapolis, in 1939.[10] While many of these studios had community support, they may be considered more properly as educational theatres since they were set up with a definite curriculum for instruction and were financed independently rather than by public funds.

[9] The 1951 Survey made by the American National Theatre and Academy.
[10] *Ibid.*

These examples of children's theatres, which were founded by educational institutions or established as private studios for instruction in the dramatic arts, indicate that the strong trend toward drama in education was continuing. The frequent references to in-school plays in periodicals of this period show that activity of a more informal nature was also taking place. In both the formal and informal drama programs, the geographical spread of institutions cited points to a national rather than a regional interest in this type of activity. And, finally, the announcement of the forthcoming American Educational Theatre Conference in December, 1938, at which a session devoted to Children's Theatre was planned, is evidence of the serious interest of educators in the nature and problems of this aspect of dramatic work.

Children's Theatre
in Community and Recreation Centers

The community theatre movement, which had gathered momentum during the twenties, likewise continued. The two directions which it had taken, activity on the part of little theatre groups and activity on the part of recreational centers, were still apparent, although in some instances several community organizations joined forces in the promotion of a particularly ambitious program. By and large, however, the two types of activity persisted into the thirties, serving, as they had in the twenties, different purposes and different needs.

Recreation during these years had undergone great expansion and quantitative growth. With this growth had come a more democratic attitude, illustrated by the participation of many persons in community affairs rather than the charitable contributions of a few philanthropists and by the supplanting of private funds with public support of the recreational centers. In addition to the continued popularity of the physical activities, there had developed many strong programs in all of the arts.

PHILADELPHIA RECREATION CENTER

The drama program of the playgrounds and recreation centers was changing somewhat as it became more sharply focused and more widespread. Articles contemporaneous with the movement indicated a shift of emphasis from the promotion of projects to the education and training of leaders. For example, a report made on the Philadelphia Recreation Center by W. D. Champlin in 1932 stated that an experimental program for dramatic directors conducted the previous year had been so successful that it was being repeated.[11] This program was oriented to fundamentals of organizational training and production in the fifteen centers maintained by the Philadelphia Bureau of Recreation. Clubs and groups in the various centers ranged in age from eight to twenty-five years, and members were reported to have participated in seventy-eight plays the preceding year. Eleven hundred players took part as members of casts, while thousands enjoyed the performances as spectators. As a part of the institute, a play-finding committee was appointed to present lists of plays suited to particular age groups and occasions. From these lists books and plays were purchased, thereby forming the nucleus of a community drama library. A central workshop for scenery and costumes was also established for the use and convenience of all.

THE BROOKLYN INSTITUTE

Another institute was held in Brooklyn during the spring of 1932. All phases of production for children from ten to fourteen were studied. Twenty-three playgrounds produced plays as a result, and in many instances it was the beginning of a summer drama program.

THE TEXAS INSTITUTE

A third type of institute was conducted in Texas in 1933 and

[11] "An Experiment in Drama," *Recreation*, Vol. XXV (February, 1932), 617, 640.

was of state-wide scope. The National Recreation Association in co-operation with the Bureau of Agriculture established a series of local institutes for rural leaders in which music, drama, and dance were included. It was apparently highly successful in educating and stimulating leaders to this type of community work. As a result of the institutes conducted in the state of Texas by some of the workers of the NRA, many rural communities were for the first time able to experience live theatre and dance.

THE WESTCHESTER COUNTY PROGRAM

Not an institute but a centralized program of activities was established in Westchester County, New York. It has often been cited for its splendid organization and community support. A centralized, efficient, and experienced organization, the Westchester County Recreation Center undertook the task of advising and helping in the local programs, conducting at the same time a year-round program of its own. Twenty-seven little theatre groups, including children and adults, were affiliated with the Westchester Dramatic Association.

MIAMI BEACH, FLORIDA

Besides the institutes and large centralized programs, successful individual activities were scattered throughout the nation. For example, Miami Beach, Florida, was said to possess an outstanding dramatic program for children and adults under the sponsorship of its department of recreation.

BOSTON PLAYGROUND PROGRAM

In Boston a pageant wagon, in the manner of its medieval forerunner, was the means of taking plays to the parks and playgrounds of the city. A huge red and yellow wagon, with one of the sides let down to make a platform, traveled for the first time during the summer of 1932 under the auspices of Boston's Community Service and the City Park Department. Two casts of children for each production provided increased opportunities for acting. Hundreds of children in the metropolitan area saw classical plays as a result of this enterprise.

MILWAUKEE MUNICIPAL THEATRE

A traveling theatre was also a feature of the Municipal Children's Theatre of Milwaukee. Organized in 1930 by the department of municipal recreation, it operated both summer and winter with an average of thirteen productions and eighty performances a year.

THE PALO ALTO CHILDREN'S THEATRE

One of the extraordinarily successful ventures planned and executed during the thirties was the Children's Theatre of Palo Alto, California. A part of the community center, it included in addition to the children's theatre an adult theatre, a children's library and museum, a swimming pool, and extensive equipment for recreation. The children's theatre, a modern and well-equipped building, was the gift of the late Mrs. Louis Stern, one of Palo Alto's leading citizens. Many articles have been written about the center during the years of its existence, but the most complete story is to be found in the book *Children and the Theatre* by Caroline Fisher and Hazel Robertson, both of whom have worked closely with it from the beginning.

The Palo Alto Children's Community Theatre began activities in 1932 in a renovated wartime USO center. A part-time director was appointed, and within a few months the first members of the advisory board had been named. There were five charter members but after the writing of the constitution, ten new members were added. Eventually there were on the board a city librarian, both public- and private-school principals, a scout representative, a university professor, social leaders, mothers, and a children's photographer. The aims set up at this time were to create a love of the beautiful by means of the dramatic arts and to afford entertainment and recreation for the children of Palo Alto by means of a permanent year-round program.

When the children's theatre was moved into its new home in 1935 it was a popular and well-organized activity. The first season in the new quarters was opened with both old and new plays of literary quality which called for colorful production. *Beauty's Beast* was the opening production and was followed by *Silver Caverns* in October, *Hansel and Gretel* in November, *Star of the Sea* (Christmas pageant) in December, *Seven Come Eleven* in January, *Jack-in-the-Box Revue* in February, and *Land of the Cards* in March. Settings and costumes were elaborate and colorful, for it was believed by the staff that children's plays needed particular emphasis on the visual effects.

Toward the end of the decade, the onset of World War II increased rather than diminished its activity. In addition to the eight plays provided during the school year, a twelve-month program was planned, to which any child could belong for a membership fee of fifty cents. While the building itself had been a private gift, city funds were appropriated for its maintenance, and the recreation department assumed responsibility for its administration. In its pioneering in city ownership of a children's theatre, Palo Alto has been called unique; it operated the only completely tax-supported children's theatre in the country. Because of the interest shown by other communities in this project, the Palo Alto Theatre prepared a documentary film which pictured and explained its method of operation.

THE CAIN PARK SUMMER THEATRE

An extensive summer program for children which began operation during this period was the Cain Park open-air theatre in Cleveland Heights, Ohio. The park, owned and operated by the city, began children's work in 1938 under the direction of Dina Rees Evans, at that time director of dramatic activities at Cleveland Heights High School. Although the Cain Park season included a full program of plays and musicals for adults, the children's offerings were an important aspect of its contribution to the community. A combined children's theatre and school, it also included classes in creative dramatics, puppetry, music, art, and dance.

OTHER PROGRAMS UNDER THE SPONSORSHIP OF RECREATION CENTERS

A few other cities were mentioned briefly in *The Playground* as having well-established dramatic programs for children under the sponsorship of their recreation centers: New Haven, Connecticut; Sacramento, California; Cincinnati, Ohio; Louisville, Kentucky; York, Pennsylvania; and Bloomfield, New Jersey. It is apparent from the number of programs cited that community interest in drama for young people was widespread. While in the majority of cases the programs were instigated by previously organized recreation centers, in a few instances they were the result of the work of civic committees. The objective, regardless of origin, was stated to be good entertainment, or dramatic programs which included good entertainment, for all of the interested children in the community.

THE WASHINGTON STATE THEATRE

A children's theatre, sponsored neither by a city nor by a community playhouse, was the Theatre of Youth located in the state of Washington, which apparently came into existence as the immediate result of the interest stimulated by the Repertory Playhouse Civic Theatre of Seattle. The Seattle theatre presented Shakespearean plays before thousands of children in Seattle and neighboring cities during the early thirties. A 1936 appropriation of $32,000 from the Rockefeller Foundation, to be used over a three-year period, financed the project, with supervision by the state department of education. A committee of citizens, teachers, and public-school officials was given the responsibility of administration. The company, described as young, vigorous, and enthusiastic, toured the state with productions of the classics.

Portrayed as the first state theatre in America, it was an experiment in the field of theatre and education. Seventeen areas were organized, with performance centers in each. Maynard Lee Daggy of the State College in Pullman, Washington, wrote of the enthusiastic reception which the first tour received in his city. Children and college students as well as citizens of Pullman crowded the auditorium for *The Comedy of Errors*. During the 1936–37 season forty-five evening performances and twenty-eight children's matinees of this play were given. Local sponsors, believing in the value of this experiment, handled the business arrangements as the company toured the seventeen specified areas.

THE CHILDREN'S ENTERTAINMENT COMMITTEE OF MAPLEWOOD, NEW JERSEY

Another program designed to bring music, drama, and art to the children of the community was located in Maplewood, New Jersey. The Children's Entertainment Committee was founded in October, 1933, as a result of discussions by the Parent-Teacher Association and the National Music League of Boston. Even though it did not emanate from a recreation center, the Children's Entertainment Committee had an advantage similar to the programs described earlier in that, from the beginning, it received wide community support.

The fourteen organizations represented at the time of its establishment were twelve Parent-Teacher Association groups, the Women's Club of Maplewood, and the Milburn Women's Club. Representatives from each of these groups, together with the elected officers, formed a committee of thirty-seven active members. The chairman of the committee was Dorothy McFadden, a Maplewood parent who was interested in securing good entertainment for her own children and those of her neighbors. For the next three years she was instrumental in guiding the program and booking the kind of attractions the community sought. This effort to provide a high-level cultural program was the first offering of a woman whose contribution to children's theatre would bring her an award for distinguished service many years later.

Performances were planned for Saturday mornings, but the enthusiastic response on the part of the young people of Maplewood made it necessary to add second performances in the afternoons. An opera, a symphony orchestra, a concert singer, a play, and a marionette show were among the first season's offerings. By having free use of the high-school auditorium it was possible to put the admission charge at ten cents; the auditorium seated two thousand and all seats were sold.

The three year period from 1933 to 1936 was a successful one for the Children's Entertainment Committee. Dorothy McFadden, working in co-operation with the National Music League, enlarged the scope of her activities by advising other communities interested in similar projects. In 1935, at her own expense, she toured the Scandinavian countries, Russia, and Germany to study entertainment offered for children abroad. Upon her return to this country she founded Junior Programs, Inc., a nonprofit organization, offering plays and operas for children throughout the United States. Since this latter venture must be classified as professional rather than community theatre, a discussion of its establishment and contribution will come later under that heading. The most interesting aspect of the Children's Entertainment Committee of Maplewood, New Jersey, is that it proved to be the first step in the development of "the miracle . . . known as Junior Programs."

SEATTLE JUNIOR PROGRAMS, INC.

A similar program, established for the purpose of providing good entertainment for children's audiences, was Seattle Junior Programs, Inc., founded in 1939. Like the Maplewood experiment, it did not stem from a recreation center but did have, from the time of its inception, the interest of leading citizens and the support of the public schools. With the help of the latter, the committee in charge was able to release publicity and distribute tickets to boys and girls throughout the city.

The purpose of Seattle Junior Programs, Inc., as stated in the bylaws of its constitution, was as follows:

The purpose of this corporation, in accordance with the agreement of association, shall be to present the junior citizens of the community educational and entertaining programs in the field of drama, music, science and interesting arts, with the purpose of raising the standards of such programs to the highest level and developing audiences of young people who will come voluntarily to enjoy the finest cultural programs, in their leisure time.[12]

During the first season, in accordance with this aim, it was said to have reached 4,200 children in Seattle with special New York attractions sent out by Junior Programs touring companies.

The war years, which had so disastrous an effect upon the road shows in America, caused the touring companies which it was sponsoring to cancel their engagements, but Seattle Junior Programs did not give up. The successful beginning as a sponsoring agency for children's entertainment was followed by a somewhat changed and considerably expanded program of activities. Since this period belongs to the postwar years, a discussion of the further developments will be postponed until a later chapter. The groundwork, however, of one of the most successful programs of its sort in the country today was carefully laid in the thirties.

THE NORTH SHORE CHILDREN'S THEATRE COUNCIL OF MILWAUKEE, WISCONSIN

In Milwaukee, Wisconsin, the desire for good entertainment for children led to the establishment of the North Shore Children's Theatre Council. This Council was composed of a group of women who had been concerned for a number of years over the lack of cultural advantages for the boys and girls of their city. The Council included among its members a representative from the Junior League and a public-school principal. The Shorewood Board of Vocational Education lent support by offering a place for the program, and the Milwaukee Players, an adult little theatre group, assisted in the promotion of the project. Like the Seattle and Maplewood organizations, the North Shore Council was a sponsoring rather than a producing agent, which directed

---

[12] Seattle Junior Programs, Inc., *Children's Theatre Manual*, 44.

its efforts toward the booking of good professional entertainment on the child's level.

The first season was highly successful in its audience response but too expensive to continue at the ten-cent admission fee which was charged. Rather than raise the price of the tickets, the Council decided to supplement the program with local attractions, including those of the Junior League and the Milwaukee Players. The interesting feature of the North Shore Council was the way in which it met both its objectives and its budget by combining local and professional fare.

BINGHAMTON, NEW YORK

A similar sponsoring organization was established in Binghamton, New York. Feeling the need for live entertainment to supplement the work of the schools and to provide a better cultural program than most of the movies being shown, a Children's Theatre Council of parents and interested citizens banded together in 1937. The committee formed at the time was the outgrowth of preliminary work done by the Junior League, which for a number of years had been producing and touring a play annually. In February, 1937, this organization conducted a Children's Theatre Institute, which in addition to covering practical aspects of production, stimulated the idea of forming a council. Gloria Chandler, the League's children's theatre consultant, encouraged the project but stressed the importance of making it a community-wide rather than an organization effort.

The result was a Children's Theatre Council composed of representatives from the department of education, the Parent-Teacher Association, the American Association of University Women, the Junior League, and two local women's clubs. The purposes agreed upon by this group were essentially those of the other groups cited.

Since much of the work would have to be carried on through the public schools, it was necessary to secure the official sanction of the superintendent and board of education. With this support guaranteed and a junior-high-school auditorium made available for the performances, the council set about finding material which it deemed worth while. Junior Programs appealed to them because of its varied offerings, and a series of three productions was scheduled for the following season.

The success of the first year was sufficient encouragement to plan for the second. By obtaining community co-operation the project grew into a popular civic institution, a description of which has been written by four members of the council. This report, compiled by Mrs. Reah Stanley Drake, outlining procedures and practices, was intended as a guide as well as a record. It shows in detail how a community enterprise, established for the purpose of enriching the lives of its children through cultural programs, succeeded and grew.

Little Theatres with Children's Programs

A somewhat different type of community children's theatre, as noted in the last chapter, was that connected with an adult little theatre group. In spite of the growing popularity and expansion of the large civic and recreation programs, this kind of activity persisted into the thirties. In some instances such groups were also affiliated with the Junior League or other similar organization, retaining at the same time their identity as a branch of the local community playhouse. The following examples are illustrative of this kind of organization.

THE NASHVILLE CHILDREN'S THEATRE

One children's theatre which actually antedated the adult producing group by about five years was the Children's Theatre of Nashville, Tennessee. Ultimately housed under the same roof, their common aim was to bring to the community the best possible theatre and to make use of the available community talent in doing so. The children's branch was established in 1931 by the local Junior League, which is still counted among its strongest supporters. In the ensuing years ticket prices were reduced and sales were conducted through the public schools, in an effort to reach more children in Nashville.

A policy of different directors during the season was thought desirable, although activities came under the general surveillance of the adult community playhouse when it was established in 1936. One of the outstanding organizations today, the Nashville Children's Theatre has held to its purpose of presenting regular programs of good children's plays, developing at the same time into a completely self-supporting group of more than four thousand sustaining members.

THE CHILDREN'S THEATRE OF WICHITA

The Children's Theatre of Wichita, Kansas, founded in 1932, had as a sponsoring agent the American Association of University Women. The program was planned to provide for both dramatic training and children's entertainment. During the first season six plays were given, with two performances of each. The prices were set at fifty cents for a season ticket or fifteen cents for a single admission, thus making possible the participation and attendance of all boys and girls between the ages of five and sixteen in Wichita. Co-operation with the libraries and the public schools helped to make this privately organized experiment a community project. Such plays as *The Blue Bird* and *The Silver Thread* were among the early productions.

THE CHILDREN'S THEATRE OF CHARLESTON

Another group established in 1932 was the Children's Theatre of Charleston, West Virginia. Five plays a year were presented under the direction of Elizabeth Wolcott. One unusual feature of this organization was the publishing plant which it maintained. Among the most successful scripts which it published during the thirties were *Little Dog Dooley*, *Rip Van Winkle*, *The Christmas Nightingale*, and *Tom Sawyer*.

THE CURTAIN PULLERS OF THE CLEVELAND PLAYHOUSE

The Cleveland Playhouse, one of the best known and most successful of the early community theatres, did not begin children's activities until 1933. In that year an experimental series of plays performed by children for child audiences was established under the direction of Esther Mullin, actress and member of the Playhouse staff. By the end of the thirties this group, the Curtain Pullers, had grown from one hundred to five hundred, had built its audience from five hundred to five thousand, and had increased its series from three plays a season to seven. The members of the Curtain Pullers received weekly lessons in dramatic arts for which no tuition was charged; they had, in addition, the opportunity of trying out for parts in the public performances. Like the parent group, the Curtain Pullers of the Cleveland Playhouse has become one of the popular institutions in the life of the city.

THEATRE WORKSHOP FOR CHILDREN, SCARSDALE, NEW YORK

During the winter of 1933–34 a theatre workshop for children was opened in Scarsdale, New York. The purpose was stated to be the unification of the creative arts through theatre. Children from five to thirteen were admitted to classes informally conducted by Don Oscar Becque, who taught dance and drama, and by Ethel Hopkins, who taught the visual arts. The policy of using guidance rather than formal direction was observed as a means of stimulating the creativity of the young participants. For this reason the term "workshop" rather than "school" was considered more applicable by the directors. *Treasure Island*, a presentation for and by children, was the first production given in the small basement quarters which served as a theatre.

CHILDREN'S THEATRE OF NORFOLK

Norfolk, Virginia, founded a children's theatre in 1935 with the help of the Junior League. Virginia Harden was one of the instigators and the first director of the group, which was considered in 1938 one of the leading children's theatres in the state. The offering of plays expanded from the four of the first season to a program of eight within three years' time.

OTHER CHILDREN'S THEATRE GROUPS

Also mentioned in newspapers and periodicals during the thirties as having established children's branches were the following community theatres: Dallas, Texas; Sioux City, Iowa; Quincy, Massachusetts; Sheboygan, Wisconsin; St. Louis, Missouri; and Waterbury, Connecticut. The survey conducted by the American National Theatre and Academy in 1951 revealed that there were several others founded during this decade which have lasted to the present time. These were the Junior Theatre of Portland, Maine (1931); the Service League of La Porte, Wisconsin (1932); Beverly Hills Junior Theatre (1933); the Children's Theatre of Columbus, Georgia (1933); the East Bay Children's Theatre in California (1934); the Children's Theatre of New Orleans under the guidance of the Junior League (1937); Youtheatre of Santa Barbara, California, suspended during the war (1938); the Lexington, Kentucky, Children's Theatre (1938); the Mansfield, Ohio, Children's Theatre (1938); and the Children's Theatre of Fairmont, West Virginia (1938).

DRAMA IN THE CHURCH

The Protestant church began extensive participation in dramatic activities during this period. Its earlier opposition to the drama gradually disappeared as the popularity of informal plays and pageants, under the auspices of churches and Sunday schools, grew. Drama returned to the church in the third decade of the twentieth century and has continued ever since, though in different directions and for various reasons.

The type of program which developed first was similar to that of the elementary school, in which the drama came as a result of current interest or learning rather than as a formally organized program. The objective in religious drama was in most instances not entertainment but a means of reaching men through the theatre arts. Obviously many nonreligious, as well as religious, plays and pageants were appropriate for presentation in the church. Despite the amount of dramatic activity which was being carried on at that time, there was little distinction between plays for children and plays for adults. A study completed in the early thirties at the Chicago Theological Seminary, in which the dramatic activities of 342 churches in 16 Midwestern states were studied, reported that 258 of the churches had produced plays. A total list of 830 plays and pageants presented annually revealed an average of more than 3 plays per church. Again, none of the churches stated that their plays were part of a formally organized program, nor did they differentiate between material suitable for children and material chosen for adults. Special occasions such as Christmas and Easter were said to be the most popular times for giving plays and pageants. In some instances they were part of the service; in others they were scheduled as separate or outside events.

Fred Eastman, writing at the time, observed that three things were needed if the church play were to make a significant contribution: skill in production (including trained leadership), adequate equipment with which to work, and plays of a better quality than the majority which were available.[13] A number of books directed specifically toward the production of the church play and pageant appeared during the twenties and thirties, indicating that the interest was general and that some qualified leaders were attempting to meet the demand for material. The art of pageantry, in which all ages can often be successfully integrated, was frequently stressed. While there was apparently considerable activity of one sort or another during the thirties, there is no published account of any genuine children's theatre program, planned and set up under the auspices of the church.

Despite the expanding recreational and playground facilities for drama, the awakening interest of the church, and the availability

[13] Fred Eastman and Louis Wilson, *Drama in the Church*, 3.

of federal and professional entertainment in a number of cities throughout the country, it is evident that the little theatres were assuming a greater share of the responsibility for children's plays by adding them to their regular program of adult activities. It has been pointed out that in some instances this was done with the help of the Junior League; in others the impetus came from parents and interested citizens. Sponsoring organizations whose concern was primarily the securing of good entertainment for children of the community were exemplified by the Maplewood, Milwaukee, and Seattle experiments. The fact that these sponsoring organizations had attractions from which to choose was the result of an increased effort on the part of the professional stage to meet what seemed to have become a national demand.

Professional Theatre for Children

Several professional companies were presenting plays for children during the thirties. Only one of these had been in existence prior to this time: the Clare Tree Major Children's Theatre, established in 1923. The others were founded during the early and middle years of the decade, with the result that professional entertainment for children was in greater supply than at any previous time.

CLARE TREE MAJOR'S CHILDREN'S THEATRE

The popularity of the Clare Tree Major Children's Theatre had been well established during the twenties. In addition to the regularly scheduled performances in the New York area, this company added a touring program, which in 1931 included twenty-five different cities. During the first few seasons engagements were limited to the Eastern seaboard, but by 1940 the touring schedule was taking plays from coast to coast. The original single company of players had tripled by 1933, and a repertory of six plays was prepared for sponsoring groups interested in booking a series. The Clare Tree Major Children's Theatre Company of New York announced its availability for performances throughout New England in repertory or for single performances. In the 1933–34 season Mrs. Major's three companies were on tour with six plays, visiting more than one hundred cities in eleven states and Canada, as far west as Michigan and as far south as Washington, D.C.

Prices for tickets were arranged by local groups, but were kept generally low. Because of the production expenses involved, admission charges had to be higher than for amateur community programs; but they could still be low enough to make possible large ticket sales, thereby attracting sponsors. Performances were booked in advance by such organizations as Parent-Teacher Associations, Junior Leagues, women's clubs, the American Association of University Women, and little theatres, which assumed local responsibility for publicity and ticket sales. Sponsors agreed to provide the auditorium and any union labor required locally, according to theatre regulations. Scenery for the plays was designed to be so flexible that it could be set up on the simplest stage. Clare Tree Major paid for the transportation of the companies, the actors' salaries, royalties, and all expenses involved in the production.

The success of this enterprise was measured by return engagements, an expanding schedule, an increased number of companies, and enthusiastic reactions from sponsoring groups. One particularly favorable comment was made by Allen Saunders, drama critic for the *Toledo, Ohio, News-Bee:*

> See to it that your youngsters see the Clare Tree Major plays. I've watched kids delightedly drinking in every syllable of a Major play and have glowed with the realization that here is being trained another generation of men and women who love the living drama and will never let it die.[14]

Children's classics and new plays made up the repertory, with a strong emphasis on international stories.

[14] Clare Tree Major, Scrapbooks, in Theatre Collection of The New York Public Library.

In 1938, Clare Tree Major celebrated her fifteenth season by extending the tours from the Atlantic to the Pacific Ocean and from the Gulf of Mexico to Canada. There were by this time six companies at work. Headquarters had been moved to Chappaqua, New York, where spacious studio facilities made possible six simultaneous rehearsals.

A 1938 article in the *Publishers' Weekly* indicated that co-operation with the booksellers throughout the country was an added and effective promotional method used by the Clare Tree Major companies:

> With a strong emphasis on local tie-ups with booksellers, the Clare Tree Major Children's Theatre is carrying on a national promotion campaign this fall for its forthcoming tour of thirty-three states. The Children's Theatre, now in its fifteenth season, is sponsored locally through committees of sponsors in each community, who are being instructed to work closely with local booksellers and are being supplied with window display material, posters and costume photographs of the six plays in the theatre's repertory. . . . Altogether the book trade tie-up is more extensive this year than ever before.[15]

The years of experience behind this group, the national reputation which it had acquired, and the interest of local organizations in sponsoring children's programs apparently enabled this company to keep on with its work, in spite of the depression and the onset of the war. The records show that the Clare Tree Major Children's Theatre emerged from the thirties as a financially stronger and larger producing company than it had been ten years before.

DOROTHY GORDON

The program of Dorothy Gordon was also available to sponsoring groups during the thirties. Essentially a singer, Miss Gordon was a dramatic artist as well, for she appeared in costume

[15] Anon., "Children's Theatre Cooperates with Book Stores," *Publishers' Weekly*, Vol. CXXXIV (August 27, 1938), 579.

and stressed the dramatic and visual aspects of her performance. Dorothy Gordon concerts were directed to children both in the United States and abroad. Her belief in good entertainment for young people was in accord with the ideas expressed by such organizations as the Children's Entertainment Committee of Maplewood (on which series she appeared), the Junior League, and Clare Tree Major. Like many of her contemporaries, she voiced her conviction that every community in the country should support a children's art theatre, where the visual arts and music as well as plays could be enjoyed. If this could be accomplished, she believed, future theatre managers would not have to worry about adult audiences.

ADRIENNE MORRISON'S CHILDREN'S PLAYERS

There appeared in New York in 1930 a professional group known as Adrienne Morrison's Children's Players. In 1931, *Drama* commented: "What Walter Damrosch has done to bring music into the lives of children, Adrienne Morrison is doing in the field of drama."[16] Great care was exercised in the selection of plays, performances of which were given on Friday afternoons in the Theresa Kaufman Auditorium. There were six plays in the series and each one ran for a month. While the inspiration for the enterprise came originally from children, the Adrienne Morrison Players were professional adult actors.

Adrienne Morrison, like Clare Tree Major, came from a theatrical family. Her childhood was spent in the theatre, where she was in constant association with the finest artists and with many noteworthy productions. The idea of founding a children's theatre did not occur to her until World War I, when she was working with the Stage Women's War Relief. Asked to present some scenes from Shakespeare for an informal program, she cast children in an excerpt from *A Midsummer Night's Dream*, and was amazed at their eager response. Realizing that this interest on the part of young people was not being satisfied by the profes-

[16] Selma Alexander, "Need for a Children's Theatre," *Drama*, Vol. XXI (May, 1931), 16.

Mary Martin in a scene from the 1955 production of *Peter Pan*. Courtesy Theatre Collection, The New York Public Library, Astor, Lenox, and Tilden Foundation.

Alice Minnie Herts, founder of the Children's Educational Theatre in 1903. Courtesy The New York Public Library.

Clare Tree Major, first producer of children's plays to tour nationally. Courtesy Marian Depew Ostrander.

Dorothy McFadden, founder of Junior Programs, Inc.

Winifred Ward, founder of Evanston Children's Theatre and the Children's Theatre Conference. Photograph by Eugene L. Ray.

The Equity Library Theatre for Children production of *Rumpelstiltskin* in the late fifties. Photograph by Priscilla M. Pennell. Courtesy Briggs Management.

"Come along with Mara to the Land of the Princess Qua Qua," in the 1960's. Courtesy Briggs Management.

Mara in *The Frog Princess*, a tale of old Russia. Courtesy Briggs Management.

Charlotte Chorpenning, eminent playwright for children's theatre. Photograph by Bergamon. Courtesy Anchorage Press.

Isabel Burger, children's theatre leader, author, and director. Photograph by Udel Bros.

Sara Spencer, founder and publisher of the Anchorage Press. Photograph by *Courier-Journal* and *Louisville Times*.

The Pocket Players of New York City in a scene from *Emil and the Detective*, directed by Muriel Sharon. Photograph by J. Pantzer.

A 1960's version of *The Wizard of Oz*, produced by the Traveling Playhouse of New York City. Courtesy Traveling Playhouse.

sional stage, she eventually set to work to establish a company which would provide the best dramatic literature in the best possible production.

Some of the plays presented by the Children's Players during their first two seasons were *The Princess Who Wouldn't Say Die* by Bertram Block; *The Happy Prince* (Oscar Wilde), dramatized by Rita Benton; *The Mad Hatter's Tea Party* (Lewis Carroll), arranged by Mrs. Burton Harrison; *Make Believe* by A. A. Milne; *The Little Princess* by Frances Hodgson Burnett; and *Aladdin* by Theodora Du Bois. Although the Children's Players attracted attention and were favorably received, there are no records of production after 1932.

JUNIOR PROGRAMS, INC.

The outstanding professional organization to appear during the thirties—indeed, in the entire history of children's theatre—was Junior Programs, Inc. The quality of material which it used, the care which it exercised in the preparation of the productions, the number of children throughout the United States whom it reached, and the enthusiastic response it received from sponsoring agents and educators placed Junior Programs in a unique position. The outgrowth of the Maplewood, New Jersey, Children's Entertainment Committee, Junior Programs, Inc., was launched in 1936 under the direction of the indefatigable Dorothy McFadden, who has been previously cited.

The thought and planning which had made the earlier local venture a success were the distinguishing characteristics in the new and much more ambitious undertaking. Junior Programs was begun as a booking agency, but because of the paucity of available material it soon went into production as well.

Although the National Music League was the organization which gave Dorothy McFadden the greatest help in the beginning, many others soon began to contribute to her new venture in an advisory way. Some of these were the National Orchestral Association, the Museum of Natural History, the Westchester County Recreation Commission, the National Congress of Parents and Teachers, the Child Study Association of America, and the General Federation of Women's Clubs. The aim of the organization was to make available at low cost to children throughout the country, entertainment of educational value. Mrs. McFadden stated her own purposes at the time as follows:

1. To make available to every child, rich or poor, productions by the finest adult artists in varied fields of entertainment, which will have real cultural value. Such entertainments should be planned to leave not only happy memories but a high standard for the child's own work in similar fields and a new stimulus and interest in various forms of art and knowledge which before had been outside of his field of vision.

2. To educate the parents and the community in general to the need for wholesome entertainment being provided at regular intervals, for every child, at low ticket prices in community supervised auditoriums, and to make them realize that such entertainment can be educationally and morally valuable as well as keeping the child off the city streets and away from harmful occupations, such as gang activities and motion pictures of the more lurid variety.

3. To act as a clearing house for programs for children, and by means of many conferences, previews and personal assistance of educators, to raise the standards of all offerings for children in the entertainment field.[17]

In accordance with these aims, each production was submitted to a careful survey by the advisory council composed of educators, child psychologists, and specialists in children's entertainment in the United States. After this, productions were given a preview before an audience of children, to get their reactions.

During the 1936–37 season Junior Programs sent productions to one hundred sponsors in twelve states and the District of Columbia. These states were Connecticut, Illinois, Indiana, Massachusetts, Michigan, New Jersey, New York, Ohio, Pennsylvania, Rhode Island, West Virginia, and Wisconsin. By the winter of 1939–40 it had more than doubled the scope of its operations;

17 Mimeographed material from the Junior Programs, Inc., Files.

companies of adult professionals were sent throughout the United States performing opera, ballet, drama, and concerts before audiences totaling approximately one million persons.

The demand for programs made it necessary to organize three separate companies: the Junior Programs Opera Company, the Junior Programs Ballet Company, and the Junior Programs Players Company. By 1939 field secretaries were operating to bring Junior Programs into more towns, where thousands of children crowded school auditoriums to see plays at an admission price of ten to twenty-five cents.

By 1940, Junior Programs had toured its productions through forty-three states, reaching audiences of nearly four million children. In addition to publicity featuring pictures and posters, a Junior Programs Educational Guidance Committee, composed of specialists in childhood education, directed the preparation of correlative materials to be used in the classroom in advance of the programs. These materials, together with instructions for their use, were sent to every sponsoring organization.

Among the programs which were particularly well received were *The Adventures of Marco Polo*, *The Bumble Bee Prince*, *Pinocchio*, and *Jack and the Beanstalk*. The ballet of *Robin Hood*, with a script by Saul Lancourt and music compiled and arranged by Margaret Carlisle, was enthusiastically received and later put on records. *Pinocchio*, a ballet danced by Edwin Strawbridge with accompanying narration, was the first production of its kind. *The Reward of the Sun God*, a play about the American Indian, was written especially for Junior Programs by John Nelson, an expert on the subject, with assistance in the dramatization by Charlotte Chorpenning.

The Adventures of Puck was a ballet based on *A Midsummer Night's Dream*, rearranged and simplified. Shakespeare's lines and Mendelssohn's music made this offering one of the classics. The score for *Jack and the Beanstalk*, prepared by John Erskine and Louis Gruenberg, had first been produced at the Juilliard School of Music; a shortened version was the one used by Junior Programs. It is apparent that both classic and new material were included, while the emphasis on international literature and plays with different historical and geographical backgrounds was maintained. Mrs. McFadden believed that the most effective way of helping American children gain insights into the peoples of other nations was through the drama.

Records of the programs given during the years from 1936 to 1940 list the following titles: operas—*Hansel and Gretel, The Bumble Bee Prince,* and *Jack and the Beanstalk*; ballets—*Pinocchio, The Princess and the Swineherd, The Adventures of Puck,* and *Robin Hood*; and plays—*The Reward of the Sun God, Run, Peddler, Run,* and *The Emperor's Treasure Chest.* The total number of performances was listed as follows: 1936–37, 158; 1937–38, 242; 1938–39, 323; and 1939–40, 558. The total number of towns in which Junior Programs played in each year was stated to be: 1936–37, 67; 1937–38, 112; 1938–39, 130; and 1939–40, 220.

It is apparent from these figures that Junior Programs, Inc., was a thriving enterprise with a steady increase in both the number of performances and the number of towns in which they were given during the first four years of its existence. Its activities continued into the next decade, when the exigencies of the war finally caused it to cease operation. A final summary of its contribution to the children's theatre movement belongs more properly to the next period, when it can be surveyed in the light of its total achievement.

GRACE PRICE PRODUCTIONS

Meanwhile, in Pittsburgh, Pennsylvania, another company had opened which was to survive both depression and war. This was Grace Price Productions, a professional group offering entertainments for children. In 1930, Grace Price, a former actress, gathered together a company of actors to put on a series of three plays a year in the Pittsburgh area. Although they performed regularly during this time, Miss Price considered 1934 to have been the founding date of her company.

Popular demand brought expansion through touring, and before long she was covering sixty-seven towns within a hundred-mile radius of Pittsburgh. There were many invitations to give her plays at more distant points, but Grace Price thought it advisable to work within a smaller area and learn to know it well.

In its repertory have been both well-known children's plays and new material; this policy has in the many years of its operation brought the group numerous original manuscripts for experimental production. While Grace Price Productions confined itself to a relatively small territory by comparison with Clare Tree Major's Theatre and Junior Programs, Inc., it was from the beginning enthusiastically received. Return engagements as well as new engagements meant financial security; Grace Price Productions was for many years the best-known company in the state of Pennsylvania.

THE AMERICAN CHILDREN'S THEATRE

The American Children's Theatre opened in New York in 1934. According to the *Literary Digest*, 1934, "Plans for a permanent professional children's theatre which will cater to the special needs and interests of New York school children, were announced recently by a newly incorporated group known as The American Children's Theatre."[18] Many leading educators were among the incorporators, and the first production was scheduled for the fall of 1934. A nonprofit organization, the theatre was designed along the lines of the state-endowed children's theatres of Europe.

The opening play, *The Chinese Nightingale*, was described as a fanciful, bright production. The performance was preceded by an address by John Dewey, who endorsed its objectives of providing wholesome entertainment of a high artistic quality for young people. Despite an auspicious beginning and apparent adult support, there are no further records to indicate any future work by this group.

[18] Anon., "Children's Theatre Planned," *Literary Digest*, Vol. CXVII (June, 1934), 32.

ALICE IN WONDERLAND

Included among the most successful offerings of the Civic Repertory Theatre of New York was a production of *Alice in Wonderland* in 1932. Under the direction of Eva Le Gallienne with Josephine Hutchinson in the part of Alice, this play was called "the month's most stimulating evening in the theatre"[19] by Morton Eustis of *Theatre Arts Monthly*. The dramatization, adapted by Eva Le Gallienne and Florida Friebus, called for many scenes, which were staged with scenery and costumes designed according to the original Tenniel illustrations. Highly praised for its script, acting, and production, this play was one of the most famous of the Civic Repertory Theatre presentations, and hundreds of school children as well as adults crowded the auditorium during the course of its run. The script was made available to nonprofessional groups, and in the forties a revival took place under the auspices of the American Repertory Theatre, of which Eva Le Gallienne was a director.

By and large, professional offerings for children had increased tremendously over the previous decade. Records of the Federal Theatre, Junior Programs, Inc., the Clare Tree Major players, and Grace Price Productions reveal that hundreds of performances were given for millions of boys and girls throughout the United States during these years. Through touring programs with local groups acting as sponsors, many communities were able to receive children's entertainment for the first time at prices low enough to make large attendance possible. While not all of the groups mentioned survived the war years, the fact that they were established with stated objectives and a plan of procedure was evidence of a genuine interest on the part of professional theatre people in this phase of entertainment. Puppets, marionettes, magic, and variety shows were also popular attractions during the thirties, but their relationship to the living theatre was apparently one of friendly coexistence rather than competition. Inasmuch

19 "Wonderland, Broadway in Review," *Theatre Arts Monthly*, Vol. XVII (February, 1933), 101.

as these activities are not a part of living theatre history, they will not be included here.

Publications for Children's Theatre

It has been stated that *Drama*, the periodical issued by the Drama League of America, ceased publication in 1931. The termination of this monthly magazine eliminated one of the important channels through which news and information pertaining to children's theatre was regularly disseminated. *The Playground* and *Recreation* magazines, as well as the *Junior League Magazine*, however, continued to give space to junior dramatic activity.

Players Magazine, official bimonthly journal of the honorary dramatic fraternity National Collegiate Players, which began publication in 1923, directed its attention primarily to problems of the college, university, and community theatres. By the thirties, however, an occasional article or note on children's theatre was included in its pages. These increased through the years until in 1937 a regular column began to appear. The first "Children's Theatre Notes," written by Sara Spencer, was followed by a longer column, "In the Children's Theatres," with Susan Welty as editor. Reviews of new plays appropriate for elementary as well as high-school students were also included in its book-review department.

THE *PLAY INDEX*

In 1931 the revised *Play Index*, put out by the American Library Association, appeared. It was edited by Aeola L. Hyatt with an introduction by Constance D'Arcy Mackay, and carried a greater number of titles than the earlier volume.

PLAYS FOR CHILDREN

Montrose J. Moses' *Concerning Children's Plays* was published by Samuel French, Inc., in 1931. It was a critical analysis of existing children's dramatic literature, which the author believed to be suffering chiefly from a condescending and moralistic attitude. Moses did, however, recommend ten plays which, he said, not only avoided these errors but possessed literary quality and dramatic appeal.

The supply of longer plays for children's theatres increased during the thirties, largely through the efforts of Charlotte Chorpenning, the Junior League, the Federal Theatre, and the individual playwrights who contributed scripts to Junior Programs, Inc. The publishers still had few titles on their lists, by comparison with those available for adult groups, but the number of published and unpublished manuscripts was being increased in an effort to meet the growing demand.

THE CHILDREN'S THEATRE PRESS

The most important date in regard to publication for children's theatre was unquestionably the founding of the Children's Theatre Press in 1935 in Charleston, West Virginia. Although operation was begun with only four titles, the list has grown through the years until today the Anchorage Press (as it is now called) occupies a unique position as one of two publishing houses in the United States devoted exclusively to the printing of books and plays for children's theatre. With Sara Spencer at its head from the beginning, the Children's Theatre Press stood for integrity and singleness of purpose. It has worked slowly and diligently in the selection of material, with the result that high quality has been consistently maintained. America's foremost writers in this field are to be found represented in its catalogues. The Press is now located in Anchorage, Kentucky.

In reviewing the children's theatre movement of the thirties, one is aware of new developments and considerable change. National organizations, recreational and community centers, professional theatrical companies, and publications of the period all placed an emphasis on this phase of the dramatic arts. By comparison with the preceding decade, the movement was spreading with an emphasis on qualitative as well as quantitative output.

In the educational theatre, there was activity on all levels. While some educators were concerned because the opportunity for participation seldom provided for the less gifted students, there was general agreement that interest in drama was widespread.

The greatest amount of activity continued to take place in the community theatres and recreational centers. The number of towns and cities reporting well-organized programs indicates that drama for children had become a popular phase of their work. Whereas fifteen years earlier the National Recreation Association had had to urge groups to include drama, now their consultation service was receiving letters from all over the country, asking questions about production and suggestions for plays. Although no actual count was made, there were probably hundreds of groups engaged in dramatic activities, most of which took the form of putting on plays.

The professional theatre, which was suffering from the depression and therefore was curtailing production for adult audiences, played its first important role in children's theatre during these years. A significant factor in the success of these groups was the sponsoring agent; though not a new idea, it functioned effectively during this time. Certainly the nationwide tours were made possible through the interest and efforts of the many local organizations and concerned individuals who gave them support.

VI

New Leadership

1940-50

The transition from depression to the war and postwar periods inevitably wrought changes in all aspects of American life. The transformation of a nation almost wholly absorbed in the arts of peace to one armed for total war created circumstances and problems which this country had not faced before. Increased population and increased production in the United States created conditions which were to engage the efforts of government, business and industrial leaders, scientists, educators, and social workers from the national to the community level.

Cultural institutions in particular felt the impact of these changes. Much has been written about the expanding enrollment in the elementary schools. Even earlier, however, community centers, serving both children and adults, were forced to augment their facilities in order to meet the demands of the thousands who flocked to such places of recreation. Many communities faced serious problems in providing essential welfare services for a great influx of industrial defense workers and their families and for army personnel stationed in near-by centers.

The professional theatre was stimulated to an extraordinary degree. People sought entertainment and the theatre responded to their need. Audiences for both Broadway and road shows were larger than they had been for many years. Children's theatre, both amateur and professional, was also affected. Increasing enrollment in the elementary schools, increasing attendance at community centers, increasing audiences for professional plays—all were to have an effect upon the quality and quantity of entertainment during the forties. With one exception—Junior Programs, Inc., which was forced to terminate its program as a direct result of the war—there was more entertainment offered for children than in any previous period.

The institutions which had been encouraging and supporting children's theatre increased their efforts, with the result that the greatest growth and expansion in the history of the movement took place during the forties.

National Organizations

The three national organizations which contributed most to the development of the children's theatre movement during the forties were the Association of Junior Leagues of America, the American National Theatre and Academy (popularly known as ANTA), and the Children's Theatre Conference.

THE ASSOCIATION OF JUNIOR LEAGUES OF AMERICA

The Junior League had been active for almost two decades; by 1940 it had a well-established program in many cities and towns throughout the United States. Virginia Lee Comer, children's theatre consultant for the organization, described at the beginning of the decade what she considered to be the unique contribution of the League. Reviewing its progress since 1921, she noted that while many changes had taken place, the touring program was undoubtedly its most successful activity. The situation in 1940 was quite different from that in 1920, when the first League productions for children were planned. A scattering of local civic and university theatres and sponsoring committees for professional entertainment were now bringing plays to many boys and girls throughout the United States. The League touring program, however, was continuing in its efforts to give theatre to communities not served by these groups. "Not only can trouping select the audiences where the greatest need exists, but it takes the easiest pattern for schools to make use of educational activities related to the theatre experience."[1]

In 1940 trouping programs accounted for at least one-third of the children's theatre activities of the League. In this year there were about forty-seven groups of League itinerant players, young women whose volunteer work in the producing of plays took them to schools, rural classrooms, settlements, and hospitals. Sometimes a small admission was charged, but frequently there was no charge when plays were done in school time or for underprivileged groups. The Newark, New Jersey, program was particularly effective. A play with thirty-five to fifty performances was given each year, with audiences totaling between twenty-five thousand and thirty-five thousand children, most of whom had never before seen a real play.

Many Leagues sponsored professional entertainment for children such as Junior Programs, Inc., thus giving support through their patronage to companies of high standards and national reputation. By the forties the children's theatre department of the League was so well organized that an annual report of all activities was compiled and published in the form of a Children's Theatre Chart. There was no set program for children's theatre; rather each League developed its program to fit the needs of the community.

It is interesting to read the carefully kept reports on the programs and audiences for each year of the decade:[2]

1939–40 Season		Number of Leagues:	127
Theatre	98	Productions	153
Puppetry	20	Performances	895
		Audience	288,375

[1] Virginia Lee Comer, "A Children's Theatre Takes to the Road," *Recreation*, Vol. XXXIV (September, 1940), 402.

[2] "Children's Theatre and Puppetry Statistics," compiled by the Association of Junior Leagues of America (November, 1956).

1940-41 Season		Number of Leagues:	111
Theatre	91	Productions	169
Puppetry	20	Performances	1,679
		Audience	592,814
1941-42 Season		Number of Leagues:	90
Theatre	76		
Puppetry	14		

26 Leagues now affiliated with Community Theatres

1942-43 Season		Number of Leagues:	55
(Breakdown not		Performances	653
available)		Audience	291,754
1943-44 Season		Number of Leagues:	61
Theatre	52	Performances	690
Puppetry	9	Audience	328,713
1944-45 Season		Number of Leagues:	70
Theatre	61	Performances	783
Puppetry	9	Audience	368,449
1945-46 Season		Number of Leagues:	81
Theatre	65	Performances	1,016
Puppetry	16	Audience	639,793
1946-47 Season		Number of Leagues:	107
Theatre	84	Performances	1,596
Puppetry	23	Audience	693,702
1947-48 Season		Number of Leagues:	118
(No breakdown)		Performances	1,845
		Audience	734,556
1948-49 Season		Number of Leagues:	149
Theatre	96	Not Listed	
Puppetry	53		

While the number of League producing groups appears to have declined, this was not actually the case, since many Leagues, according to the 1946-47 Chart, merged their efforts with their communities and were thenceforth governed by a community board or council. In general the total number of productions and the total audiences actually increased tremendously between 1940 and 1949, indicating the spread of League work in the field of children's theatre.

THE AMERICAN NATIONAL THEATRE
AND ACADEMY

The American National Theatre and Academy, chartered in 1935, had been dormant for the first ten years of its life. In 1945 it was reactivated, and in 1946 set forth its aims and plans for the future. Vinton Freedley was the first president, with five hundred members located in twenty states.

While ANTA has always been primarily concerned with adult theatre, both professional and nonprofessional, it has taken a sympathetic interest in the children's theatre movement. To this end it conducted two surveys during this ten-year period to determine the number of producing groups, persons and institutions connected with them, the scope of their activities, and the types of plays they produced. While ANTA is a service organization rather than a research agency, the results of its findings are in the ANTA files of the New York office, for the use of any organization or individual who wants to consult them. The first survey, made in 1948, was announced in *Theatre Arts Monthly* of that year. It listed over 1,500 children's theatre projects throughout the country.

This report also mentioned the names of two women, Winifred Ward and Charlotte Chorpenning, to whom it gave much credit for the growth of the movement. Winifred Ward, through her writing, administration of the Evanston Children's Theatre, and leadership in the Children's Theatre Conference, and Charlotte Chorpenning, through her contribution to the field of juvenile dramatic literature, were credited with leading the movement which in the forties became a lively and important institution in American community life.

THE AMERICAN EDUCATIONAL THEATRE ASSOCIATION

While the American Educational Theatre Association (AETA) directed its attention largely to the problems of college, university, and high-school drama programs, it was cognizant of the children's theatre movement and sympathetic to its aims. From the time of the founding of the Children's Theatre Committee in 1944, a full report of the annual conference of this group has been included in the December issue of the *Educational Theatre Journal*, the official publication of AETA. Other news items and articles pertaining to children's theatre have also appeared in its pages from time to time. Through the Children's Theatre Committee, a newly formed division of AETA, increased support and direction were given to hundreds of educational and community drama groups throughout the country.

THE CHILDREN'S THEATRE COMMITTEE

The Children's Theatre Conference, established as the Children's Theatre Committee in 1944, has dedicated itself to the children's theatre movement. Unlike other national organizations, it was founded for the express purpose of promoting more and better theatre for children throughout the United States and has maintained an expanding program of activities directed toward this end.

At the invitation of Winifred Ward, members of the Children's Theatre Committee of the American Educational Association gathered for a summer meeting on the campus of Northwestern University, Evanston, Illinois, in 1944. Some eighty leaders of children's theatres from all over the country attended the conference. Because of the similarity of its objectives, program, and personnel, the group retained its affiliation with the AETA; but because of the growth and complexity of its work, a special category was later given to it in the structure of the parent body. It was first recognized, however, as the Children's Theatre Committee of the American Educational Theatre Association and was known by this name throughout the forties.

Annual meetings are held either on the campus of some interested college or university or in a hotel when the meetings are held in urban locations. Frequently meetings are preceded by workshops of several days, during which time special topics are studied. At the first conference, the following objectives were listed in the printed program: new materials and ideas, a rethinking of recreational standards to fit wartime and postwar needs, a renewed confidence in the field of children's drama, and a basis for a regional children's theatre organization.

The original conference was part of a Program in Speech Arts for the Elementary Schools; since that time the Children's Theatre Committee has met as an independent body. The first chairman to be elected was Hazel Robertson of the Palo Alto Children's Theatre. Other chairmen during the forties were Virginia Lee Comer, drama consultant of the Junior League; Burdette Fitzgerald, director of the Children's Theatre of Oakland, California; and Campton Bell, director of children's theatre in the University of Denver. The varied backgrounds of these leaders illustrated the spread of interest.

A Children's Theatre Directory prepared by the Children's Theatre Committee (later the Children's Theatre Conference) has been published and distributed by AETA. This directory, brought up to date every two years, made authentic and useful information available to workers in the field. Questionnaires were sent out to groups and persons whose names were obtained from AETA and the Junior League listings.

A Play Standards Committee was organized to set up standard requirements of good plays for children and to help arrange trial productions of all promising new works. A Children's Theatre Bibliography was prepared in which books and articles on children's theatre subjects were listed. In 1950 a newsletter with a national coverage of children's theatre news was first published; thereafter it appeared four times a year. Finally, a Placement

Service was inaugurated, through which both producing groups and directors could be served to mutual advantage.

Members of the Children's Theatre Conference were from the beginning persons engaged in children's dramatic work in schools, colleges, universities, community centers, Junior Leagues, and professional companies. Delegates from these various institutions and organizations have always been in attendance at the annual meetings, thus insuring a consideration of various types and phases of children's dramatic activity. Programs of these meetings have included speeches, group discussions, demonstrations, meetings on specialized subjects, productions of plays followed by evaluations, and social events in which members of the conference could become acquainted.

In 1949 between 200 and 300 permanent children's theatre groups were operating in the United States, according to the combined figures of the AETA and ANTA. These groups were under the guidance of colleges, community theatres, the Junior League, municipalities, drama schools, churches, and professional organizations. In addition to these regularly producing agencies, some 1,000 other groups produced children's plays sporadically. In the period from 1944 to 1949 an estimated 1,000,000 children saw living theatre, which was nearly a 100 per cent increase over the five years preceding. At the 1949 meeting in New York City there were in attendance 248 delegates concerned with better scripts, better direction, and better understanding of child audiences.

In addition to its primary concern with the furthering of good children's entertainment in this country, the Children's Theatre Committee in 1947 passed the following resolution in regard to UNESCO (United Nation's Educational, Scientific, and Cultural Organization):

Whereas, children's theatre fosters the enrichment of personality development and influences the social attitudes of the child, both as a participant in the drama process and as an audience member; and whereas, children's theatre is a basic and dynamic force for sowing seeds of peace through intercultural understanding, there-

129

fore, *Resolved*, that it is the sense of this meeting that children's theatres of the United States support the aims and programs of the UNESCO through local activities and through whatever practical assistance may be given to children's theatre programs elsewhere in the world.[3]

The resolution, made jointly with the Thespian Dramatic Arts Conference, was passed on to Robert Kase, president of AETA. He gave it to Rosamond Gilder of *Theatre Arts Monthly*, who was attending the UNESCO Conference in Paris in July. It is interesting that this concern for children's theatre throughout the world eventually led to the formation of an international body to be known as Association Internationale du Théâtre pour l'Enfance et pour la Jeunesse).

The increasing membership in the organization, the publications which it sponsored, and the widening scope of its activities indicate that by the end of the forties the Children's Theatre Committee had become a strong and influential body. It is also significant that while different types of organizations were represented in it, the colleges and universities have been host to its meetings and have assumed the major share of the responsibility for its growth and development.

The four national organizations which concerned themselves with children's theatre during the forties are not only still in existence but have strengthened each other by a close co-operation. The Association of Junior Leagues of America, which had pioneered for twenty years in this field of activity, joined with both ANTA and the Children's Theatre Committee in an effort to carry on its work in the best interests of the communities in which the Leagues were located. AETA, as the parent body of the Children's Theatre Committee, lent support through its organization, yet permitted freedom for specialized action through a relationship which led to virtual autonomy. The Children's Theatre Committee, by welcoming into its membership directors

[3] Burdette Fitzgerald, "Children's Theatre Conference," *Players Magazine*, Vol. XXIV (December, 1947), 64.

and teachers of educational and community groups of every sort, established an organization which could reach and help everyone engaged in children's theatre work. And finally, ANTA, through a program which embraced professional and nonprofessional theatre for adults and children, was able to function as a service organization for each.

Educational Theatre for Children

It is apparent from the role played by the colleges and universities in the Children's Theatre Committee that educational institutions were active in the movement during this time. A direct expression of the attitude of educators is to be found in an address given by Sara Shakow before the National Progressive Education Association in February, 1940. Implicit in her statement is a belief in children's theatre as an effective and worth-while cultural force:

> A children's theatre today, if it hopes to justify its right to existence, cannot confine its aim to merely furnishing amusement. A children's theatre today, if it expects to exercise its rightful function as a developmental agency and serve effectively as an instrument of education and culture, must offer more than sheer diversion and clean entertainment.[4]

She went on to say that a children's theatre could no longer serve its community by producing plays sporadically but must be established as a permanent institution, regularly presenting plays of artistic merit at nominal admission charges. A long-range program with definite objectives designed to satisfy the emotional and recreational needs of children is essential. Moreover, it should integrate its program with those of other social and educational agencies in the community so as to plan jointly for leisure-time activities.

Proof that educational institutions were acting in accordance with these beliefs was evidenced by the fact that an increasing

[4] Sara Shakow, "Children's Theatre in a Changing World." (Mimeographed copy in the ANTA Children's Theatre files.)

number of colleges and universities were adding courses in children's theatre to their curricula. In many instances the drama program was organized with the needs of community institutions in mind.

As early as 1940, there were announcements of children's plays on the school and college levels. Some which received specific and frequent mention were the following private institutions, all in New York: the Dalton School, the Nightingale-Bamford School, the Hewett School, the Little Red School House, the Rudolph Steiner Schools, the Friends Seminary, and the Spence School. Many public institutions were doing equally fine work.

Extensive programs in children's theatre were being developed on the university rather than on the elementary level. In some cases a close relationship between the university and the public-school system existed. This trend, which was noted during the thirties, was continuing with apparent success.

THE UNIVERSITY OF MINNESOTA

A number of colleges and universities established children's theatres as a part of their drama programs during the forties. One of these, whose children's theatre today ranks among the leading groups in the country, was the University of Minnesota. The program began officially in 1940, although a production of *Peter Pan* the year before started activities. The popularity of this experimental production caused the establishment of the Junior Community Theatre, which was to serve both Minneapolis and St. Paul. Kenneth Graham's leadership and the co-operation of a wider group of civic organizations in 1941–42 brought about changes resulting in the establishment of the Young People's University Theatre. It was the first university theatre in the country whose plays were attended by school children during school time. Saturday matinees and evening performances have been offered in addition, while study aids to teachers provided correlation between the work of the university and the curriculum of the schools. Drama was thus accepted as warranting a place among the arts in elementary education.

According to a Children's Theatre Conference *Newsletter*[5] in 1955, the Young People's Theatre of the University of Minnesota had just celebrated its fifteenth anniversary with a gala production of *Hiawatha*. A luncheon honoring citizens and public-school officials who had given time and effort to this enterprise was part of the celebration of one theatre which has achieved the respect and co-operation of the community.

DENVER CHILDREN'S THEATRE

The Denver Theatre Department assisted in the organization of Denver Junior Entertainment, Inc., and the department continued to play an active part in its development. It also inaugurated one of the first children's theatre touring companies in the Rocky Mountain area in 1949. Under the supervision of Campton Bell, who was director of the Children's Theatre Committee in that same year, the university added special courses in children's theatre techniques, a workshop in creative dramatics for children from seven to thirteen, and a course in original script-writing for children by advanced students in the department.

THE CHILDREN'S EXPERIMENTAL THEATRE
OF BALTIMORE

One group which underwent extraordinary growth during the forties was the Children's Experimental Theatre of Baltimore. The project had been the outgrowth of creative drama classes held at Johns Hopkins University as a laboratory for teachers. Activities were initiated in 1940–41 by Isabel Burger, who set up creative drama sessions for five different age groups. In 1943 the Children's Experimental Theatre was officially established with eighty families, whose children had participated in the Johns Hopkins classes, as charter members.

Other civic-minded people joined as sponsors and within a year four plays had been given at the museum and at the Vagabond Theatre (the name given to their playhouse), and a concentrated

[5] (Summer, 1955).

teacher-training course was established. Requests from youth-serving agencies and Parent-Teacher Associations for demonstrations, lectures, and leadership training came as the reputation of this popular group spread through the community. In 1948 the Children's Experimental Theatre was forced to move to larger quarters in a hundred-year-old carriage house. Repairs and decorations took nearly a year but by 1949 an attractive new home was ready for occupancy. This playhouse was soon crowded with activities and the following year a suburban branch was set up in Catonsville. The Children's Experimental Theatre stated in its own brochure that four full-length productions a year were given, with at least sixteen regular performances of each.

THE REEDER SCHOOL, INC.

One of the schools which frankly patterned its program after the King-Coit School in New York was the Reeder School, Inc., a children's school of theatre and design in Fort Worth, Texas. It was founded in 1944 as an educational project using the theatre and its related arts as a cultural and recreational outlet for children from four to thirteen years of age. Some of the plays chosen for their literary value were *The Happy Hypocrite*, *The Rose and the Ring*, *Kai Khrosu*, *Aucassin and Nicolette*, *The Tempest*, and *Lady Precious Stream*. Throughout the year classes in acting, pantomime, painting, and dancing were conducted, with the play, the climax of the year's work, in mind. Each year audiences traveled from great distances to see the work of the Reeder School. Like the King-Coit School, this institution placed an emphasis on good literature, studied and produced with the highest artistic standards.

BRIGHAM YOUNG UNIVERSITY CHILDREN'S THEATRE

The School of Education of Brigham Young University in Utah officially launched its program in 1947. The program arose from the need for drama for elementary-school children in the area and the belief in children's theatre training for prospective teachers. The theatre was conducted in co-operation with the public schools and was reported in 1950 to have become successful and satisfying to both audience and players.

THE UNIVERSITY OF DELAWARE

In 1947 also the University of Delaware began its children's theatre program. With the public schools for audiences, the venture was successful and led to extended tours throughout the area. Each spring since 1947, children's plays have been toured to communities throughout the state and to a few adjoining ones. According to the director, Robert Kase, campus performances alone have attracted audiences equal to the average audience for any of the regular adult productions.

BAYLOR UNIVERSITY CHILDREN'S THEATRE

An unusual program was undertaken by the Baylor Children's Playhouse in Waco, Texas. A Negro children's theatre had been opened in 1947, with financial backing and transportation between the theatre and their schools provided for the actors by the Junior League. Baylor University permitted the use of its theatre building and assigned two instructors to work with the twenty-five talented children who made up the group.[6] Classwork and rehearsals for forthcoming productions were carried on.

DENISON CHILDREN'S THEATRE

The Denison Children's Theatre began in 1948 under the joint sponsorship of Denison University and the central Ohio branch of the American Association of University Women. The group was active from the start in touring plays to near-by Ohio towns. Probably the most interesting enterprise of its career to date was the transporting of a production of *Grandmother Sly Boots* to England and Scotland in 1954. While this took place at a later

[6] Mary Brinkerhoff, "Talent Unlimited," *Recreation*, Vol. XLIII (February, 1950), 534.

period, the foundations of a well-organized touring program which could handle so ambitious a project were laid in the forties.

PORT WASHINGTON CHILDREN'S THEATRE

In Port Washington, Long Island, a highly successful school and community project was initiated in 1947. The idea originated with the principal of the Main Street School, who believed that there should be some sort of local theatre for children in which adults played the adult roles. The result was an elaborate annual production of a well-known children's play. The unique feature, which has contributed to community interest as well as satisfactory casting, has been the age range of the participants. Children from the fifth grade through senior-high school were combined with adult actors once a year in a series of performances given at the junior-high school. Molly and Elmer Tangerman, residents of Port Washington, were instrumental in the development of the project from the beginning, although there has been a sharing of the directional responsibility from time to time.

Two organizations were established, with separate duties: the Main Street Home and School Association was to handle promotion, ticket sales, and auditorium management; the Port Washington Play Troupe, a local adult dramatic society, was to give support through the lending of actors and the assuming of backstage responsibility. Parents and interested citizens joined the committees of each group as the annual children's play became a popular winter tradition. While ticket prices were kept low (fifteen cents for children at the beginning and thirty-five cents later), the plays were self-supporting, with the Home and School Association handling finances and receiving whatever profit was made.

Some of the plays presented over the years were *The Reluctant Dragon, The Wizard of Oz, Alice in Wonderland, Snow White and the Seven Dwarfs, Peter Pan, Cinderella, Aladdin, The Emperor's New Clothes,* and *Jack and the Beanstalk.* Visual and technical effects were given special attention, for it was the conviction of the adults in charge that color, beauty, and spectacle were important elements of children's entertainment. While the

136

number of performances increased from two to five, no more than one production a year was given. This one, however, increased in extravagance and attracted much interest in neighboring suburbs as a worth-while type of school and community project.

It is apparent from the number of colleges, universities, and private studios which began work in the forties that the interest of educational institutions in children's theatre was spreading rapidly. It is significant that each children's theatre cited was either founded in conjunction with another community organization or shortly after its founding began work in co-operation with the public schools. With the exception of the private studios, the work was carried on as a public service. These private groups, by drawing audiences from the areas in which they were located, served the cultural interests of the community also, in a somewhat different way. It is interesting to note that the activity was not confined to any one section of the country but was taking place in all regions, urban and rural.

Community Theatre for Children

Community theatres for children under the sponsorship of civic playhouses or recreation centers likewise continued their activities with unprecedented growth. The following report for 1941 was made in *Recreation*:

> Plays had been given in 300 American cities during the preceding year.
> There were listed 211 dramatic clubs, 172 festivals, 108 little theatre groups, 296 plays, 213 puppet and marionette groups and 509 programs of story-telling.[7]

By 1943 hundreds of playgrounds all over the country were giving boys and girls the excitement and educational opportunities to be found in recreational dramatics. The point was often made that no other activity offered so many possibilities for self-

[7] Anon., "Chart of Recreational Activities Reported in 1941," *Recreation*, Vol. XXXVI (June, 1942), 136.

development along with wholesome pleasure. For this reason drama, in one form or another, was one of the most important offerings of the playground and community center.

Many of these organizations were described in *Players* and *Recreation* during the forties. A number of them were started by the Junior League and later turned into community projects. Whereas during the preceding decades, community theatres for children could be identified either as a branch of an adult civic playhouse or as a part of a municipal recreation department, during the forties this distinction could no longer be made. In the majority of cases various civic groups and agencies joined together for the sake of a stronger organization, which could, as a consequence, reach more children in the community.

DULUTH CHILDREN'S THEATRE

Duluth has been cited earlier as one of the pioneers in children's theatre activities. Since it not only continued but reorganized with the changing times, further mention must be made of it here. "The Duluth Children's Theatre, a venerable institution (as such things go) with ten years of successful producing to its credit is enjoying renewed vitality."[8]

The reorganization consisted of sponsorship by the City Council with assistance from the WPA Recreation Department. A board appointed by the mayor supervised the work while the WPA supplied the personnel. This shift in status from a civic theatre branch to an institution under municipal sponsorship seems further evidence of the trend toward the large community enterprise and away from the small semiprivate organization.

CHILDREN'S THEATRE OF ROANOKE

The groundwork for the community children's theatre in Roanoke, Virginia, was laid in the spring and summer of 1940. Prior to this the American Association of University Women had spon-

[8] Welty, "In the Children's Theatres," *loc. cit.*, 16.

sored Clare Tree Major's productions and the Junior League had given plays. Believing this program to be inadequate, the League approached clubs and civic groups in the city in an effort to stimulate the formation of a more extensive program. By the fall of 1940 a board of directors had been appointed, a director named, and a constitution written. In addition to civic organizations, the schools and department of recreation were included among the sponsors. A theatre school was established and a series of three plays was presented publicly each season. In 1941 both the tuition for these classes and the admission prices to the plays were lowered in an effort to serve a greater number of children in the city.

WAUWATOSA, WISCONSIN

An unusual type of program was established in Wauwatosa, Wisconsin, in 1940. A community project, in which nonprofessional adults put on the plays exclusively for children, it achieved immediate success. Parents originated the ideas and interested the superintendent of schools and the Parent-Teacher Association in the plans. Fathers, mothers, and teachers put on the plays; the WPA made the costumes; the Boy Scouts of Wauwatosa ushered; and the entire community participated in the promotion of the enterprise. Season tickets were sold and plays were put on in the high-school auditorium. Questionnaires sent to school children for their reactions to the plays helped the adults to determine the content of the program.

THE LOS ANGELES RECREATION PROGRAM

The Los Angeles Children's Theatre, founded and operated by the recreation department, has been described in an earlier chapter. Further mention must be made of it at this time, however, since by 1941 the one center had been increased to seven, all of which were offering weekly matinees. The popularity of the original summer programs led to the establishment of a winter one; thus a year-round theatre for children was available for boys and girls in all parts of the Los Angeles metropolitan area.

LAKEWOOD, OHIO, CHILDREN'S THEATRE

In Lakewood, Ohio, a drama program took shape under the auspices of the recreation department. Begun in 1941, by 1945 it included ten classes of fifth- and sixth-grade children, three classes of junior-high children, one of senior-high students, and many adult classes. The younger children met in the school buildings and the older ones in the recreation center. While the objectives were primarily social, the quality and popularity of the work brought this group to public attention.

CHILDREN'S THEATRE CONFERENCES

Such growth as has just been reported in all parts of the country led to conferences, two of which were held in 1941. One was a state-wide meeting in West Virginia. The purpose was stated to be the giving of cohesion to the rapidly growing drama programs in the state. Another conference was sponsored jointly by Stanford University and the Palo Alto Children's Theatre. Attending were directors and teachers from throughout the northern part of California.

THE SUMMIT, NEW JERSEY, PROGRAM

In an effort to meet the wartime need for children's entertainment, Summit, New Jersey, installed a traveling playhouse. A project of the recreation department, it toured the five playgrounds of the city for the first time in the summer of 1941. Children from each center prepared plays which were subsequently given in the other four. While not a new idea, the extraordinary success of the trailer theatre, as a means of developing and sharing projects among an increasing number of children in the community, caused it to be described in *The American City* in 1942.[9]

BURLINGAME, CALIFORNIA

Burlingame, California, organized children's theatre activities

[9] H. S. Kennedy, "Children Need Recreation in Wartime," *The American City*, Vol. LVII (July, 1942), 64.

in 1941 and increased its offerings almost immediately to meet the wartime demand for local recreation. Municipally subsidized, the Burlingame Children's Theatre was a special division of the recreation department, which agreed to appropriate an operating budget for the theatre and pay the salary of the director. From the first the enterprise was practically self-supporting, with low admission charges of ten cents for children and twenty-five cents for adults at each performance. A lay board was established to handle the box office, to usher, and to act as air-raid wardens. Children from five to fourteen worked on scenery and costumes as well as acting in the plays.

A large carriage house on the property of the recreation center housed the theatre. Since it seated only eighty-two, at least four performances were necessary to take care of the crowds of boys and girls in Burlingame who wanted to see the plays. Plays with large casts were given in the public schools, which readily gave their support to this popular project.

RICHMOND, VIRGINIA

"Richmond's Children's Theatre—Second Edition" was the title of a 1943 article in *Recreation*, describing the rebirth of a popular community institution. Some fifteen years before, a group of Richmond high-school students had organized a club which gave public performances of well-known children's stories. The recreation association had sponsored the project, which flourished for several years. As the original members grew up and left the community, the group dwindled and finally died. In 1942, however, another group made its appearance. Assisted in its efforts by the Parent-Teacher Association, the Junior League, the Musicians Club of Richmond, the Virginia Museum of Fine Arts, and Miller and Rhoades Department Store, a brand new children's theatre was born. So successful were its offerings that in 1946 summer tours were added.[10]

---

[10] Patricia Royal, "Children's Theatre Goes Traveling," *Recreation*, Vol. XXXIX (January, 1946), pp. 535–36, 550–51.

JACKSONVILLE, FLORIDA

A children's theatre which resulted from a wartime need was established in Jacksonville, Florida, in 1942. Because camping and the usual vacation activities had been curtailed, a summer dramatic program was started to occupy the leisure hours of the children of the city. The activity was so popular that in September a delegation of parents prevailed upon the director of the program to continue the work, thus forming a regular junior theatre.

SEATTLE JUNIOR PROGRAMS, INC.

The founding of Seattle Junior Programs, Inc., has been described in an earlier chapter; however, a major change which took place as a result of the war caused 1941 to be an important date in its history. Originally set up for the purpose of sponsoring local performances of such traveling professional companies as Junior Programs, Inc., the Seattle group found itself suddenly without productions to book. Rather than give up what had become a popular civic attraction, it changed its policy and in 1941 began sponsoring only local productions. In 1942 it persuaded an adult acting group in the city, the Seattle Repertory Playhouse, to present two series of plays: an elementary series appealing to children in grades one through six, and a senior-high-school series. The University of Washington Division of Drama agreed to supply the junior-high series for children in grades seven, eight, and nine. Another group which contributed was the May Ann Wells School of Ballet.

Despite the success of the new policy, in 1944 Seattle Junior Programs, Inc., was again about to close. Another project was added in that year, stimulating new interest and increased activity. This was the playwriting contest for children's plays which George Savage of the University of Washington helped to initiate. Prizes were awarded to the three winning plays, which were selected from entries from throughout the United States. By 1949 the playwriting contests had added twenty-five new children's scripts to the repertoire of juvenile dramatic literature, besides arousing local and national interest. Figures showed that in addition to this nationally publicized project, classes sponsored by Seattle Junior Programs were growing in popularity and audiences for performances had increased from 4,200 in 1938-39 to 15,000 in 1948-49.[11]

ST. LOUIS, MISSOURI

The St. Louis children's theatre was organized in 1944 under the sponsorship of the Community Playhouse, which had been presenting plays for adults for nearly twenty years. Need for children's entertainment in that city caused the opening of a series of three productions a year for boys and girls. Participation in the public performances was handled with adults in adult roles and children in children's parts. The type of organization did not follow the pattern of the majority of children's theatres reported during the forties; as a branch of a little theatre group already in existence, it resembled some of the earlier ventures in which sponsorship was handled by the adult playhouse rather than by municipal or civic organizations.

JUNIOR ENTERTAINMENT, INC., OF DENVER

An organization which concentrated on the procurement of the best live entertainment for children of all ages was founded in 1943; it was known as Junior Entertainment, Inc., of Denver, Colorado. Like the Seattle group, it enlisted the co-operation of civic and educational institutions; the Denver Public Schools, the Denver Symphony Orchestra, the Denver Art Museum, the Parent-Teacher Association, the Junior League, and the University of Denver have all been active participants. Both professional and nonprofessional entertainment were included in its offerings, for which 2,000 season tickets were sold annually. While the

[11] Mrs. George Savage, "The Business Side of It," *Theatre Arts Monthly*, Vol. XXXIII (September, 1949), 54.

whole city contributed support, the University of Denver remained its strongest ally.

FORT WORTH, TEXAS

In Fort Worth, Texas, a similar organization was sponsoring children's programs. This was the Bureau of Children's Entertainment, to which six local civic and service organizations contributed. These were the American Association of University Women, the Association for Childhood Education, Administrative Women in Education, Classroom Teachers, the Junior League, and Principals and Vice-Principals. The aims of this group, like the others mentioned, were to provide wholesome entertainment and cultural opportunities for the boys and girls of the city. By obtaining the support of the organizations listed, successful promotion was possible and financial backing was assured.

MEMPHIS, TENNESSEE

A "theatre for and by children" was described before the National Recreation Association in 1943 as one of the most exemplary groups in operation at the time. It was said to be an unusual organization for the following reasons: It was theatre for children and by children; the playing space was extremely small; it was complete in every detail, from box office to scenery workshop; and the presentations varied in age offering and appeal.[12]

The room in the Peabody Community Center, in which plays were presented, was of average size but attractively decorated with murals depicting the story of Hansel and Gretel. Children were on all of the committees, even to the printing of the tickets. Children of nine took part in the Saturday matinees; children from ten to twelve participated in the half-hour dramatic radio show put on by the recreation department; and teen-agers had a choice of activity, including all phases of backstage work. With a minimum of guidance by adults, this junior enterprise flourished during the war years.

[12] Alice Gilbertson, "Curtain Going Up," *Recreation*, Vol. XXXVII (November, 1943), 432–34.

AUSTIN, TEXAS

Children played an important part in the Children's Theatre of Austin, under the auspices of the recreation department. It was opened in 1943 with a director of plays and a program of classes held in the Austin Athletic Club. Children from nine to fourteen were included, but within a few months another class for six- to eight-year-olds was added. By 1944 it had produced three plays, with boys and girls active in the backstage staff as well as in the casts. With performances in winter and summer, the children's theatre of the recreation department was one of the recognized cultural institutions in Austin.

PORTLAND, MAINE

A highly successful trailer theatre was established in Portland, Maine, in 1944. A joint project of the Parks and Recreation Department of Portland and the Portland Children's Theatre, it was given further assistance by Virginia Lee Comer of the Junior League. Plans were laid the preceding year, so that when it started to travel in the summer of 1944, its itinerary was carefully charted. Tuesday and Friday performances in the greater Portland area from the beginning of the summer until Labor Day constituted the first season's engagements.

The small stage was built in sections to rest on the floor of the trailer; it could be opened up into a platform with an apron in front and dressing rooms on the sides. A crew of 15, including the actors, went with it on its tours of the city. By 1948 it was said to have traveled 250 miles throughout the Portland area, presenting 27 performances of 2 plays to 20,000 children in playgrounds, housing projects, and parks. In September, 1949, it went as far afield as Central Park in New York City, where it was one of the features of the Children's Theatre Conference being held in the city at that time.

WESTCHESTER CHILDREN'S THEATRE GUILD

The Westchester Children's Theatre Guild, established in 1944 by the county recreation commission, was highly successful in its appeal and contribution to the community. Facilities and a plant in which to work were given to the group, in return for which a certain number of performances were expected. The project included regular classes in drama, creative dramatics, stagecraft, and dance. "Arts in Action" was dedicated to the principles underlying the teaching of all the arts. While the objectives were primarily educational and social, public performances of plays were the climax of a term's work.

JUNIOR THEATRE OF MARIN COUNTY

Marin County, California, was the scene of an enterprise founded in 1945 by a group of mothers who wanted live theatre for their children. Professional entertainment was procured and performances were scheduled in the seven areas of the county. The two purposes behind the planning were the presentation of good professional theatre for children during the winter at low cost, and the teaching of good theatre to children during the summer at no cost.

To these ends, one over-all director was given charge of educational work, with individual unit directors in each of the seven areas. According to the ANTA questionnaire six years later, the educational and cultural objectives had been fulfilled through this kind of organization.

JEWISH THEATRE FOR CHILDREN IN
NEW YORK CITY

In 1946 the Jewish Education Committee of New York and the United Parent-Teacher Association of Jewish Schools established the Jewish Theatre for Children. Plays dealing with Jewish history, folklore, and tradition were emphasized, and public performances were offered every Sunday afternoon at 2:30 from November through March in New York City. With Samuel Citron as director, this group made a successful beginning and has maintained its program as a community service every winter since its founding. A play contest evolved in later years; a prize of $1,ooo is offered for the best full-length play for children in English based on a Jewish theme.

BIRMINGHAM JUNIOR PROGRAMS

The Birmingham Junior Programs originated in Birmingham, Alabama, in 1947 as a result of Junior League and Parent-Teacher Association effort. Backed financially by the League the first year, the project became very successful. Through the co-operation of the public schools, the high-school auditorium was made available, dates were arranged, and ticket sales were facilitated. A program of five plays and a symphony orchestra constituted a season of quality entertainment, with an admission charge of thirty cents for a single performance. Hence the objective of good drama and music for the young people of Birmingham was achieved by means of community co-operation.

MADISON SQUARE CHILDREN'S THEATRE

One of the most active and colorful theatrical enterprises in the East was located on the lower east side of New York. This activity was the work of the Madison Square Boys' Club, which began sponsorship of the group in 1947. Robert Oberreich, the director, was a former soldier and a graduate of the American Academy of Dramatic Arts and Theatre Wing Professional Schools. Over five hundred boys and girls from forty different nationalities were among the participants. These children assumed responsibility for all phases of backstage work as well as acting in the plays, with the major objectives of social integration and good theatre. The group was reported to have done such outstanding work that dozens of its members appeared subsequently in movies, radio, and television in New York.

THE HOUSTON CHILDREN'S THEATRE

The Houston Children's Theatre, Inc., of Houston, Texas, was founded in 1948 in recognition of the need for good children's entertainment and in appreciation of the part that the Houston Civic Theatre had contributed in the past to the cultural development of the youth of the city. With the good will of the city behind it, the organization was able to formulate ambitious plans which included not only a program of legitimate plays but a puppet theatre, radio studio, and extension work for children beyond an easy commuting distance.

RALEIGH CHILDREN'S THEATRE

The children's theatre of Raleigh, North Carolina, established in 1948, was a widely supported community project. Nancy Stamey, the director, contributed numerous magazine articles on children's theatre as well as assuming an active part in the Children's Theatre Conference. Her report on the Raleigh Theatre, which appeared two years after its founding, gave the following details. A board was composed of representatives from eight organizations in the city: the Junior League, the Junior Women's Club, the Raleigh Little Theatre (an adult dramatic society), the Girl Scouts, the Parent-Teacher Association, the school system, the city library, and the recreation department. Each agreed to furnish a service, with the recreation department handling the budget and the director's salary. Elementary-school children performed in the plays and high-school students acted the adult roles. Three productions a year and a summer theatre during the vacation months constituted the program.

BINGHAMTON CHILDREN'S THEATRE COUNCIL

Although the Children's Theatre Council of Binghamton, New York, has already been described, further mention of its work seems pertinent since in 1948 the publication "Promoting Good Theatre for Children in Binghamton" was brought up to date. Reviewing its ten years of service, the statement was made that this "Council is still Binghamton's only agency with the primary purpose of providing the best in all forms of cultural entertainment for children."[13]

148

At the end of ten years the program was said to be the most extensive in its history, the balance in the bank at its highest, and the membership larger and more enthusiastic than in any previous season. Unlike many of the other children's theatre groups, the organization of the Council had remained virtually the same during the ten years of its existence. Its membership included representatives from the groups who initiated the enterprise: the American Association of University Women, the Civic Club, the Department of Education, the Junior League, the Monday Afternoon Club, the Parent-Teacher Association, and a member from the Jewish Sisterhood. Co-operation from the schools had made for a happy relationship, which, in turn, helped immeasurably in the promotion and sale of tickets and the orientation of the audience to the program.

A venture into radio was inaugurated in 1943, since the war was curtailing the number of stage productions. With a Council member in charge, children from various schools took part in the *Lady Tell in Storyland* series of thirty-eight programs, all of which were prepared by "Lady Tell," a Council member, and the Department of Education. Another series, *Books Bring Adventure*, a group of Junior League recordings, was produced in 1946–47. The co-operation of the public libraries of Binghamton added to the interest of the community in this phase of the Council's work.

In concluding the chapter on organization, the Council expressed its hope that its report might show how one community had pooled its resources to realize certain ambitions. During the past ten years, the Council had become less and less an entity unto itself and much more the agent through which the entire town worked to enrich the cultural life of its young people.

In addition to the groups which have been described above, many other children's theatres under community or municipal administration were reported in the ANTA Survey of 1951. Each year of the decade gave birth to a greater number than had the year before.

[13] Mrs. Reah Stanley Drake and others, "Promoting Good Theatre for Children in Binghamton," 1.

From the larger number of community theatres which either described or acknowledged activity during the forties, it is apparent that the children's theatre movement in the communities of America was spreading and gathering strength. The pooling of resources and the combining of sponsorship have made it impossible to draw hard and fast lines between different types of community organizations. While there were a few which were strictly little theatre groups (such as the St. Louis Playhouse Children's Theatre) and a few which were strictly playground groups (such as the project in Summit, New Jersey), the majority were joint enterprises of two or more civic organizations. In some instances several sponsors joined in the sharing of responsibility and promotional work. In such cities as Binghamton, Richmond, Denver, and Raleigh, virtually every important civic organization contributed to the project, thus ensuring not only a sounder financial backing but a wider interest on the part of the citizens at large.

The frequent reference to co-operation between university and community, and public schools and community, indicates that the educational and community theatres were not operating as separate entities. Interdependence strengthened rather than weakened the programs of each, as in the case of Seattle Junior Programs and the University of Washington, Denver Junior Entertainment and the University of Denver, and the Universities of Delaware and Denison and their respective communities. Altogether, larger programs, reaching more children and carried on under the auspices of more than one civic organization, seemed to be a definite trend among community children's theatres during the forties.

Professional Theatre for Children

It has been implied through the activities of sponsoring organizations that professional children's theatre was available during this decade. One company, Junior Programs, Inc., whose outstanding contribution was described in the last chapter, was active at the beginning of this period but was forced to cancel its tours because of wartime conditions. Clare Tree Major's company, on the other hand, managed to weather the obstacles and continue production. In addition to those two well-known groups, there were several other professional companies which began work during the forties and so were available for booking throughout the United States.

JUNIOR PROGRAMS, INC.

Junior Programs, Inc., continued its touring of plays, ballet, and opera through the season of 1942-43. Because of the shortage of gasoline during this last season, it was thought advisable to amalgamate the three companies in order to keep going. In addition to regular sponsored performances, Junior Programs also had recordings made of *Marco Polo, Robin Hood, Hansel and Gretel,* and *The Bumble Bee Prince.* These were put out by Victor Records and became available in stores throughout the United States.

Dorothy McFadden held to a firm belief that theatre for children in wartime was important. "We may be able through the means of music and drama to influence our children toward a greater pride and a sincere unshakable faith in their American democracy."[14] In spite of this belief and the effort to conserve gasoline by combining the three companies, there were obstacles which could not be surmounted. Male members of the casts were drafted and many parents, particularly in New York City, feared having their children in large public auditoriums. Operations were suspended in 1943, and America's largest professional company presenting children's plays closed. According to the records, 102 performances of plays were given in the last season in which the three companies were touring.

During the seven years of its existence 1,300 performances were given by its casts, 700 performances were given by other companies which it booked, and over 4,000,000 children made up the total audience in 43 states.

In reviewing their work, Junior Programs was the first organi-

[14] "The Future of Professional Children's Theatre," *Players Magazine,* Vol. XX (February, 1944), 9.

zation to take opera for children on tour and present it with a variety of forms and dramatic techniques. In the field of dance the use of the stylized-narrator technique was introduced in such fantasies as *Pinocchio* and *The Princess and the Swineherd*. For these innovations particular credit was due Saul Lancourt, managing director. In *The Adventures of Marco Polo* songs and dances were carefully integrated to further the plot. It was Dorothy Mc-Fadden's dream that someday productions for young people might be given as much serious consideration as those for adults. While many children had been reached, it was still only a fraction of the potential audience. ". . . up to now comparatively few parents or other grown people have been awakened to the fact that the theatre for children should be as beautiful and as well acted and well produced as theatre for older folks."[15]

Some of the techniques first used in Junior Programs have been used in subsequent music dramas, and many of the young actors and dancers were next seen in the successful production of *Oklahoma!* How many adult theatregoers were first introduced to music, dance, and drama through Junior Programs would be only conjecture; however, in the seven years of its existence this organization reached the largest audience of young Americans to date.

CLARE TREE MAJOR

Clare Tree Major during the forties not only continued her tours of children's plays but added a National Classic Theatre which gave performances on high-school and college campuses. During the 1947–48 season seven companies embarked on nation-wide tours. In their repertory were such favorite old plays as *Alice in Wonderland, The Sleeping Beauty, Robin Hood, Heidi, Penrod, Mrs. Wiggs of the Cabbage Patch,* and *Hans Brinker*.

Her school, the National Academy of Theatre Arts, located at Pleasantville, New York, offered a two-year course for young actors preparing to work in her company and a summer school for teachers. Both the tours and the school managed to survive,

[15] *Ibid.,* 9.

although wartime restrictions presented greater problems than had the depression years.

EDWIN STRAWBRIDGE

A dancer whose name has been linked with Junior Programs, Inc., but who actually began his own touring company in 1940 was Edwin Strawbridge. Strawbridge had been a concert performer during the twenties and thirties. His introduction to children's theatre came when he was booked by Dorothy McFadden for Junior Programs. This led to the organizing and touring of his own small group of dancers whose work was directed to audiences of children. His success in this field brought him continued engagements and recognition as one of America's foremost entertainers of juvenile audiences. Among the heroes he has brought to life through dramatic dance interpretation were Christopher Columbus, Daniel Boone, and Johnny Appleseed; among the story-tale characters were Pinocchio, Simple Simon, and Little Red Riding Hood. His tours were seasonal from September to May, with two companies frequently appearing simultaneously.

Strawbridge's belief that children were his most appreciative audience caused him to devote the rest of his life to their entertainment. His philosophy that theatre is vital to the development of a sense of values, standards, and attitudes was expressed in his brochures.

AMERICAN THEATRE FOR CHILDREN IN LOS ANGELES

Another professional company founded in 1940 was the American Theatre for Children in Los Angeles. Sara Shakow and William Loewe were coproducers of this nonprofit professional group of adult actors. Their purpose was stated to be: "To provide worth-while entertainment for children of the community; to function as a genuine cultural center."

To these ends they gave what they considered to be vital contemporary plays, which were a reflection of the times and which should stimulate thinking on important issues of the day. The fairy tales and well-known children's stories were avoided in an effort to meet this aim. Four series of plays were planned, including plays for six- to eight-year-olds, nine- to eleven-year-olds, twelve- to fourteen-year-olds, and fourteen- to sixteen-year-olds.

On the governing board were two psychologists, two educators, one children's librarian, one author of children's books, two child-welfare workers, and two representatives from religious groups. These persons worked with the theatre staff on selection of plays and the children's reaction to them.

Radio programs and classes in the arts of the theatre were added as this enterprise developed. From its stated objectives and organization the American Theatre for Children bore more resemblance to the Federal Theatre than to such professional companies as Junior Programs or Clare Tree Major's Company. This was also an instance of attention paid to the age level of the audience.

PROVINCETOWN CHILDREN'S THEATRE

A professional group which began activity as a summer theatre for children during the 1946 season and ten years later became a year-round organization was the Provincetown Children's Theatre of New York. Under the leadership of John Grahame, who wrote and staged the plays, and Alexander Maissel, who composed and directed the music, the Provincetown Children's Theatre first presented its plays near Monticello, New York. The audiences during the first ten years were composed of children from camps and summer resorts. Demand for a winter program of a similar nature caused the management in 1956 to expand its offerings, which according to box-office records were as popular during the winter as they were during the summer months.

Certain specific objectives were held by this group. The belief that children should be treated with respect was a guiding principle. The combining of music and drama in a modern musical-comedy form suitable for children was a second aim, and, according to the directors, it was very well accepted by audiences ranging in age from three to fifteen.

The stories selected for this type of production were traditional; they included *Rip Van Winkle, Cinderella, The Prince of Egypt*, and *Aladdin*. The fact that the performances were consistently well attended at a ticket price of $1.50 indicated two things to the management: there was need for professional children's theatre in the downtown area of Manhattan, and the musical-comedy form was a good medium in which to work. The children's theatre, far from being a side line, was an important part of the Provincetown Theatre, which for many years had offered off-Broadway plays for audiences of adults.

MAE DESMOND'S COMPANY IN PHILADELPHIA

Mae Desmond's company, which toured the East, North, and Middle West, was founded in 1941 in Philadelphia. This group began with a series of six plays which were presented at the Philadelphia Town Hall. The war interfered with operations and for two years activity was suspended. When production was resumed, it was on a touring basis with four new titles added to the repertoire each season. Such favorite children's plays as the following were presented by the Mae Desmond company: *Snow White and the Bear, Robin Hood's Treasure, King Arthur's Magic Sword, The Arabian Knights*, and *Kit Carson and the Indians*.

CHILDREN'S WORLD THEATRE

"One of the brightest hopes of the children's theatre in America has been a very fine professional company, the Children's World Theatre."[16] This statement by Sara Spencer, head of the Children's Theatre Press, was made in 1955; the Children's World Theatre came into being in 1947. Its aim, according to the founders, was to instruct but above all to give good entertainment.

The six founders of the Children's World Theatre were Monte Meacham (president), Jo Ann Sayers Bliss, Bette Butterworth,

16 *Children's Theatre Conference Newsletter*, Vol. V (October, 1955), 7.

Sarah Newmayer, Julie Thompson, and Sheldon Thompson. It was set up originally as a nonprofit membership corporation organized to establish a permanent repertory theatre for children with adult professional actors. Its fundamental purpose was stated to be: arousing children's imagination through active entertainment; inspiring with the best in movement, speech, art, and music; and increasing their understanding of other national cultures and customs.

The opening performance was a production of *Jack and the Beanstalk* at the Barbizon Plaza in New York. Evidence of the serious purpose of the company was their invitation to the well-known and highly respected Charlotte Chorpenning to come to New York to direct this production. High praise from critics as well as from educators greeted the new venture, which subsequently sent shows on the road in addition to the regularly scheduled performances at the Barbizon Plaza.

Little Red Riding Hood was the first play to tour. Before long, engagements up and down the East Coast and as far west as Cincinnati, Indianapolis, and St. Louis were part of the itinerary. Among the sponsors were the Junior League, the Association for Childhood Education, and independent community groups. According to all reports, the company was greeted with as much enthusiasm on tour as it was in New York.

Monte Meacham's and Bette Butterworth's background included training at Ohio State University, the University of Missouri, and the American Academy of Dramatic Arts. Work in professional stage, radio, and television productions, in addition to serving on the board of directors of AETA, acting as consultant to the Junior League, and membership in ANTA, further equipped Meacham for the role he was to play in children's theatre between the years 1947 and 1955. Bette Butterworth, actress and art director for the company, and a professional staff not only emphasized beautiful productions of worth-while plays but studied their audiences for reactions.

Sheldon Thompson, graduate of the Philadelphia Museum School of Industrial Arts, was admirably equipped to handle the technical aspects, whereas Julie Thompson had come to Children's World Theatre with a rich background of specialized training in dance and acting for children. Formerly a member of Clare Tree Major's company, she had the reputation of having played more children's heroines than any other actress in the United States. All six, however, doubled in brass—the production was of primary importance, with no job too menial to be done for the sake of a fine and finished result.

An article in the *New York Times* described the observations of the writer, who was vice-president of the company. In it she commented that "children are invariably on the side of goodness . . . children like beauty, cleverness, certain kinds of comedy, secrets, magic, suspense; are bored with aimless fooling; hate cheating and injustice."[17] These observations were indicative of the approach of the new company, trained in the theatre arts and sensitive to the needs and responses of children.

Enthusiasm on the part of the Children's Theatre Committee, praise from such critics as William Rose Benet and Brooks Atkinson, and the response of young audiences from the beginning marked the Children's World Theatre as one of the significant contributions of the forties, if not of the century. It was the combined abilities and idealism of the six founders, rather than the strength of any one person, which accounted for the immediate success of this group. It was to claim a prominent place in the history of the movement despite the relatively short span of its existence.

NATIONAL YOUTH THEATRE IN NEW YORK CITY

A professional group which began activity in 1949 was the National Youth Theatre of New York City, originally called Pam Productions. Organized by Joel Gray and Phil Arnold, this company purported to supplement the school program by bringing to life famous historical and literary characters and building appreciative audiences for the future.

[17] Sarah Newmayer, "For Children It Is Not Make-Believe," *New York Times Magazine Section* (December 5, 1948), 24–26.

A series of four plays, which were scheduled to tour from New York to Denver, through Texas and the South, was available for booking. *Marco Polo* was the first production to travel to small towns and cities of the United States. Low ticket prices and economical production made it possible for this group to realize its aim of reaching young audiences in many small towns throughout the country.

THE CARAVAN THEATRE OF DORSET, VERMONT

The Caravan Theatre, originating in 1949, was a resident stock company at the summer playhouse in Dorset, Vermont. It was opened as a professional group but was not affiliated with Actor's Equity. Operating only during the summer months in the beginning, its purpose was the entertainment of children during the vacation period. Successful, well-attended performances encouraged the Caravan Theatre to tour its plays; however, an extensive program of touring did not develop until the next decade.

THE TRAVELING PLAYHOUSE

The fall of 1949 was the founding date of the Traveling Playhouse of the Young Men's Hebrew Association, in New York City. Directed by Kay Rockefeller, who had charge of dramatic activities there, the Playhouse was opened for the purpose of offering good entertainment to the children who came to this center. Grants of $2,000 apiece from the Rockefeller Foundation and the Young Men's Hebrew Association enabled this group of adult professional actors to launch its program.

The Traveling Playhouse established the custom of giving a first performance of each play in the Kaufman Auditorium of the "Y," after which touring engagements in the East were accepted. Plays, dances, and music were among the offerings on the subscription series for children at the Young Men's Hebrew Association, of which the Traveling Playhouse was at this time a part.

Other professional groups reported to have begun activity during this decade were Salome Gaynor's company in Philadelphia, the Children's Drama Guild of New York (semiprofessional), the Bunny and David Show Party of New York, and the Young Actors' Company of Hollywood.

Judging from the number and success of the producing companies mentioned, professional theatre for children increased steadily during the forties. In spite of the difficulties encountered by reason of wartime restrictions, only one company, Junior Programs, Inc., closed. One, the Clare Tree Major Company, which had been in existence previously, survived; and several others began operation between the years 1940 and 1949. In nearly every instance both entertainment and education were stressed. High standards and concern for the child's ethical and moral values were listed among the objectives.

The frequent mention of sponsoring groups indicates the support that these professional touring companies had in planning their programs, which included most of the United States. Educational institutions and organizations, as well as the Junior League, were among the most active supporters of children's entertainment, a fact which shows a greater unity among these groups than was apparent in any previous period. Finally, the listing of professional companies among the membership of the Children's Theatre Committee is proof that professional and nonprofessional, as well as educational and community producing groups, were engaged in the sharing of problems related to play selection, production, and audience.

Publications for Children's Theatre

During the forties more publication for children's theatre was needed to keep pace with the increasing interest in the movement. Some groups, such as the Junior League, continued to write their own plays. Special writers were called in to help with Junior Programs scripts, while Charlotte Chorpenning's name was found with increasing frequency on the printed programs of many producing groups.

In 1940 the American Library Association announced a *Subject Index to Children's Plays*, prepared by a subcommittee of the American Library Association Board on Library Service to Children and Young People, and compiled by Elizabeth D. Briggs. This was an indexing of plays under such headings as plays with historical background, plays about foreign countries, and plays on American life. There were 202 collections of plays listed for grades one through eight. Altogether, nearly 783 subjects were included.

In an effort to secure new material, ten organizations during the forties began offering prizes for new scripts, with the promise of a complete production to the winners. First to do this was Seattle Junior Programs, whose play contest has become a national event.

Caroline Fisher and Hazel Robertson's *Children and the Theatre*, an account of the Palo Alto community theatre, appeared in 1940. The interest of many communities throughout the United States in the extensive program and singular success of this enterprise served to make the book a guide as well as an account of achievement.

In 1947–48 the Children's Theatre Council of Binghamton, New York, revised the detailed record of its work, "Promoting Good Theatre for Children in Binghamton," an unpublished account which was at the same time a practical guide for other sponsoring agencies. It was a record of significant achievement and an excellent guidebook.

The first edition of Winifred Ward's *Playmaking with Children* appeared in 1947; while this was basically a text for creative dramatics, it was written by one of the leaders of children's theatre in the United States and was therefore an important publication for educational and recreational groups. Articles, as well as plays, by Charlotte Chorpenning, stressed the special techniques involved in writing for young audiences. Whereas good literature had long been emphasized by previous groups, the analysis of specific writing techniques did not appear in publications until the thirties and forties. According to Charlotte Chorpenning, the

key to writing good plays for children's theatre was the understanding of a child audience. She stressed certain fundamentals,
such as identification with the story and the hero or protagonist,
no interruption of the story, a worth-while basic experience, character and meaning in terms of the story, and exercise spots for the
audience.

In 1947 Kenneth Graham of the University of Minnesota completed his doctoral dissertation: "An Introductory Study of the
Evaluation of Plays for Children's Theatres in the United States."
For the first time a comprehensive piece of scholarly research was
done on available plays, including questions asked of experts and
publishers. The data were analyzed with respect to the purpose
which children's plays should serve and the special dramatic techniques which should be applied to the elements of a children's
play.

While the Federal Theatre writers had analyzed children's
plays with respect to their audience, it seems significant that the
foremost writer of juvenile dramatic literature, Charlotte Chorpenning, and an educator, Kenneth Graham, prominent in the
children's theatre field, were concerning themselves with techniques as well as content.

The Children's Theatre Press, meanwhile, was adding new
titles annually and becoming known as the only publishing house
in the United States devoted exclusively to the publication of
plays and books for children's theatre.

From its remarkable expansion during the forties it is apparent
that the children's theatre movement had become a vigorous institution in American community life. On all levels from the elementary school through college, there was evidence of interest,
participation, and support on the part of educational institutions
in this aspect of drama. The national organizations, the American
Educational Theatre Association and the Children's Theatre
Committee, were offering their services through meetings, publications, research, and promotion. *Players Magazine*, published by

the National Collegiate Players, and *Educational Theatre Journal*, published by AETA, both began giving space regularly to announcements and problems related to children's work.

George Freedley, stressing the audience aspect of adult and children's theatre in the perspective of the entire field, said that the training of an audience cannot begin too early. "Children who become theatre-goers will continue all their lives to have an interest in the dramatic arts, whether they participate actively or not. Our theatre, professional and non-professional, commercial or subsidized, can never develop into the Great American National Theatre unless it has a trained audience."[18] The future of the American theatre, according to Freedley, will be influenced by what is done in children's theatre. The forties demonstrated that much was being done, and that it was taking place for the first time in the history of the movement in an organized and unified way.

[18] Virginia Lee Comer, "Highlights of the American Educational Theatre Association Children's Theatre Conference in Seattle, Washington, August 1-5, 1946."

VII

Becoming Professional

1950-60

The trend toward unification of children's theatre activities through national and local organizations, which appeared in the forties, continued into the fifth decade of the twentieth century. Intensification and expansion of program rather than change characterized the movement during this period, in which at least three significant events took place. First was the Mid-Century White House Conference in 1950, at which children's theatre was a topic of consideration. Second was the change in status of the Children's Theatre Committee, which after 1952 became officially the Children's Theatre Conference, a division of the AETA, operating more or less autonomously and publishing its own newsletter for members. Finally, there was the establishment of sixteen regional organizations under the aegis of the Children's Theatre Conference. These were important milestones of the first five years.

In schools and colleges throughout the United States drama had become a frequently included and a valued part of the educational program. Surveys made by the AETA during these years proved that many colleges had added curricular offerings in children's theatre as well as plays to prepare teachers and directors for work in this field. Community and recreation centers were likewise expanding steadily. Since drama had long since become an important inclusion in many of these centers, the growth of community organizations and resources affected the growth of children's theatre.

Finally, the professional theatre, which had evidenced a keener interest in entertainment for young people during the forties than in any previous period, continued to grow. Reports from Briggs and Haynes Management, theatrical booking agencies in New York, showed both supply and demand to be at their highest thus far in the fifties.

Support for the claims of children's theatre advocates existed even in the Office of Information and Educational Exchange of the State Department in Washington by the mid-century. In 1950 children's theatre activities were said to be a definite part of the program at the American information centers in Germany and Austria. With local, national, and international attention directed toward the movement, children's theatre had unquestionably come of age.

The White House Conference

The Mid-Century White House Conference on Children and Youth brought to Washington in December, 1950, some six thousand delegates from the states, national organizations, and local agencies. This was the sixth such conference called by a President at ten-year intervals. Past areas of study had included child welfare, security, health, and preparation for citizenship. The significance of aesthetic experience and artistic expression for healthy personality development was the topic in 1950; this subject claimed the attention of leaders in educational and community theatres from various parts of the country. Implications for children's theatre in this conference were to be found in the following statement: "The very essence of theatre lies in the interrelation of human beings and used properly in the educational process, drama can richly aid healthy personality development in children and youth."[1]

1 Virginia Lee Comer, "The White House Conference and Educational Theatre," *Educational Theatre Journal*, Vol. III (October, 1951), 222.

Objectives which grew out of this conference were the securing of recognition and more effective functioning of drama in the total educational scheme; the encouragement of opportunities for children to see and participate in theatre during leisure hours; the development of a sound body of knowledge; and an attempt, basically, to deepen the understanding of life.

Representing children's theatre at this conference were Virginia Lee Comer, Sara Spencer, Rose Cowen, and Sybil Baker. A special report on "The Value of the Theatre in the Emotional Development of Children" was prepared by Burdette Fitzgerald, Charlotte Chorpenning, and Sara Spencer. The inclusion of children's theatre on the agenda of the White House Conference was tangible evidence of its importance to the educational and recreational leaders of the United States in 1950.

After the conference, the Mid-Century Committee for Children and Youth was organized, with Leonard W. Mayo as chairman. Its plans included the publication of a bulletin and providing of information and field services for interested groups throughout the United States. Leaders of the educational theatre named three areas in which a contribution might be made. These were the self-evaluation of both individuals and groups, a more effective functioning through closer ties and co-operation with community groups, and a long-range program of research on activities already established. Since children's theatre was included in the educational theatre program, the implications for its future contribution were stated in these aims.

National Organizations

It has been stated that delegates from national organizations were in attendance at the White House meeting. Among the organizations which offered particular leadership during the fifties were the Junior League, the Children's Theatre Conference, and ANTA.

THE ASSOCIATION OF JUNIOR LEAGUES
OF AMERICA

A catalogue from the Children's Theatre Press in the fifties stated that many an American city owed its community children's theatre to the local Junior League. Conditions had changed since the first entrance of the League into this area of community service, but Leagues throughout the country had experimented and adapted their activities to meet these changes, thereby providing a special kind of entertainment. According to their own record of achievement, many Leagues became active members of the Children's Theatre Conference and were regularly represented at the annual meetings.

The grouping program continued to be an important contribution, with noteworthy co-operation from the public schools. League plays were presented over television in Amarillo, Colorado Springs, El Paso, Seattle, and Macon, while in Philadelphia the League established a Drama Library to serve the recreation centers. Here a "package" could be borrowed with script, sets, costumes, properties, and lighting equipment—everything needed to produce a show. An example of co-operation with the educational theatre was the Toledo Junior League, which accepted an invitation from the University of Toledo to assist in a six-week summer session on children's theatre for teachers. Such diverse activities as these indicate the extent to which the Leagues co-ordinated their activities with those of their communities.

Statistics from the Junior League headquarters in New York reveal the scope of individual dramatic offerings between 1950 and 1955. By the 1955–56 season over 100 Leagues reported plays presented for children annually. The 144 productions offered in the 1955–56 season included 87 different play titles. Those reported by four or more Leagues were *Cinderella, Hansel and Gretel, Beauty and the Beast, Pinocchio, Rumpelstiltskin, Puss in Boots*, and *The King's Balcony*.

In 64 Leagues, children's theatre was trouped to schools; frequently productions were also taken to hospitals, orphanages, settlement houses, homes for children, museums, recreation centers, and other institutions.

Eleven Leagues presented children's theatre productions on television and one League on radio. In addition, seventeen Leagues used radio and television for children's theatre publicity, giving excerpts from plays and interviewing members of the cast.

The record of Junior League activities indicates both the interest of the organization in this area of community service and the extent to which its offerings in drama for children have developed. In recognition of its achievement, the Children's Theatre Press dedicated its 1956 catalogue to the Association of Junior Leagues of America. A pioneering organization, the Junior League had maintained the longest consistent program of dramatic entertainment for children to be found in the history of the movement in this country.

THE CHILDREN'S THEATRE CONFERENCE

The Children's Theatre Committee, established in 1944, underwent several major changes during the fifties. In 1950 the organization was renamed the Children's Theatre Conference; it was recognized as a division of the AETA in 1952. During the AETA convention in December of that year the Advisory Council approved both the recommendation that the committee be made a division of AETA and the operating code which had been drawn up. The title of "chairman" of the Children's Theatre Committee was changed to "director" of the Children's Theatre Conference.

Certain work projects undertaken by the Children's Theatre Conference (or CTC) have been mentioned in an earlier chapter. These projects were the work of the following subcommittees: Bibliography, Play Standards, Directory, Resolutions, Publicity, Curriculum, and Costume Exchange Index. By 1953 some others had been added: College Survey, Mass Media, New Plays, International Children's Theatre, Newsletter, Placement Service Liaison, Regional Organization, and Royalty Investigation.

The establishment of regional organizations, through which greater unity could be attained, took place in 1952 as a result of the annual conference held in August in Madison, Wisconsin. A system set up by ANTA was adopted with minor changes. This system provided for the following regional divisions: Regions 1 and 2—California, Arizona, Nevada; Region 3—Washington, Oregon, Montana, Idaho; Region 4—Utah, Wyoming, Colorado, New Mexico; Region 5—Texas, Louisiana, Oklahoma, Arkansas; Region 6—Kansas, Nebraska, Missouri, Iowa; Region 7—North Dakota, South Dakota, Minnesota; Region 8—Illinois, Wisconsin; Region 9—Ohio, Michigan, Indiana; Region 10—Kentucky, Mississippi, Tennessee, Alabama; Region 11—Georgia, Florida, North Carolina, South Carolina; Region 12—Virginia, West Virginia, Maryland, Washington, D.C.; Region 13—Western Pennsylvania, Delaware, New Jersey; Region 14—New York, Connecticut, Eastern Pennsylvania; Region 15—Maine, New Hampshire, Vermont, Massachusetts, Rhode Island; and Region 16—Canada.

The report on the Eighth Annual Children's Theatre meeting stated that through this type of organization with local officers and programs, the aims and objectives of the Children's Theatre Conference could be carried out to much better advantage. The objectives of the CTC were as follows:

1. To promote the establishment of children's theatre activities in all communities by educational, community and private groups.
2. To encourage the raising and maintaining of high standards in all types of children's theatre activities throughout America.
3. To provide a meeting ground for children's theatre workers from all levels through sponsorship of an annual national meeting, regional meetings and conference committees throughout the year.

Pamphlets published by the CTC provided further information for prospective members:

1. *What*
   The Children's Theatre Conference is a Division of the AETA, a non-profit organization, encouraging the development of theatre in education.

2. *Who*
   Directors of plays for children, teachers, leaders of community recreation, Junior Leagues, civic theatres, service clubs, church groups, etc. all may belong.
3. *Where and When*
   The annual meeting of the Children's Theatre Conference is usually held the last week of August, by the hospitality of some interested college or university. The location of the annual meeting is shifted, from year to year, to different geographical locations, to give all areas an opportunity to attend and participate.
4. *Why*
   A. To receive helpful publications like:
      The Educational Theatre Journal
      Survey of college courses in children's dramatics
      List of published American plays for children
      Bibliography of books on children's theatre
      Manual for directors of children's theatre
      Directory of AETA membership
   B. To receive services from:
      The Placement Service
      The New Plays Committee
      The Regional Organization
      The Committee on Rights and Royalties
      The Audio-Visual Aids Committee
   C. To attend the annual meetings
   D. To help promote children's theatre through:
      Distributing information
      Encouraging productions in college, school, community
      Reduction in admissions taxes
      Widespread releases on scripts

Some of the special topics which have claimed attention at the annual meetings have been "Psychological Aspects of Child Audiences," "The Impact of Mass Media on Children's Audiences," "Training for Children's Theatre," "Children's Drama in Religious Education," and "International Children's Theatre." Regular sessions devoted to problems of plays, various aspects of production, and audience have been conducted for the membership, which by 1955 had reached nine hundred individuals and organizations. Book and technical exhibits, photography displays, and unpublished manuscripts were added attractions for delegates between the scheduled events. The workshop preceding the conference has been a successful adjunct for which, in 1955, college credit could be received. At these conventions professional theatre people, educators on all levels, and volunteers have worked together in harmony and with singleness of purpose. This dedication to a common goal has contributed to the uniqueness of this organization and accounts in large part for the spread of its influence.

The Children's Theatre Foundation, Inc., was established in 1958. Its aims were to bring speakers for conferences, to provide scholarships for graduate study in children's theatre for students of demonstrated ability, and to award travel grants to United States representatives to international councils. Increased membership will provide income for additional projects in the future.

Dorothy Schwartz, co-ordinator of regions and later national director of the Children's Theatre Conference during this period, commented on the responsibilities which fell to the heirs of the first Children's Theatre Committee. She spoke of the responsibility to provide the richest possible drama experience for children, but added that it was equally important that the work be interpreted through constant clarification of aims. The second responsibility which she stressed was the strengthening of the national organization; toward this end, contribution at the regional level was not only important but vital.[2]

As a national organization which grew enormously in size and strength during the short span of its existence, the CTC stood as the foremost agency supporting and unifying children's dramatic activities and maintaining the high standards set by its founders. Unquestionably, the Children's Theatre Conference was one of the most effective and successful organizations in America dedicated to the happiness and development of children.

[2] "Report," *Children's Theatre Conference Newsletter* (January, 1956), 1.

THE AMERICAN EDUCATIONAL THEATRE ASSOCIATION

With the Children's Theatre Conference established as a division, the AETA had given approval and support to its various activities. The annual conference continued to be reported in the December issue of the *Educational Theatre Journal*, and Geraldine Siks was made the first regular children's theatre editor in the year 1955.

THE AMERICAN NATIONAL THEATRE AND ACADEMY

The American National Theatre and Academy continued its program of service to both professional and nonprofessional organizations. By 1955 there were two thousand members in forty-eight states, Hawaii, and the Canal Zone. The listing of projects on the ANTA program for the fifties included Productions; National Theatre Service; the ANTA Albums; the ANTA Play Series; Experimental Productions; ANTA, UNESCO, and the International Theatre Institute; the International (Theatre) Exchange Program; and Publications. Under Publications were Bibliographies on Children's Theatre and the Children's Theatre Directory, based on a national survey conducted in 1951.

With the help of ANTA and Rosamond Gilder, children's theatre was represented for the first time at a UNESCO conclave. In 1952 in New York a panel discussion was held on the subject "UNESCO and the Theatre: Appraisal and Planning." Among those representing children's theatre were Sara Spencer, Robert Kase, Winifred Ward, Virginia Lee Comer, Frances Cary Bowen, Dina Rees Evans, Dorothy Allen, Monte Meacham, Bette Butterworth, and Isabel Burger.

In the spring of the same year a Paris conference on "Theatre and Youth" was called under the auspices of the International Theatre Institute (ITI). Rose Cowen of Washington, D.C., and Leon Miller of Cincinnati, Ohio, were the American representatives at this meeting which was the first of its kind. A full report of the meeting was included in the December, 1952, issue of *World Theatre* which featured children's theatre activities throughout the world. One important outcome of this broadening of interest was the observance of International Theatre Month, designated as March of each year. Educational and community theatres throughout the United States were urged to give plays of other than American background during this time. Lists of plays, international in origin and suitable for audiences of children, could be obtained from both ANTA and the CTC, along with posters and other publicity with which to advertise them.

Reports on children's theatre activities throughout the world indicated that the interest of American teachers and directors had gone beyond the local scene to encompass the dramatic activities of young people in all parts of the world. From its activity in regard to UNESCO and the International Theatre Institute, it was apparent that ANTA in the fifties was embracing an even wider program: the sharing of ideas and publication through the cultural experiments of UNESCO and ITI.

The Educational Theatre

It has been stated that during the forties the educational theatre was assuming leadership of the children's theatre movement. This trend continued with the combination theatre and school of the theatre a popular *modus operandi*. At the eighth annual CTC held in 1952 the college and university delegates discussed ways of co-ordinating classes of children with the children's theatre program and the children's theatre curriculum of a university. Three types of laboratories were found to be prevalent: university students observing or participating in the public schools; children paying nominal tuition and meeting at the university; and the use of the university demonstration school for observation by university students. Several types of course offerings were mentioned: separate courses in children's theatre and creative dramatics, a combined course under the general heading of "Dramatic Activities for Children," and children's theatre as a small unit in a general speech program.

One of the important projects undertaken by the CTC during the fifties was a survey of children's theatre courses offered in American colleges and universities. Mouzon Law of the University of Texas acted as chairman of the investigating committee, and the report was published in 1954. Sixty-nine colleges and universities in twenty-seven states reported that course work was being offered in either children's theatre or creative dramatics or both. All parts of the country were represented; there were nine different institutions in both New York and Illinois which reported some kind of curricular offering in this field.

According to the report of the College Curriculum Survey Committee, 1,060 questionnaires were mailed; 346 were returned, signifying a response of 33 per cent. Of the total number returned, 219 indicated that no work in the field of children's theatre was then being offered. Of this total (219), 86 indicated that there was interest in the establishment of such a program. Of the total number returned, 127 reported that some attention (courses or productions) was being given to children's theatre or creative dramatics. The committee pointed out the fact that each year more colleges were adding courses in one or another phase of children's theatre work in order to meet the growing demand.[3]

During the fifties news of particular institutions continued to be reported in the periodicals, but the chief source of information was the *Children's Theatre Conference Newsletter*, which began publication in 1950. In the *Newsletter* programs, both established and new, were cited along with facts concerning plays, directors, and types of audiences for which productions were given.

THE UNIVERSITY OF WASHINGTON

At the University of Washington, where extensive work in

[3] Mimeographed Report of the College Curriculum Survey Committee of the Children's Theatre Conference, 1953. See also Mouzon Law, "A Directory of American Colleges and Universities Offering Curricular Programs in Children's Theatre," *Educational Theatre Journal*, Vol. VI (March, 1954), 40–46.

drama was being done, two new developments were reported. One of these was the establishment of Creative Dramatics as a required course for recreation majors as well as for education majors in the university. The other was the inauguration of a touring program of children's plays, the purpose of which was stated to be introducing live drama into the northwest communities which otherwise might never see a stage play.

The May, 1958, issue of the *Educational Theatre Journal* carried a report by Agnes Haaga entitled "Directory of American Colleges and Universities Offering Training in Children's Theatre and Creative Dramatics." This survey revealed that 220 were offering work of some kind, as compared to 127 in 1954. Thirteen offered children's theatre as part of a course; 103, creative dramatics as part of a course; 93, graduate work in the field; 98, laboratory work with children; 12, production for children's audiences only; and 12, occasional work.[4]

THE EVANSTON CHILDREN'S THEATRE

The *Newsletter* for January, 1955, carried the announcement of the thirtieth birthday of the Evanston Children's Theatre of Northwestern University. One major change had been made two years earlier in regard to its program. This was the setting up of two series of plays, one of which was designed for the upper elementary grades and the other for younger children. Each series included three plays. Whereas the former continued to be acted by a combined cast of university students and elementary-school pupils, the latter was performed by seventh and eighth graders who had had four years of creative dramatics work.

TUFTS COLLEGE CHILDREN'S THEATRE

At Tufts College in Medford, Massachusetts, a summer drama program for children was organized. The announcement which appeared in the *New England Children's Theatre Bulletin*, 1955, described the Tufts Magic Circle as an outstanding project in the

[4] Vol. X (May, 1958), 150–63.

New England area. There twenty-five children, led by five experienced staff members, produced three plays in five weeks, presenting two performances each week. The children who attended came from the Boston metropolitan area and ranged in age from nine to fourteen. Actually a day camp in which drama was given the major emphasis, the program included recreation and rest with a noon meal served in a college dining room.

The Tufts Magic Circle was reported to be the only day camp of its kind in New England. Auditions were required for admission, but programs presented by the young actors on Thursday mornings were open to the public at a moderate charge. The plays were given on the Tufts area stage and included *The Magic Fishbone*, *The Blow Hard* by Adele Thane, *The Dragon* by Lady Gregory, *The Man Who Married a Dumb Wife* by Anatole France, *The Sleeping Beauty*, *The Emperor's New Clothes*, and *The Rose and the Ring*.

ST. PETERSBURG JUNIOR COLLEGE

In 1951 the Junior College Playmakers of St. Petersburg Junior College in Florida began producing plays for children. A 1955 article in *Players Magazine* described their production of *The Wizard of Oz*, in which over one hundred students were involved, as a satisfying example of community and college co-operation.

TAMPA CHILDREN'S THEATRE

A 1951 *Newsletter* mentioned the Tampa Children's Theatre in Florida which was growing rapidly. The unique feature of this group was its policy of presenting only original plays. The production described in this issue, *Iridessa*, included music and dance.

ONEONTA STATE TEACHERS COLLEGE

The show-wagon idea, which had been used by a number of community groups as a means of touring plays to different parks and recreation centers, was adopted by the Oneonta State Teachers College in New York. Under the title "The Dragon Wagon," this portable stage began transporting a repertory group of college actors in 1950. Casts were composed of potential elementary-school teachers for whom this project was a valuable aspect of their training. The Dragon Wagon functioned, therefore, both as an educational instrument and as a community service.

HUNTER COLLEGE OF NEW YORK

During the forties and the early fifties Hunter College in New York City sponsored an active program of children's drama. Charlotte Perry, who later retired, not only developed a program of creative dramatics and children's theatre but contributed new scripts, one of which was mentioned as having been given a *première* production at the Perry-Mansfield School of the Theatre in Colorado. This was *The Cockney Cats*, later presented at Hunter College.

SAN FRANCISCO STATE COLLEGE

San Francisco State College, which was the scene of some of the earliest children's theatre activity, continued to be a leader among educational institutions. A Creative Arts Division presented programs for young people, including both productions by its own students and outside entertainment. Under the direction of Burdette Fitzgerald, who has been an active member of the Children's Theatre Conference since the time of its founding as well as a frequent contributor to *Players Magazine*, this department has become well known not only in California but throughout the country. Besides the regular performances in the college theatre, the casts of the children's plays toured on weekends for two months every spring.

THE CHILDREN'S EDUCATIONAL THEATRE
OF MARYLAND

A change in the policy of Johns Hopkins University during the fifties caused the children's theatre which it had sponsored for a number of years to become a community organization known as the Children's Educational Theatre of Maryland. It continued under the direction of Frances Cary Bowen. According to the *Newsletter*, the enrollment increased and plays were presented for audiences in and around Baltimore.

HOBART COLLEGE

At Hobart College in New York children's theatre was inaugurated in 1953. Paul Berkowsky, a senior student, produced *Rumpelstiltskin* as a class project with the intention of touring it. The first performance was apparently highly successful for the play traveled 350 miles in a period of three months, appearing in ten western New York communities, and played to 7,000 children between the ages of five and ten.

PORTLAND, OREGON

Mention was made in *Theatre Arts Monthly*, 1953, of the new facilities for the high-school drama program in Portland, Oregon. A million-dollar wing in which to house dramatic activities, including children's theatre, was built as a result of eight years of outstanding work. The first play in the new auditorium was *Alice in Wonderland*.

THE UNIVERSITY OF CALIFORNIA AT LOS ANGELES

An announcement of a new program, "Show Time at UCLA," under the sponsorship of the Los Angeles Junior Programs, appeared in the October, 1955, *Newsletter*. The Fine Arts department of the University of California at Los Angeles planned a varied series, including dance, theatre, music, opera, and movies, designed especially for children from seven to twelve. Performances were to take place every third Saturday afternoon for eight consecutive months. The 1955–56 season, a pilot program for the western area of the city, was aimed at giving the children of Los Angeles "an opportunity to experience the best in all the arts" at a minimum charge. This project was another example of co-operative planning between a university and a community-service organization.

OTHER CHILDREN'S THEATRES UNDER THE AUSPICES OF EDUCATIONAL INSTITUTIONS

According to the ANTA survey conducted in 1951, children's theatres had been established at Texas Christian University, at Endicott Junior College in Beverly, Massachusetts, and at Wheaton Community High School in Wheaton, Illinois, in 1950. Reported in the *CTC Newsletter* between 1950 and 1955 were programs of children's plays at more than thirty institutions in all parts of the United States. A bulletin from the New England Regional Conference of the CTC listed also Bennington College, Lasell Junior College, Radcliffe, Harvard, and the University of Vermont.

WORKSHOPS IN CHILDREN'S THEATRE

During the fifties workshops were becoming a popular method of introducing children's theatre on college campuses. The July, 1955, *Newsletter* referred to several which had been held recently. The University of Pittsburgh conducted a six-week workshop in creative dramatics and children's theatre under the direction of Barbara McIntyre. At the University of Alabama, Kenneth Graham and Dorothy Schwartz held a two-day workshop; at Kent State, Winifred Ward led a summer-session program designed for elementary-school teachers. At the University of Utah, where the annual Children's Theatre Conference met in 1955, course credit could be obtained through attendance at the Young People's Institute in August preceding the meeting.

The most active workshop leader was unquestionably Winifred Ward, who, after her retirement from Northwestern University, was available for both long- and short-term workshops throughout the United States. She traveled to all parts of the country, teaching and advising educational and community groups in this area of theatre work. Cincinnati, Atlantic City, Louisville, Kansas

City, Washington, D.C., and Ohio Wesleyan University, Macalester College, and National College of Education were the scenes of some of her workshops.

From reports and announcements in *Players Magazine*, the *Educational Theatre Journal*, and the *CTC Newsletter*, it is apparent that the children's theatre under the auspices of educational institutions was a popular and growing activity. Both productions for children by college and university groups and course work in children's theatre and creative dramatics were being offered, though the former seemed to be more widespread than the latter. Conferences, national and regional, were a means of publicizing, interpreting, and unifying activities. Workshops of varying lengths were becoming a popular means of introducing the subject or initiating programs; these were conducted by well-known leaders in children's theatre on college campuses or in recreation centers.

Community Theatre for Children

The recreation movement in America was expanding rapidly at mid-century. Many references in periodicals between 1950 and 1960 pointed to the fact that the dramatic program had become an important area of activity. Numerous individual projects were cited; some of these have been described previously, but others were just being set up as a result of community interest.

SEATTLE JUNIOR PROGRAMS, INC.

Seattle Junior Programs, Inc., has been described earlier but must be mentioned again as an unusually successful enterprise. By the early fifties it was serving an area of half a million people and had secured co-operation from the Junior League, the public-school system, the University of Washington, newspapers, and radio stations, as well as private citizens. As a sponsoring organization, Seattle Junior Programs, Inc., presented plays produced by the University of Washington School of Drama and ballets from a local dance studio. Subsequently the program was enlarged to include professional children's theatre touring companies.

The playwriting contest, classes in creative dramatics, touring performances, and publication of a practical guide for sponsors, *Children's Theatre Manual*, have earned this organization a national reputation for initiative and imaginative planning. News of its activities have been regularly reported in the *Children's Theatre News*.

CHICAGO, ILLINOIS

For over forty years the National Recreation Association had kept in close touch with the development of the park and recreation service of Chicago. In 1950 the comment "Recreation at its best" was made in describing the quality of the work. Drama was one of its important contributions and included both plays for children and Shakespearean drama by the Actors Company of Chicago.

A Children's Theatre Festival was held in Chicago in 1950 as a part of the Chicago Fair. Plays were presented six times a day between June 24 and September 4 by the Goodman Children's Theatre, the National Youth Theatre of New York, and the Children's World Theatre. Richard Beckhard was in charge of the project, which attracted attention and favorable comment from children and adults.

ROCHESTER, NEW YORK

The Rochester Community Players, Inc., of Rochester, New York, has been mentioned earlier in regard to children's work. In 1951, ten years after the founding of the program, dramatic classes were added for children and young people from eight to eighteen. An annual Easter production was the culminating project of a semester's study.

EVANSVILLE, INDIANA

The caravan or trailer-theatre idea had been adopted by a number of communities as a means of taking plays to various parts of a city. Evansville, Indiana, in 1954, was authorized by the Public Recreation Commission to establish a "show wagon" on which children's plays, talent shows, and equipment for street dances could be transported. Through co-operation with the public schools and Evansville College, the recreation department promoted the drama program; seventh- and eighth-grade pupils from four elementary schools in the city were used in the plays. Under the direction of Howard Hill, drama professor in the college, the entertainment provided for the children was said to be a popular summer activity.

KEENE, NEW HAMPSHIRE

One of the programs often cited in periodicals of the fifties was the Keene Children's Theatre in New Hampshire. Under the direction of Susan Ott, this enterprise was said to have provided outstanding community service. A donation from the community chest and the free use of municipal buildings helped to finance the activities from the beginning. Classes for one hundred children, teen-agers, and adults comprised the educational program, and a series of plays in school hours at the high school were an important outcome of the work. Students from Keene Teachers College assisted in production, and ticket prices were set low enough to ensure a large community participation.

WEST VIRGINIA

A 1950 *Newsletter* included several items of information regarding children's theatre activity in West Virginia. In Charleston a series of four plays for the 1950 season was announced; in Parkersburg the Children's Theatre Bureau was sponsoring children's entertainment; and in Oglebay the Junior Theatre, previously mentioned, was continuing the series of plays for young people set up in 1947. A newsletter, "The Children's Theatre and Radio Council of West Virginia," was established as a means of spreading information and unifying activities within the state.

MONTGOMERY COUNTY, MARYLAND

An adult theatre, producing plays for children, was established in 1951 in Montgomery County, Maryland. This enterprise, the Adventure Theatre, was highly successful in its initial efforts. A production of *The Sleeping Beauty*, written by Elizabeth Goodwyn and Helen Jordan, coproducers, was scheduled for seven performances in November and December, 1955, an increased schedule which had come about as a result of community interest.

YAKIMA, WASHINGTON

Players Magazine, in 1951, carried an account of the newly organized children's theatre in Yakima, Washington. The proximity to Seattle, where an extensive program had been in operation for a number of years, was said to have been responsible for the success of the idea. By the mid-fifties high schools, community theatres, and the University of Washington were bringing plays regularly under the sponsorship of Junior Programs of Yakima, and many of the plays were given in school time.

In 1950, Junior Programs of Yakima and the metropolitan park district combined talents, money, and physical assets for the purpose of extending the program to the parks.

HARWICH JUNIOR THEATRE

An experiment in summer theatre for children was begun on Cape Cod in 1951 by Betty Bobp, director of dramatic arts at Wheelock College in Boston. This was the Harwich Junior Theatre, described as the only summer theatre on the "straw hat circuit" devoted exclusively to producing plays for children. Established as a nonprofit self-supporting community theatre, the Harwich project served the community by offering entertainment and an opportunity for experience and participation in the dramatic arts. Children from nine to fourteen staged the plays under the direction of a small staff of adults. Moderately priced tickets were sold through local bookshops and stores, and the Harwich Recreation Council sponsored the project.

Children's classes were a part of the program and these were taught by well qualified adults. Although children performed in the plays, and a high standard of performance was demanded, the aim of the theatre was not to develop young "stars" but rather to stimulate appreciation of live theatre and to develop creativity.

UTICA, NEW YORK

In 1952 the Utica Community Theatre, one of the oldest adult community theatres in the country, added children's work. A staff of six instructors, with classes for children from eight to thirteen, was part of the expansion program.

HARRISBURG, PENNSYLVANIA

The Caravan Theatre of Harrisburg was a popular organization composed of children and adults. Founded and directed by Edwin Shade, this group played to numerous audiences of children in and around Harrisburg. *Marco Polo, Tom Sawyer*, and *The Emperor's New Clothes* were offerings of the 1951 season.

THE JUNIOR CIVIC THEATRE OF
PORTLAND, OREGON

In the season of 1944–45 the Portland (Oregon) Junior Civic Theatre began a program which grew steadily. By the mid-fifties it had expanded its program to include nine major productions, an arena presentation, and a city-wide contest of scenic and costume design, open to high-school and drama students. In order to serve the entire community, blocks of seats were reserved for children in outlying suburbs and towns. Tickets were handled through the schools, and children were brought to the theatre on weekends in their own school buses.

The Junior Civic Theatre was part of the Civic Theatre School, and more than 150 young people were enrolled. Adult members of the theatre staff were in charge of directing, designing, and costuming the plays.

MUSKEGON, MICHIGAN, CHILDREN'S THEATRE

Another community enterprise which was developed during the fifties was the Junior Division of the Muskegon Civic Theatre. This organization included three departments: a primary department (second- and third-grade pupils), an intermediate department (fourth-, fifth-, and sixth-grade pupils), and a junior department (seventh-, eighth-, and ninth-grade pupils). Under the direction of Louise Durham these groups presented plays as well as received training in the dramatic arts.

DES MOINES COMMUNITY PLAYHOUSE

A third community playhouse, in which children's activities became an important adjunct, was described in periodicals at this time. This was the Des Moines Community Playhouse, which employed a full-time director for the Children's Workshop. Classes for boys and girls from seven to seventeen gave instruction in dance, stagecraft, acting, and speech correction. In 1955–56 over 100 children participated in the public performances of 2 plays which were seen by more than 3,600.[5]

CHILDREN'S THEATRE OF WASHINGTON, D.C.

The Children's Theatre of Washington, D.C., under the direction of Rose Cowen, was among the most active groups in the fifties. Its observance of International Theatre Month in 1952 was described in a *Newsletter* as "probably the most ambitious children's theatre offering." The offering referred to was a performance of Aurand Harris' *Simon Big Ears*, of which four performances were given for the benefit of the Korean War Orphans and the Israeli Youth Services. Supplementing the regular cast of actors were forty children from various embassies.

PHOENIX, ARIZONA

In Phoenix, Arizona, the opening of the Tree House Children's

[5] Alice Griffin, "Theatre U.S.A.," *Theatre Arts Monthly*, Vol. XLI (February, 1957), 67.

Theatre was announced in 1955. Classes in creative dramatics, pantomime, voice and diction, and body movement augmented the series of plays, which during the first season included *Hansel and Gretel* and *The Emperor's New Clothes*. Don Doyle was founder and director of this theatre-in-the-round for the boys and girls of Phoenix.

KARAMU HOUSE IN CLEVELAND

Karamu House had been one of the first settlements to establish children's theatre as an important offering in its program. In the fifties a renewed emphasis was placed on the work. With Ann Flagg in charge of children's drama, classes on four levels were set up: a beginners' class for children from nine to fourteen; an advanced class for children of the same age; creative dramatics for children from six to eight; and student theatre for young people from fourteen to nineteen. A series of plays for child audiences on Saturday afternoons constituted the public part of the program.

While the educational values were held to be of primary importance, quality of production was also stressed. Some of the plays chosen for public performance were *The Blue Bird*, *The Sleeping Beauty*, *The Gooseherd and the Goblin*, *Paul and the Blue Ox*, *The Clown Who Ran Away*, *Robin Hood*, *The Apple of Contentment*, *The Magic Whistle*, and *The Emperor's New Clothes*. The Karamu Theatre, for both children and adults, continues to be one of America's significant community projects, attracting attention and respect both at home and abroad.

HENRY STREET SETTLEMENT IN NEW YORK

At the Henry Street Playhouse in New York City a unique program was developed. While the settlement was one of the first in this country to recognize the performing arts, it was not until the fifties that an extensive program including professional dance-drama for children's audiences was offered. The first production, *Fable of the Donkey* and *Lobster Quadrille*, was presented in 1949 for the *New York Times* Book Fair. The response to this program was so enthusiastic that regularly scheduled performances throughout the year resulted.

Under the direction of Alwyn Nikolais the Concert Group presented programs for adults and occasionally for children. Another company, the Repertory Group, under the direction of Ruth Grauert, performed exclusively for children. In addition to the appearances at Henry Street, both groups accepted touring engagements in other parts of the country as well as in the metropolitan area. During some seasons as many as seventy-five performances were given. The primary objective, since the casts were composed of professional adults, was a fine quality of entertainment, with the educative value in the product rather than in the process.

The performances of the adult professional companies were generally given on Sunday afternoons. Another program called "Saturdays at Three" was instituted. This series included magicians, marionettes, singers, dance-plays, clowns, and films. Some of the offerings in the series were an outgrowth of the classes in drama and dance at the settlement.

These classes, in which sound and movement rather than specific plays were stressed, were a means by which creative productions were built. In 1955 over 550 children were enrolled. Low tuition fees and admission charges made the Henry Street programs available to neighborhood children as well as to outside groups which helped to fill the Playhouse auditorium on weekends. While the presentations of the two companies, the Concert Group and the Repertory Group, could be classified as professional entertainment, the fact that they were part of the settlement program, which is a community offering, makes the inclusion of their activities under "Community Theatre for Children" equally appropriate.

THE BOSTON CHILDREN'S THEATRE

The Boston Children's Theatre was founded in 1951 by the Community Recreation Service of Boston for the purpose of providing "Better Plays for Children," the slogan of the organization.

It was one of the few programs of its kind in which both training and productions were stressed as a part of the recreational and cultural offering of the city. Creative dramatics and acting classes for children from eight to ten, ten to twelve, and twelve to fourteen met once a week under the guidance of the director and assistant director of the theatre. About 125 boys and girls were registered regularly for the three-month terms, and from these children the plays were cast. Five plays were produced during a season, with an average of three performances of each play in the New England Mutual Hall in Boston. Although two union stagehands were employed at these times, children were given an opportunity to assist backstage.

Salaried personnel included the director and assistant director (who were employed on a year-round basis), the publicity representative, costumer, business manager, ticket sellers, and stagehands, as well as the executive director of the Community Recreation Service. Admission to the plays was kept within a popular price range to encourage attendance of all children. An advisory committee of prominent citizens, which met once a year, approved the repertoire of plays selected by the director.

In 1953 a "Stagemobile" was inaugurated for the purpose of taking plays to sponsors in the Boston area. The success of the first summer caused this to be a regular adjunct to the winter program. Administrative costs were absorbed by the Community Recreation Service. Some of the plays selected for presentation during both winter and summer seasons were *Once Upon a Clothesline, The Prince and the Pauper, Racketty-Packetty House, The Wizard of Oz, The Bird's Christmas Carol, Tom Sawyer,* and *Peter and the Wolf.* While many familiar titles appeared in the list, the Boston Children's Theatre was interested in new plays so long as they met the requirement of "Better Plays" which was the reason given for its existence.

CHILDREN'S THEATRE IN THE CHURCH

During the fifties the church began showing interest in children's theatre as a part of its educational program. The church not only encouraged play production among young people and children's groups but began to include the dramatic arts in the training program of its religious leaders. Mentioned specifically in a 1953 *Children's Theatre Conference Newsletter* were Union Theological Seminary in New York and the Religious Drama Workshop held at Green Lake, Wisconsin, which included children's theatre in its summer meetings. The latter began work in 1949 and included such subjects as direction, production, creative dramatics for children, rhythmic choir, playwriting, play evaluation, and basic philosophy of religious drama. Delegates who attended the week's workshop participated actively in various phases of dramatic production, "working together to find deeper meaning and insight and to develop skills in this means of expression of Christian faith and belief." Newsletters, describing the activities of the workshoppers, were issued throughout the year; while there were many reports of children's dramatic activities, creative drama rather than children's theatre appeared to take precedence. On both adult and child levels, the effectiveness of this means of expression was stressed. More fine plays were said to be needed, as well as more trained leaders to share the responsibility.

Professional Theatre for Children

With the fifties came increased offerings in professional theatre for audiences of children. Three important companies described in earlier chapters continued to offer entertainment; a number of new companies also emerged. In nearly every instance productions were of a touring nature and were sponsored by schools, Parent-Teacher Associations, Junior Leagues, and community children's theatre councils. The two principal agencies which assisted in the promotion and scheduling of performances were Briggs Management, directed by Frances Schram, and Haynes Management, directed by Ellen Gephart, both of which were located in New York. Through those offices varied programs of dance, drama, music, and puppetry were sent throughout the country in an efficient, well-organized manner. While individual scheduling of performances still took place, the records of these two offices testify to a widespread use of this means of obtaining children's entertainment.

There was a greater interest in live entertainment than in puppets and marionettes, a greater demand for performances in newly developed suburban communities than for the centralized downtown show, and a tremendous increase in bookings as compared to the preceding decade. Briggs Management during the season 1955–56 offered the following attractions for young people: Children's World Theatre (three plays in repertory), Dorothy White's Fun with Music program, the Playhouse Dance Company, Tom Two Arrows' Rhythms of the Red Man, Judith Carrell and Don Reid's Young Folks Theatre, Kay Harwig's Party Entertainment, and Jim Powell's Characters Unlimited. Haynes Management during the same season offered these additional programs: Mae Desmond's Children's Theatre (five plays in repertory), Mara and Her Dancers, and John Begg's Ballet Carnival. Besides these, both companies managed puppet, marionette, magic, and variety shows. Since Briggs and Haynes were the two agencies specializing in entertainment for children, their offerings comprised the bulk of what was available in the professional field in the East.

CLARE TREE MAJOR'S CHILDREN'S THEATRE

The name of Clare Tree Major had been connected with children's theatre in the United States for three decades. Her work of carrying plays to young audiences throughout the country continued into the fifties, but just preceding her death in 1954 this oldest theatre for children was closed. Newspaper articles paying tribute to her spirit and enterprise stated that in taking children's plays to remote places, she inevitably created a nation-wide children's theatre audience and indirectly established the need for a national children's theatre organization. Never active in the Children's Theatre Conference, she nevertheless shared the same objectives of more and better entertainment for young people and to that end devoted thirty years of her life.

THE EDWIN STRAWBRIDGE COMPANY

Edwin Strawbridge's Company, which began programs for children in 1940, had increased offerings by the mid-century. In the fourteen years of its existence this group had covered 450,000 miles, had crossed the United States 18 times, and had played to 4,000,000 children in its September-to-May tours. In 1953, Strawbridge aligned himself with Actors' Equity Association, the first producer of children's entertainment to take this step.[6]

Strawbridge's programs were different from the usual children's plays in that they were a blend of ballet, theatre, and music. With six members in each of the two companies, a Broadway scenic artist to handle stage effects, and a stage manager to direct the running of the show, this was a professional enterprise whose work made a significant contribution to children's theatre in America.

During the 1955–56 season the Strawbridge offerings included *Doodle Dandy of the U.S.A.*, *The Shepherd King*, *Toby Tyler or Ten Weeks with the Circus*, *Peter and the Wolf*, and *The Nutcracker*. They were described by Strawbridge as "miniature musical comedies"; while they were primarily dance, they were billed as children's theatre.

CHILDREN'S WORLD THEATRE

The Children's World Theatre of New York had met with high praise at the time of its inception. This group continued to offer a variety of plays both locally and on tour until the summer of 1955, when its founder and director, Monte Meacham, was killed in an accident. The company kept its summer engagement at the Minnesota State Fair, but in September notified its sponsors of the permanent closing of the theatre.

[6] Stanley Richards, "450,000 Miles of Children's Theatre," *Players Magazine*, Vol. XXXI (December, 1954), 66–67.

Meacham had been an active member of ANTA, had been a member of the CTC governing board, and had played a part in upgrading this branch of the theatre in the brief but bright period that Children's World Theatre existed.

THE CARAVAN THEATRE OF DORSET, VERMONT

The Caravan Theatre of Dorset, Vermont, has been mentioned as a resident stock company which began operation in 1949. Operating as a non-Equity professional group, it continued its summer offerings for the following six seasons. In 1955 it extended its program to include winter touring engagements through the New England states, New York, New Jersey, and Pennsylvania. A production of *Winnie the Pooh* marked the entrance of this company into the area of year-round entertainment for children.

THE TRAVELING PLAYHOUSE

The Traveling Playhouse, directed by Kay Rockefeller, began activities in 1949 under the sponsorship of the Young Men's Hebrew Association of New York. The reputation of this group multiplied its touring engagements until by 1955 it was presenting from fifty to one hundred performances a year in the metropolitan area, upper New York state, New Jersey, Pennsylvania, and New England.

In 1955 sponsorship by the Young Men's Hebrew Association was officially ended; the Playhouse no longer needed this kind of support and was able to carry on as an independent company. Performances are still given in the Kaufmann Auditorium, however, and the YMHA maintains an active interest in the work. A special feature of this group is its production of a new script each season; these scripts are obtained as a result of the Aline Bernstein playwriting contest. This contest was begun in 1951 at Aline Bernstein's suggestion, for the purpose of stimulating the writing of plays for children. The Junior Entertainment Committee of the YMHA continued it as a memorial after her death in 1955, and presented the winning script as an expression of appreciation for her interest in children's theatre. A cash award went to the winner, who might be either a professional or a nonprofessional writer in any part of the United States.

THE MERRY-GO-ROUNDERS

Another professional company was established in the fifties under the aegis of the Young Men's Hebrew Association. This was the Merry-Go-Rounders, a dance-drama group which placed an emphasis on audience participation. Bonnie Bird was director with Doris Humphrey, supervisor.

Members of this company were adults; some also belonged to other dance groups in New York City. Some ten performances were given in the Kaufmann Auditorium, but, like the Traveling Playhouse, many more were given outside. While its contribution was largely in the field of dance, the dramatic character of the performance placed it just as appropriately among professional offerings in children's theatre.

CHARACTERS UNLIMITED

Characters Unlimited was a unique organization whose watchword was flexibility. Originally organized as a one-man show by Jim Powell, it expanded into a small group of players who accepted touring engagements in the New York area. In response to requests for a different type of entertainment for parties, conventions, and programs, this group became a complete producing unit which traveled to other parts of the country. Shows for children and adults, with settings which could be carried by hand, were given for the *New York Times* Book Fair, on television, in Town Hall, at the Metropolitan Museum, and at the Brooklyn Institute of Arts and Sciences.

Offering a variety program rather than straight drama, this company became known throughout the East and Midwest. In 1955, however, the accident in which Monte Meacham was killed

Goodman Theatre of Chicago production of *The Magic Isle*, by Wesley
Van Tassel, 1968. Courtesy Goodman Theatre.

Karamu Youth Theatre of Cleveland, Ohio, presented *Mean to Be Free* in 1969. Courtesy Karamu Youth Theatre.

Another scene from Joanne Kraus's *Mean to Be Free*, at Karamu Youth Theatre. Courtesy Karamu Youth Theatre.

Hote Casella, Cherokee Indian performer for children, in the 1950's and 1960's.

Tony Montanaro, the distinguished American mime. Courtesy
Frances Schram, Artists' Management.

The Paper Bag Players exhibit some of their scenery and props. Courtesy
Judith Martin.

Big, Little, and In-Between, as presented by the Children's Theatre International of New York City, 1969–70. Courtesy Vera Stilling.

also claimed the life of Jim Powell. Characters Unlimited was forced to disband.

JUNIOR THEATRE IN NEW YORK

A company of professional child-actors was established during the fifties by Phyllis Chalzel in Carnegie Hall in New York. The group offered well-known children's plays at regularly scheduled times throughout the year: Thanksgiving, the Christmas holiday season, and in the spring.

This company did not go on tour, but blocks of seats as well as individual-admission tickets were sold to schools and organizations. Prices of tickets were $1.50 and $2.00, higher prices than those paid for most plays during this period. Rehearsals rather than classwork comprised the activity of this group between productions.

EQUITY LIBRARY CHILDREN'S THEATRE

Equity Library Theatre was founded by Actor's Equity, the professional actor's union, and the New York Public Library system. A nonprofit organization, it was set up for two purposes: to give professional actors an opportunity to act and to bring theatre to the neighborhood. Shows were first given in the public libraries, but the need for a permanent home led to the establishment of headquarters at the Lenox Hill Playhouse.

> The Equity Library Theatre project has demonstrated how the neighborhood life . . . can be enriched by bringing live acting and good plays to people who otherwise would never have had the opportunity to enjoy dramatic productions. Furthermore this public-spirited organization has proven that it can produce a play without spending a million dollars.[7]

Equity Community Theatre was formed as a result of the success of this enterprise. With Equity Library Theatre and the New York Board of Education as coproducers, four shows yearly were

[7] "Equity Library Theatre for Children." Comment by Newbold Morris, chairman of New York City Center.

taken to communities in the metropolitan area. Out of this activity came Scrapbook Productions for young people, assembly-length programs of scenes from great plays. Thousands of junior- and senior-high-school students became acquainted with classic drama from Shakespeare to O'Neill through Scrapbook Productions.

A subsequent development of this organization was Equity Library Theatre for Children, which came into being in 1955. Funds from the National Council for the Living Theatre, an organization composed of ANTA, the Theatre Guild, and the League of New York Theatres, were approved for its use. Under professional direction Equity Library Theatre for Children presented full-length children's plays with careful attention to sets and costumes.

Large and enthusiastic audiences greeted the work of this group as they did the earlier organizations. Bookings were arranged through Briggs Management in New York.

THE KNICKERTY KNOCKERTY PLAYERS OF PITTSBURGH

The Knickerty Knockerty Players were located in Pittsburgh, although they played for audiences all over the United States and in six foreign countries during the fifties. A touring children's theatre composed of adult professional actors, this group gave a *première* of each production at the Pittsburgh Miniature Playhouse. Margot Frye, formerly of Grace Price Productions, was producer, and Madge Miller, children's playwright, directed. The group played a full season five days a week, including performances in the schools during school time.

Literary quality and careful production were stressed with the help of an advisory board of educators, writers, and civic leaders. Some of the plays selected for the repertory of this group were *The Emperor's New Clothes, Androcles and the Lion, St. George and the Dragon, The Red Shoes,* and *Rapunzel.*

THE PAPER BAG PLAYERS

In 1958 a new group captured the attention of New Yorkers

who saw its first public performance. This group called itself the "Paper Bag Players." Although its work belongs more properly to the next decade, it must be mentioned here because of its immediate success, due not merely to technical skill but to an imaginative and revolutionary approach to children's theatre. Instead of using familiar stories or fairy tales, the Paper Bag Players under the leadership of Judith Martin introduced original sketches, songs, and dances created by the company and based on children's own experiences, interests, and humor. In place of traditional costumes and scenery, this company wore black leotards, with flashes of color and the everyday objects with which children play: paper bags, cardboard cartons, shower curtains, etc. The appeal was to the child's imagination. The "Bags" were, from the first, singularly successful in reaching the preschooler as well as the older child through this new medium. A small group of young artists, the Paper Bag Players presented a true innovation in children's theatre.

STORY TIME DANCE THEATRE

Another company offering dance in the form of dance-plays was the Story Time Dance Theatre, which opened in 1959 under the direction of Sheila Hellman. Based in New Jersey, this group performed in schools and community centers, using as material such classics as *Aladdin,* with original music, costumes, and scenery. Programs ranged from thirty minutes to an hour in length so as to adjust to school-assembly programs.

THE MERRY WANDERERS

The Merry Wanderers Children's Theatre of New York opened in 1954 and played for several seasons as both a resident and a touring company. Under the combined direction of Gian Pace and David Dunham, this group offered children's classics by a professional cast. Gian Pace's background as a dancer made for an emphasis on movement, although the group performed plays and worked in the theatre tradition.

THE MERRY MIMES

One professional company which performed regularly off Broadway in New York during the late fifties and early sixties was Blanche Marvin's Merry Mimes. Located in the Cricket Theatre, a small auditorium housing adult productions in the evening, this group emphasized style and new ways of presenting familiar material. The Cricket, seating under two hundred, was in many ways ideal for children's performances; every child could see and hear well, and the director believed in physical comfort, charm, and cleanliness. The Merry Mimes were unique in adhering to a program of weekend performances and no touring engagements.

NATIONAL CHILDREN'S THEATRE ASSOCIATION

While much of the activity in the professional theatre was taking place in New York, a very successful company was founded in the Southwest. This was the National Children's Theatre Association of Dallas, Texas. Fiske Miles and his wife, Ruth Gilley Miles, had been booking agents in New York for a number of years. Among the companies they handled was Clare Tree Major's theatre. In 1955, following Mrs. Major's death, Fiske Miles decided that the tradition which she had carried on so long should continue and that he was the one to do it. Three years later, at a time when he might have contemplated retirement, the Mileses began a new career in Dallas: the establishment of a children's theatre company which had bookings in thirty-five towns during its first season. Tours ran from October to May and included in its repertory a fairy tale, a legend, and a historical play, all designed for children from kindergarten through sixth grade.

By the early sixties the National Children's Theatre Association was covering 10,000 miles, from Texas to Wisconsin and from New Mexico to Mississippi and Tennessee, and playing to 150,000 children each season. Actors were sought in New York and Chicago, and scenery and costume design were particularly stressed by the producers. Fiske Miles's belief in the importance of theatre in the life of a child included the joy derived from watching a play on the stage as well as the learning, the discrimination, and the standards of taste which resulted from experiencing good literary material.

TOM GLAZER

Among the solo performers of the fifties mention must be made of three artists, who have performed widely and who have added a new dimension to children's theatre. The first of these is Tom Glazer, folk singer, who has been acclaimed by the critics for his warmth, his ability to hold large audiences of children, and his skill in stimulating audience participation. The critics, by and large, have ignored children's theatre; Tom Glazer is the exception. He has not only been reviewed but praised in the *New York Times* as ". . . a man who knows how to captivate children with his voice and guitar . . . audience participation by the youngsters was spontaneous and unselfish."

HOTE CASELLA

An artist whose first appearances before children's audiences took place in the fifties is Hote Casella. Miss Casella, herself a Cherokee Indian, had accumulated a large repertory of authentic Indian songs and legends, which she was urged to bring to young audiences. Wearing native dress and using drums or piano accompaniment, Miss Casella went beyond music (she had been trained as a concert singer) and designed a program both educational and entertaining, which would hold the interest of the older child. While she has always worked alone, the dramatic style of her performance places it as appropriately in the area of theatre as in the area of music. Originally appearing in New York, Miss Casella during the sixties was to tour the United States, bringing a program of high quality to schools, concert halls, and television.

CHARITY BAILEY

Third of the solo performers seen in New York during this period was Charity Bailey. Miss Bailey, whose background was in music and dance, was singularly successful in her appearances before children's audiences; she involved the audience in active participation. She has also appeared on several television programs, and has become well known to thousands of children. Educational values have always been of primary importance to Miss Bailey, as they have been to Miss Casella.

THE LITTLEST CIRCUS

An entertainment which captivated audiences at the close of the decade was Wolfgang Roth's *Littlest Circus*. With a company of seven, staged and designed by Roth with choreography by Nelle Fisher, it offered an imaginative concept of the small European circus. Animals, ballerinas, clowns, and ringmaster performed in dance and mime to the music of a hurdy-gurdy and a one-man band at the Phoenix and the John Golden theatres in New York and subsequently on tour. Though this show could not qualify as drama, it was undeniably theatre, presented with tasteful simplicity and professional skill.

OTHER GROUPS OFFERING PROFESSIONAL CHILDREN'S ENTERTAINMENT

In addition to the companies offering regular plays, a number of other professional groups, which were primarily dance or music, opened during the early fifties. Mention will be made of them since they constituted live entertainment for audiences of children and stressed the dramatic appeal of their presentations.

JOHN BEGG'S BALLET CARNIVAL

John Begg opened his first Ballet Miniatures in the 1949–50 season. Described as "story book dance," these productions emphasized "beauty of story, dance, costumes, decor and music." Both Begg and his company had previously been associated with the classic ballet as well as with Broadway musicals.

There was reorganization resulting in a change of name; under the title of John Begg's Ballet Carnival, the group's later offerings included *Cinderella, The Three Bears, The Frog Prince, St. George and the Dragon,* and *The Big Top.* An unusual feature of the program was a costumed narrator who introduced and carried the thread of the story, which was presented in dance form.

MARA

Mara and Her Dancers likewise introduced drama in programs which were essentially dance. The country's foremost authority on Cambodian and Siamese dances, Mara gave her first dramatic dance performance for children at the Young Men's Hebrew Association Dance Center and the Henry Street Settlement in New York in the 1954–55 season. Little-known legendary material from the East and extravagant costumes made for performances which elicited praise from both dancers and educators. Subsequent programs have proved Mara to be a performer of stature, whose work blends authenticity with a high degree of technical skill.

CHILDREN'S DANCE THEATRE

Erika Thimey, who directed and co-ordinated activities for the Dance Theatre in Washington, brought stories in dance form to audiences of children in various parts of the country during the fifties. Productions were imaginatively costumed and choreographed, and combined the elements of dance, acting, speech, and classical as well as modern music.

TOURNABOUT, JUNIOR

Tournabout, Junior, a project of the nationally known Tournabout Theatre of Los Angeles, offered plays for young audiences for the first time in the summer of 1951. The group performed under a tent in the Farmers' Market, where it was enthusiastically received. Plans were made to continue the program the following summer, but there is no further record of activities.

THE CHILDREN'S THEATRE OF THE WEST

Another professional group established in California during the early fifties was the Children's Theatre of the West. This company, based in Sacramento, toured its plays through the states of California, Oregon, Washington, Montana, Idaho, Texas, Nevada, New Mexico, Arizona, Wyoming, and Colorado. Tours were booked in advance with local organizations such as Parent-Teacher Associations and schools.

Among the productions which were given were *The Emperor's New Clothes*, *The Sorcerer's Apprentice*, *The Giant of Knockmany*, *The Bremen Town Musicians*, and *Johnny Appleseed*. Special attention was paid to settings and costumes.

Casts for the plays were composed largely of young people graduating from western schools who wished to go into the professional theatre, teaching, or recreation work with children. While Wilma Murphey was producer and manager, Burdette Fitzgerald of the San Francisco State College directed the productions. During the mid-fifties, the Children's Theatre of the West played to audiences totaling 1,400 at the college and to around 10,000 regularly during a season's tour. While this company was not known throughout the country, it was extremely popular and successful in the region covered by its tours.

With the appearance of so many new professional groups in the fifties, there was a greater interest in children's entertainment performed by adults. Music and dance as well as drama were among the available offerings but even with such companies as Mara, Edwin Strawbridge Productions, the Children's Dance Theatre, and the Merry-Go-Rounders, a dramatic approach was emphasized. Agencies booking professional entertainment were responsible for bringing many of these attractions before sponsoring organizations, and both supply and demand increased within the decade. A warning note was sounded at the Eighth Annual Children's Theatre Conference, however, when the point was made that if these new professional companies were to survive, they must be supported and should be included in the seasonal programs planned by sponsoring organizations.

REGION 14 SHOWCASE

A regional project which was to become an important event of the sixties was inaugurated in New York City in the spring of 1955. This was the Region 14 Showcase, originally planned as a feature of a small annual conference sponsored by CTC. Inasmuch as a number of professional groups were based in New York, a showcase was an opportunity for the Region to render a double service: to recognize some of the more interesting work being done by the professional companies and to give sponsors an opportunity to become acquainted with work of superior quality. The showcase format was an overwhelming success, and the following year the spring conference was organized around this feature and held in the Kaufmann Concert Hall of the 92nd Street Young Men's–Young Women's Hebrew Association.

Each succeeding spring more companies were represented in the Showcase, which was drawing larger and larger crowds. Delegates from surrounding states as well as from the New York metropolitan area attended, representing sponsors as well as educators. A Showcase Committee was set up and a screening process known as "previewing" was carried on throughout the year. The growing number of professional companies, however, posed a problem as the Region promised to preview all plays (if requested by the producers) and then present the best. The solution was the presentation of excerpts rather than complete performances of plays; in this way as many as six companies could be shown in one day. By the end of the decade the spring conference, including Region 14 Showcase, had been extended to two days and was an established event, attracting delegates from several states as well as from local cities and communities. Both well-known and new producers wished to be previewed in the hope of being chosen for presentation.

Region 14 has always been unique among regional chapters in the diversity of its membership. It has from the first included educators on all levels, recreation leaders, actors, producers, writers, agents, and sponsors. The Showcase was, therefore, a natural activity to have developed in this area, serving the interests of many as it grew to proportions undreamed of by its founders. Among the Showcase presentations during the first five years of its existence were Equity Library Theatre for Children, the Merry Wanderers, Red Thundercloud, Edith Stephens Dance Theatre, the Traveling Playhouse, the Paper Bag Players, Hote Casella, and Tom Glazer. Although many small professional companies opened and closed during these years, the majority of these companies survived to become well-established groups by the sixties.

The Region 14 Showcase has been given credit for bringing many new groups to the attention of sponsors; it is also possible, although the purpose of Showcase was never commercial promotion, that the future financial stability of some companies resulted from this opportunity to be seen and heard.

PETER PAN ON BROADWAY

In addition to the entertainment planned specifically for children, the fifties also included two productions of *Peter Pan*, different in many ways from the earlier ones mentioned. The first, starring Jean Arthur and Boris Karloff, with music by Leonard Bernstein, was presented in 1950. Like the preceding productions, this was an elaborate Broadway offering to which both adults and children responded enthusiastically. The critics compared it favorably with the Maude Adams production and agreed in general that it was superior to the Marilyn Miller version of the twenties.

The second production in the 1955–56 season was the Mary Martin musical version, a spectacular interpretation which was later repeated for television audiences. While the music was described as disappointing, the play enjoyed a four months' run and was attended by both children and adults. Neither production was planned with an appeal to young people as the primary consideration; nevertheless, these two productions of a well-loved classic made a rich contribution to the normally scanty fare for children on Broadway.

Publication for Children's Theatre

The growth of children's theatre in the United States stimulated the writing of both plays and books useful to directors and teachers working in this area of drama. Many of the plays most frequently mentioned by producing groups were published by the Children's Theatre Press in Anchorage, Kentucky. When this company was founded in 1935 it listed just four full-length plays for children; it is now the foremost publisher of children's drama, with over one hundred titles in its 1969 catalogue. The criteria for publication of plays were popular appeal and a wholesome influence which met high dramatic standards. In addition to the plays, the Children's Theatre Press engaged a group of leaders in the field to write six books of theory, method, procedure, and repertoire. These books included Winifred Ward's *Stories to Dramatize*, Charlotte Chorpenning's *Twenty-One Years with Children's Theatre*, Winifred Ward's revised edition of *Theatre for Children*, Vern Adix's *Theatre Scenecraft*, Madge Miller's *Miniature Plays*, and Seattle Junior Programs' *Children's Theatre Manual*.

The New Plays Committee of the Children's Theatre Conference compiled criteria for evaluating plays for children. These criteria, published in the catalogue of the Children's Theatre Press, include the worth and content of the story, good dramatic construction, an admirable hero or protagonist, opportunity for audience identification with this hero, the development of character and story through interaction, naturalness of dialogue, avoidance of technical difficulties in staging, the handling of adaptations so as to retain the essential elements of the story, and a consideration of the finished play in regard to purpose, clarity, and appeal.

From the beginning the Children's Theatre Press has been guided by an advisory board including such leaders as Winifred Ward, Charlotte Chorpenning, Dorothy McFadden, Harold Ehrensperger of Boston University, the late Earnest Bavely of the National Thespian Organization, George Savage of the University of California at Los Angeles, and Helenka Adamowska

Pantaleoni of the Association of Junior Leagues of America. Some of the playwrights whose work has been published by the Children's Theatre Press are Rosemary Musil, Nora McAlvay, Aurand Harris, Geraldine Brain Siks, Madge Miller, James Norris, Martha King, and Albert O. Miller.

Since the Children's Theatre Press serves groups presenting plays for child audiences rather than in-school dramatization, it observes a policy of publishing only full-length dramas and plays designed for trouping. The editor of this publishing company is its founder, Sara Spencer, who was also director of the Children's Theatre Conference during the years 1953–55.

OTHER PUBLISHING HOUSES OFFERING PLAYS FOR CHILDREN

By the fifties a number of other publishing houses were advertising both full-length plays and one-acts for school and children's theatre use. According to the ANTA listing of 1954 there were twenty-seven companies which were either regularly or occasionally engaged in printing children's plays. Most of these were nonspecialized publishing houses which included collections of plays from time to time. Seven of them, however, published drama as the major part of their business and included some plays for children. Only two, the Children's Theatre Press and the Coach House Press in Chicago, concentrated entirely upon the juvenile field.

INTERNATIONAL BIBLIOGRAPHY

An *International Bibliography on Youth and the Theatre*, prepared by the International Theatre Institute, was published in 1952. A seventy-two-page booklet, edited by Oliver Perrin, it listed the best material available on theory and the specialized techniques of educational theatres as well as lists of plays which can be performed by and for children. Prefaces by John Allen of Great Britain, Campton Bell of the United States, and Leon Chancerel of France added interest and clarification of objectives.

The following statement by Chancerel contains a frequently mentioned aim of children's theatre, for the first time publicly shared by leaders from fifteen nations of the world:

> I am profoundly convinced that productions of real human, artistic and technical quality specially conceived and carried out for children and adolescents, in collaboration with their teachers, by artists and craftsmen, conscious of their high tasks and responsibility, can contribute largely to the progress of peoples, and to the extension of culture and taste.[8]

Fifty-three delegates contributed to a bibliography which grew out of the first International Conference on Youth and the Theatre, held at UNESCO House in Paris. The result was a profusely illustrated issue of *World Theatre* with the text in both English and French.

As in the children's theatre activities of the fifties, publication during this period appears to have been better organized, better publicized, and better co-ordinated with other theatre practices. The election of an editor, Sara Spencer, as head of the Children's Theatre Conference emphasized the closer relationship between a leading source of dramatic literature and the various producing groups. While there was still a greater demand for plays than had been met, the discussions on material and standards at the Children's Theatre meetings, the establishment of nationally advertised playwriting contests, and the growth of specialized publishing houses as the Children's Theatre Press and the Coach House Press indicated progress in the area of publication.

The report on the 1959 annual meeting, held in Michigan City, Michigan, proposed two goals for the sixties. These included a stronger effort to raise the standards of children's theatre throughout the country and a concerted drive to promote the arts in the curriculum. Mayo Bryce, specialist in Fine Arts Education with the U.S. Office of Education was the keynote speaker at this conference, and he sounded a theme which was to be heard again and

---

[8] "Youth and the Theatre," *World Theatre*, Vol. II (December, 1952), 3.

often in the future: "We have spent much time educating only one-half of ourselves, the intellect. We must balance this by educating our emotions."[9] After a decade of emphasis on the so-called solid subjects, the recognition of human feelings was an idea with fresh implications for the arts.

A survey of the fifties points to increased activity in each of the areas mentioned and to the dedication of the groups supporting and leading them. Evaluation and restatement of purpose marked much of the writing. Progress reports described what had been accomplished, but a new emphasis on standards distinguished the fifties from all of the preceding decades.

[9] Marcella Oberle, "Children's Theatre Conference at Michigan City," *Educational Theatre Journal*, Vol. XI (December, 1959), 296–303.

VIII

Angels: Public and Private
1960-70

Ｉf the fifties brought unprecedented expansion in children's theatre, the sixties brought changes of a different sort. Funding programs, new concepts and new art forms, community co-operation, and the building of arts centers, which included children's theatre, were among the more important developments. Most significant was the advent of grants from public and private sources.

Money, a perennial problem in children's theatre, became available to many communities in the late sixties through government funds on both state and national levels. For the first time since the days of the Federal Theatre the arts were given government subsidy for the establishment of new programs and for the support of others already in operation. Unlike the Federal Theatre, which was a relief measure, the federal funding programs of the sixties represented the first mandate in American history for direct support of the arts. It is too early to tell how many of these programs will become permanent, but there is no doubt that government funding distinguished the sixties from all other decades in the history of children's theatre.

This financial assistance appeared at a critical juncture. Both community and professional theatres were feeling the effects of inflation, and some were facing inability to meet operational expenses in the face of rising costs. The educational theatre was better off than either of the former in that it was subsidized by the college or university and was, therefore, not dependent upon box-office receipts for survival. Financial assistance from government agencies, as well as from business and private foundations, may prove to have been a turning point in the history of children's theatre in America.

An overview of the sixties must of necessity be more general than specific. In the first place, the very proliferation of activities would make a description of each group run literally into volumes. In the second place, the comprehensive *Directory of Children's Theatres in the United States,* compiled by a committee under the direction of Professor Jed H. Davis and published by the American Educational Theatre Association, lists all known groups with pertinent information on location, auspices, and type of operation. It would be premature to attempt to cite the most important or influential groups; time will prove which were the most significant. There are, however, some highly successful enterprises, which have grown since their founding or which have claimed public attention in the past ten years for their innovative programs. These will be cited. The immediate past, like the present, is the concern of the critic rather than the historian and can be evaluated properly only in perspective.

A study of the period reveals a dichotomy. This decade in the history of our country was one of material prosperity, a new awareness of social problems, exploration of space, and concern with the educational system. On the other hand, there were frustration over the continuing war in East Asia and serious conflicts at home. Children's theatre was affected by all of these conditions. Funds, heretofore not available for the arts, were for the first time allocated to dramatic activities stimulated by public interest. There was an effort to take theatre to the disadvantaged child as well as to the affluent; in some instances this meant literally taking theatre into the streets.

For the first time in the history of the children's theatre movement, serious questions were raised concerning the relevance of traditional material in a time of social change, and efforts were made to find new scripts with greater meaning for today's children. Violence, decried heretofore, was now viewed in a somewhat different light; while criticism of television and film programs persisted, there were some adults who spoke out against a diet of fairy tales and inevitable "happy endings." Why, it was asked, could there not be children's plays which dealt with contemporary themes? Why not sympathetic and realistic treatment of ghetto problems as well as stories of the privileged and beautiful? What about new staging techniques for an audience which had known professionalism on the television screen from birth? Why not black theatre for black children?

Children's plays did not change radically as a result of these questions, but for the first time since the thirties there were some scripts with contemporary social themes and many others which showed the influence of the adult theatre, particularly the musical. By the end of the sixties the commercial theatre for children was overwhelmingly musical—some of it presented in a modern, almost "camp," idiom. It was in the techniques of production rather than in the literature that the greater change took place. Nevertheless, some new ideas as well as new styles emerged along with the encouraging news that funds were available to communities and groups which could prove the validity of their programs. To anyone closely associated with children's theatre for two or more decades, the sixties were indeed different.

Government Aid to the Arts

The long-cherished dream of government aid to the arts finally materialized in the sixties. Although far from evenly distributed at the time of this writing, federal funds are available to all states and territories, and all states now have organizations through which to apply for grants-in-aid. Some states have gone far in the establishment of arts councils, with the result that many fine programs have been launched. Children's theatre in the United States has received a share of these monies thus far through a variety of federal and state agencies.

In many countries of Europe today—indeed, throughout history—state and city governments have had a part in enriching the lives of the people through support of the arts. America has traditionally preferred to give aid through private philanthropies rather than through government agencies. President John F. Kennedy, therefore, took a radical step in 1962, when he named August Heckscher as his special consultant on the arts. In 1964, President Lyndon B. Johnson appointed Roger Stevens to organize and direct the administration's cultural program. In the same year the National Council on the Arts was established, with the following specific responsibilities: to recommend ways to maintain and multiply the cultural resources of this country; to encourage private initiative; to advise and consult with local, state, and federal departments on the best ways to co-ordinate the existing facilities; to conduct studies; and to make recommendations for the future. This was the beginning of an extensive program of aid to the arts through various agencies set up to help educational and community programs, including individual artists and performing groups.

FEDERAL AGENCIES

The most important and far-reaching programs were the National Foundation on the Arts and Humanities Act of 1965, the two branches of which are the National Endowment for the Arts and the National Endowment for the Humanities; and the Elementary and Secondary Education Act (ESEA) of 1965, administered by the Department of Health, Education, and Welfare. Under ESEA's Title I and Title III a number of children's theatre activities have been made possible. In addition, there was the Economic Opportunity Act of 1964, which also contributed to children's drama; it included the Headstart Program for preschoolers and the Upward Bound Program for teen-agers, both of which embraced drama among cultural benefits for disadvantaged children. The Housing and Urban Development Act of 1965 was established to upgrade cultural programs, and to that end contributed to the improvement of certain aspects of drama programs. In the same year a sum of $31,000,000 (one-half from federal funds and one-half matching funds from private sources) was realized for the construction of a National Center for the Performing Arts in Washington. It is hoped that children's theatre will one day be housed in this center.

The National Endowment for the Arts operates under the guidance of the National Council on the Arts, a group of twenty-six private citizens recognized for their knowledge and expertise in this area. The Council is responsible for assisting in a variety of services, including pilot projects in the arts, and advisory and consulting services for foundations, educational institutions, public and private groups and councils.

The programs administered by the Endowment on the Arts are set up to:

1. Stimulate enjoyment and appreciation of the arts by creating the widest possible audience for arts activities of substantial artistic and cultural significance.
2. Encourage and assist individual performing and visual artists to achieve standards of professional excellence.
3. Develop and expand the capacity of independent arts institutions and organizations for imaginative and substantive programs.
4. Explore the problems of the arts in America in order to develop new programs and institutions to meet existing and future needs.
5. Encourage imaginative arts programs in the field of education.
6. Support international arts events.[1]

The National Endowment for the Arts receives and allocates private as well as government funds to establish programs or implement programs of grants-in-aid to public agencies, nonprofit, tax-exempt groups, and state arts agencies and individuals. A program of matching grants-in-aid to states enables state arts agencies to develop their own community programs and services. This large-scale recognition of the arts on the part of the federal government is indicative of a new direction in the nation's cultural growth.

[1] Judith Gault (comp.), *Federal Funds and Services for the Arts*, Introduction.

In December, 1969, President Richard M. Nixon asked Congress to extend the legislation which created the National Foundation on the Arts and Humanities Act for an additional three years beyond its expiration date of June 30, 1970. He further proposed that Congress approve $40,000,000 in new funds for the National Foundation, double the level of the preceding year. Music, theatre, dance, and literature would thus be brought to millions of people who could not otherwise afford them. While children's theatre is only one aspect of the performing arts, it is covered in the program and in certain areas of the country has been aided extensively.

The American Educational Theatre Association has urged that the Endowment become a permanent agency. Many theatre programs, initiated during the sixties, indeed may fail without this continued support. Money alone cannot make an arts program; imaginative planning and the people's belief in the arts are of primary importance. With the availability of government funds, however, there is an opportunity for people to enjoy the arts in their daily lives rather than as occasional and expensive experiences. It is hoped that continued exposure will effect the realization that the arts are necessary to a rich and full human life.

The second important piece of legislation was the Elementary and Secondary Education Act, designed to improve and enrich education. Children's theatre has benefited from this legislation as well as from the Endowment on the Arts. Title I funds are authorized for special projects and activities to help meet the needs of disadvantaged children. Programs include supplementary cultural activities. Title III, on the other hand, authorizes funds for supplementary educational centers and services not available to the community and provides for the establishment of exemplary elementary- and secondary-school programs. It is under Title III that children's theatre has benefited principally.

An analysis of the proposals submitted for Title III grants reveals that although they are drawn up with individual communities in mind, they fall into one of several general patterns. There are projects designed to meet the needs of the inner city, the rural area, the school system, and the suburban or small-town community. Some programs are state-wide; some, country-wide; others are confined to a single school district or area. Some include instruction in the arts; others, attendance at plays and concerts; many of them, both. Some offer in-service education for teachers, while others provide for educational materials and/or research. The size of the grant and the length of its duration are obviously determining factors in the size and scope of the program.

In 1966 the United States Department of Health, Education, and Welfare listed thirty PACE projects (Projects to Advance Creativity in Education) which had received Title III planning or operational grants for programs including children's theatre and creative dramatics. There were additional projects in the arts, in which dramatic activities comprised one aspect, but the former are obviously more significant in an analysis of the movement. These projects varied in size, scope, length, and method of operation and were located in all regions of the United States. The following year, 1967, there were twenty-four theatre projects listed, and in 1968 there were six.[2] Title III funds have made possible programs of such magnitude that the future of children's theatre in America may well be altered as a result.

Exposure to living theatre, the opportunity for direct participation in creative dramatics, professional leadership, and the experience of working with artists-in-residence, resources, and materials—these are the components of programs which touched the lives of thousands of elementary-school children in the last five years of the decade. Even in this short space of time there has been so much activity that a comprehensive treatment in a specialized book is prohibitive. A description of a few of the larger projects which were approved in different parts of the country is essential, however, if we are to gain a concept of the stimulation which children's theatre received. The following show the variety of ways in which the performing arts were introduced into or co-ordinated with the elementary-school curriculum.

[2] *Pacesetters in Innovation*, I, II, III.

OPERATION AREA ARTS

A large after-school program, designed to serve approximately 57,000 elementary- and secondary-school students and 1,200 teachers in Green Bay, Wisconsin, was among the first approved in the country. A fine arts program, it included the visual arts, music, dramatics, dance, and creative writing. Materials, exhibits, and instruction were to be integral parts of the project. Dramatic activities included programs by both local and touring companies, in-service education for teachers, classes in dance, theatre, and music, and a publication in which student writing could appear.

HUNTINGTON, NEW YORK

Huntington, New York, was the scene of one of the largest in-school projects in the arts made possible by a planning grant under Title III. As a performing arts curriculum enrichment program, it brought performing artists of top quality into the instructional program of a school district. Based on the conviction that the arts are for the many rather than the few and that they belong in the center rather than on the periphery of society, a program of performances and artists-in-residence was planned for school children from kindergarten through grade nine for a period of four years. Over 240,000 children and 11,000 teachers were served.

THE CULTURAL ENRICHMENT PROJECT

In Chicago a large program funded under Title III made it possible for over 550,000 children to experience the performing arts during the two-year period from March, 1967, to March, 1969. More than 1,000 live performances of plays, dance programs, puppet shows, and dramatic readings were attended by elementary- and high-school-age pupils, most of whom could not have afforded or even have had access to these offerings. Known as the Cultural Enrichment Project, this program was developed by the Board of Education of the City of Chicago to give an opportunity for children to attend quality presentations suitable to their various age levels, backgrounds, and needs; to correlate live theatre performances with classroom activities in order to widen and enrich the curriculum and stimulate innovative teaching techniques; to provide participating teachers with helpful material (guidelines and reprints) to suggest before-and-after activities; and to sponsor in-service workshops for teachers, orienting them to different aspects of the performing arts and suggesting ways in which the arts can be integrated with the regular curriculum.

Recognizing the need for experiences that would give pupils a sense of pride in their various cultures, the project included performances by ethnic groups whenever available. Theatre trips offered children the added opportunity to widen their horizons as they visited other parts of the city and mingled with young people from other schools. Guidelines were prepared by the staff and by such organizations as the Illinois Arts Council, the Illinois Foundation for the Dance, and the Stratford Festival Theatre of Canada.

The teachers' workshops were conducted by theatre experts. Indirectly, thousands of students will continue to benefit from the new insights which their teachers gained through this added enrichment. Indeed, the success of this aspect of the Chicago program led to the planning of a third workshop for the 1969–70 season. The concept of learning about the arts while enjoying them for their entertainment value was characteristic of the Title III project planning of the sixties. The belief that knowledge leads to a deeper appreciation was a basic premise; it is still too early to evaluate the results, but the validity of the premise cannot be faulted.

THEATRE RESOURCES FOR YOUTH

Theatre Resources for Youth, or Project TRY, was inaugurated in New Hampshire in 1967 with an operational grant under Title III. It was conceived and developed as an outgrowth of programs begun in the Drama Department at the University of New Hampshire. A variety of services included classes for teachers on both elementary- and secondary-school levels and tours of productions to elementary schools. A large staff administered this project, which was designed to make the widest possible use of resources available in the region. TRY could serve as a model for the development of similar projects in the region or the nation. TRY was unique in that it was devoted exclusively to state-wide development of theatre arts programs in the elementary schools.

Teachers in elementary schools were given training in creative dramatics techniques. High-school teachers were given college credit for instruction in play production, and high-school students were given an opportunity to perform for elementary-school children. In addition, there were touring performances of children's plays to 143 schools; bussing was deemed impractical as too costly and too hazardous in the New England winters. Both professional and nonprofessional plays were presented. New Hampshire's two professional theatres, the Players' Theatre and the Theatre by the Sea, provided half of the total number of performances each year. Other plays were provided by out-of-state professional touring companies, five colleges, and two community theatres.

Fees for plays were handled in varying ways. During phase one, the local school received one performance without charge; during phase two, the school contributed a portion of the cost for the second performance; and in phase three, the school paid the total cost for the third performance. According to Judith Kase, director, TRY reached more than 50,000 children during the two-year span of its operation, 1967–69. This ambitious program was given a regional citation by the New England Theatre Conference for enriching the lives of youngsters in the state of New Hampshire. It has been described in some detail here because of its focus on the theatre arts.

LIVING ARTS PROGRAM

In Dayton, Ohio, an operational project designed to advance creativity in education was financed under Title III. Its stated purposes were "to identify, nurture and evaluate the creative potential of youngsters, whose interests lie in the fine arts, creative writing, dance, drama, music and visual arts; and to assist in developing the creative perceptual, aesthetic and social growth of youngsters through the fine arts." This program was begun in June, 1967, and continued for a three-year period.

The program, under the direction of Jack De Velbiss, differed from the others cited in that it took children of demonstrated talent and devoted special attention to them by means of after-school and Saturday classes. Children were given a chance to work with professional artists in a large warehouse renovated for this specific purpose. In addition to classes, there was an opportunity to hear music and to see performances of theatre by professional companies. These performances were given in the schools so that thousands more than the eight hundred selected pupils could enjoy them.

During the first year of its existence there were 30 guest artists and presentations in 154 schools with more than 53,000 children in the audiences. During the second year there were 45 guest artists. With a budget cut in the third year the number was reduced, but it was estimated that over 15,000 children and adults were involved. Among the guests who came into the schools were John Ciardi, Agnes Moorehead, Lee Evans, Erick Hawkins, and Mara. The community expressed tremendous enthusiasm for this program, which brought an exciting dimension to the education of the children of Dayton.

There were many other imaginative projects developed at this time; the above are included here as representative of different types of planning—the after-school program, the in-school program, a creative arts emphasis, and drama as the single focus. Unlike the majority of enterprises in the past, reports are available giving full information on objectives and methods of operation.

In addition to the programs made possible by Title I and Title III, there were others which owed their existence to active and imaginative state arts councils. A product of the sixties, the arts councils have grown at different rates of speed and in proportion to local interest and enthusiasm.

STATE ARTS COUNCILS

The formation of state arts councils preceded the federal Endowment legislation. New York state was the first to establish a council in 1960, as a temporary commission in the beginning and as a permanent agency in 1965. New York was followed by several other states, including Missouri, California, and Illinois; by 1968, three years after the National Foundation on the Arts and Humanities Act, every state and territory had its own council or commission. Some have impressive accomplishments to their credit; others have done little thus far. A 1969 government report noted that in the preceding year forty-six state arts agencies had received Endowment grants and had launched approximately 1,100 projects. Some of these were for children.

The state councils encourage participation in and appreciation of the arts by giving professional advice and financial support. Long-range programs are encouraged, with the common objective of bringing a high level of artistry to the people at a reasonable cost. By the end of the sixties thirty-four states had reported children's theatre as an area of interest, though programs have varied widely in scope. The most popular projects have been support for touring performances of plays, workshops for teachers, conferences, and aid to individual children's theatres. In a few instances councils have met the individual needs of local communities in other ways. The state of Washington, for example, voted the sum of $1,000,000 to continue the performing arts programs originally brought to school children through Title III.

One of the most comprehensive programs is New York State's, entitled "The Professionals Teach the Performing Arts." Established in 1965 by the New York State Council, it is administered by the Division of the Humanities and the Arts of the State Education Department. The program supplies one-third to one-half of the expenses involved in bringing outstanding performing artists to schools. An artist-in-residence program for periods of one or two weeks is an added attraction; many schools have enjoyed not only performances of music, dance, and theatre but the rich experience of instruction by the artists as well. A brochure from the Department of Education in Albany lists the dozens of artists and performing groups available to the schools in the state.

"SUMMER ON WHEELS"

The New York State Council created a particularly imaginative project in the summer of 1969, by which high-quality professional groups with material geared to ghetto children would be taken to inner-city neighborhoods. This was street theatre and was given the title "Summer on Wheels." All performances took place out of doors—in parking lots, in parks, and in closed-off streets. Prior consent was obtained from both municipality and black community before performances were scheduled. "Summer on Wheels" reached 60,000 children in its first summer. According to the Council, the idea was not to "cool things" but rather to give children a chance to see artists to whom they could respond. The next step was the organization of workshops and seminars. It is hoped that this highly successful street theatre will lead to year-round performing arts workshops to develop young talent which would not otherwise be discovered. Among the attractions offered in the first two years of operation were the Afro-American Folkloric Troupe, Dance Caravan, Dancemobile, Jazzmobile, Moviebus, New York Free Theatre, Pickwick Puppet Theatre, Playhouse in a Box, Soul and Latin Theatre, and Sounds Unlimited. Ethnic music, dance, and folklore were emphasized in performances which experimented with modern techniques and styles.

PENNSYLVANIA PROJECTS

In the three years of its existence the Pennsylvania Council on the Arts has developed two programs which have attracted wide attention. One of these is street theatre aimed at reaching people of all ages, children included. Traveling throughout the city, the Society Hill Street Theatre is a professional group with a deep sense of responsibility to the community. During the summer of

1968 more than 17,000 persons in deprived areas responded to the arrival of the truck with its loudspeaker and brightly painted signs. The following year 30,000 persons saw sixty performances. Material was written or selected especially for the mobile unit; it touched on love, war, law enforcement, and humor, and was designed to involve and hold a fluid audience.

Both government and private enterprise co-operated with the Playhouse (Society Hill Playhouse); in 1969 funding came from the Pennsylvania Arts Council, the Philadelphia Urban Coalition, the Samuel S. Fels Fund, and the Department of Recreation. The organizers saw theatre not as a means of confrontation but as a way of stimulating activity as well as entertaining the summer audience.

In addition to this experimental program, the Free Children's Theatre of the Germantown Theatre Guild was established in the same area to meet the needs of children aged five to fourteen. Housed in a pre-Revolutionary carriage house during its first season (1968–69), it was moved the next year to a school with excellent year-round facilities. The Theatre Guild is an integrated group of actors, who have made a particular study of the techniques and disciplines involved in performing for children. Children's classics have comprised the offerings enacted on an open or thrust stage.

FREE STREET THEATRE IN CHICAGO

The Illinois Arts Council, together with the Art Institute of Chicago, has also used the street-theatre idea with success. Though aimed at a somewhat older age level, children of elementary-school age are in the audience. Like its counterparts in New York and Philadelphia, the Chicago Street Theatre was intended to develop cohesiveness in the inner-city community, to stimulate appreciation of the theatre as the most effective form of public communication, and to encourage creative talent which had been denied expression. To achieve these ends a two-part program was set up in 1961: a Street Touring Company, which would go into the neighborhoods; and workshops in drama. It is hoped that the latter will generate theatres which will express the life of the people. It was estimated that over 125,000 persons were reached during the first summer.

"PROJECT CREATE"

A unique project was conceived by the Education Committee of the Connecticut Commission on the Arts, in which theatre was the major vehicle used to introduce elementary-school children to all the art forms. "Project Create" was a two-year program, introduced in 1967 in nine communities across the state; during an entire school year all pupils and teachers in the selected schools experienced or actively participated in the arts under the guidance of professional consultants.

Among the producing groups which took part were the Paper Bag Players; the Eugene O'Neill Memorial Theatre Center, which produced *The Hide and Seek Odyssey of Madeleine Gimple*, a play written especially for the project by Frank Gagliano; and the Hartford Conservatory, which mounted Benjamin Britten's music-drama, *Noah's Flood*. During the second year of "Project Create" the Paper Bag Players developed a new production, *Dandelion*, based on a theme of evolution and man's environment which the company had previously explored with the children. Children's Theatre International was commissioned to do a similar residency program in the spring of 1969; members of the company worked directly with children in the classroom, then performed their Kabuki play, *A Box of Tears*, which stimulated school-wide interest in the arts of the Orient. Theatre was chosen by "Project Create" because it incorporates all of the arts and is therefore a springboard to creativity in every aspect of the curriculum.

The programs cited were among the first inaugurated under state councils; it is to be hoped that the next decade will see many more conceived according to regional interests and needs. The state arts councils, in brief, offer communities the chance to establish and strengthen their local programs in a variety of ways. It is too early to tell which or how many of the programs given such assistance will be continued, but the fact that government support now exists on all levels indicates recognition of the arts as a humanizing force in society.

National Organizations

Newest of the national organizations involved in theatre is the Associated Councils of the Arts. It is described here because its services relate directly to those of the preceding organizations.

THE ASSOCIATED COUNCILS OF THE ARTS

The similarity of the names of the various organizations and agencies is somewhat confusing, but the Associated Councils of the Arts performs a specific service in relation to the state arts councils. Based on the assumption that public support of the arts is in the public interest, this private, nonprofit organization works with all state arts councils to strengthen and guide them. It assists in planning and administering programs, stimulating public interest, and recommending methods of raising funds. Every two years the Associated Councils of the Arts holds a conference, which interested citizens may attend, to participate in discussions and hear outstanding speakers and see unusual or high-quality performances.

The Associated Councils of the Arts publishes *Cultural Affairs*, a quarterly journal, and a monthly newsletter in addition to a publications program, which has already released seven books, with a film and other books in the planning stage. As a national organization, it serves all of the states and is able to aid communication more expeditiously than the states could on their own. The organization is still very new, inasmuch as the state arts councils are all products of this decade.

Meanwhile, the national organizations which were responsible for the growth of children's theatre in the fifties continued their support. Oldest in years of service was the Junior League. Although the changing times influenced the program in some respects, the energy and involvement of League members did not diminish.

THE ASSOCIATION OF JUNIOR LEAGUES OF AMERICA

Annual reports for the sixties revealed nationwide involvement in children's theatre. In 1960 activity was reported by 104 Leagues; in 1970, by 113. The major changes which took place during this period were increased sponsorship of professional touring companies instead of, or in addition to, League production, and co-ordination of League activities with other community programs. In some cities individual trouping was phased out in an effort to obtain a higher quality of production for a greater number of schools.

A 1970 report called attention to some of the more significant developments. The Atlanta Children's Theatre, spearheaded by the Junior League of Atlanta, was the first resident professional company for children in the United States. The Junior League of Minneapolis commissioned a study of resources and needs in the area and a long-range developmental plan. The presentation of the plan resulted in a steering committee of the League and the community to set up an arts council. In Oakland, California, the Junior League was involved in a project to bring live theatre of superior quality to high schools in low-income areas and to provide an orientation program for teachers.

In San Diego pupils in grades seven through twelve were enabled to attend performances of the Shakespeare Festival. The Junior League of St. Louis worked with the Title III MECA Project, described later in this chapter, in an administrative capacity to take plays to the schools and to conduct workshops in improvisations for teachers; it also provided some financial aid for the program.

The Junior League of Pittsburgh reported the establishment of an ambitious cultural enrichment program for elementary-

223

school children. In Springfield, Illinois, the Junior League established an arts council, which was to be turned over to community leaders by 1970. A great variety of programs were made possible under Junior League sponsorship for thousands of boys and girls throughout the country during this period. The emphasis on serving the disadvantaged continued but on a larger scale than at any other time in Junior League history. Indeed, the policy was to see that no child be denied theatre experience for reason of color, creed, ability to pay, or geographic location.

AMERICAN NATIONAL THEATRE AND ACADEMY

Although the American National Theatre and Academy has been primarily concerned with adult theatre, it has sponsored children's theatre on occasion and has served as an information center for interested persons both at home and abroad. It is too early to tell whether the reorganization of ANTA in 1968 will have any effect on theatre for children, but ANTA's new association with the National Council on the Arts is viewed as a strengthening change in structure. The 1969–70 season in New York saw the first subscription season of regional theatre productions as a result of this new program. No plays for children were included, although several plays were appropriate for high-school students who attended them. Plans to expand ANTA's service to the cultural life of the nation are presently being formulated.

AMERICAN EDUCATIONAL THEATRE ASSOCIATION, INC.

The American Educational Theatre Association, by the end of the sixth decade of the century, boasted an international membership of 7,000. In addition to the individual members who work as teachers, scholars, writers, dancers, critics, technicians, directors, and volunteers, there were more than 600 separate theatrical organizations. Over 1,400 libraries subscribed to AETA publications. An office in Washington was established and is administered by a full-time staff.

224

AETA's three major divisions, the Children's Theatre Conference, the Secondary School Theatre Conference, and the American Community Theatre Association, serve the special interests of members; a new division, the University Resident Theatre Association, was added provisionally in 1969. AETA now sponsors over twenty theatre projects, ranging from overseas productions and study tours to research. One of the most exciting developments was the establishment of the annual American College Theatre Festival in 1968. Each spring ten companies are chosen and brought with all expenses paid to Washington, D.C. Each of these companies participates in a week of activities and performs three times during the Festival period. There are plans to expand the Festival by adding examples of high-quality work from community, high-school, and children's theatres in the near future. These plans illustrate the place which children's theatre has at last come to occupy in the college and university theatre.

In the sixties students were invited to participate in national conferences, not only as participants in demonstrations but as panelists and members of discussion groups. This recognition of the student's role in the educational theatre was in line with current campus efforts to establish dialogue and co-operation between the professional and the student of the discipline. From all reports this was a highly satisfactory innovation.

In 1966 a new award was established by AETA to be given to some professional group or individual for "excellence in children's theatre." This was the Jennie Heiden Award, named for a CTC member whose efforts in Brooklyn, New York, were thought to have influenced immeasurably the calibre of professional children's theatre in the nation. This recognition, by way of an annual award, reflected the organization's respect for this branch of theatre.

The 1969 AETA convention in Detroit had as its theme "Theatre for Educational Values," with the subtext "What has been done, what might be done—to make learning of and through theatre more meaningful?" General dissatisfaction with the *status quo* and an earnest desire to find better solutions to urgent problems made this one of the most challenging conferences in the history of the organization. Keynote speaker, Kathryn Bloom, director of the Arts in Education Program of the John D. Rockefeller III Fund, described pioneer programs made possible by public and private funds and pointed out the need to develop integrated arts programs in the schools if art, including drama, is to occupy a significant place in the lives of the American people. At the present time AETA is undergoing a critical self-examination for the purpose of reorganizing in order to meet the needs and interests of its members more effectively.

ARTS IMPACT

One example of the kind of co-operative enterprise to which the sixties gave birth was Arts Impact (Interdisciplinary Model Program in the Arts for Children and Teachers). The project was funded under the Education Professions Development Act and administered by the U.S. Office of Education. A million-dollar experiment, Arts Impact was launched by AETA, the Music Educators National Conference, the National Arts Education Association, and the Dance Division of the American Association for Health, Physical Education, and Recreation. Five states were selected as a network to develop and implement teacher-training and curriculum-improvement programs in the arts to be tested in the schools. The states selected were Alabama, California, Ohio, Oregon, and Pennsylvania. Overseeing the project for AETA during the initial two-year period was Brian Hansen from the staff of CEMREL (Central Midwestern Regional Educational Laboratory, Inc., in St. Louis).

Arts Impact was national rather than regional in scope and is cited here because of the size and implications of its program for the future. Specific objectives of the program were stated as follows:

> To reconstruct the school's educational program and administrative climate in an effort to achieve better balance between the arts and other instructional areas, and in the learning process, between feelings or emotions and acquiring knowledge;

To develop high quality visual arts, music, dance and drama education programs in each participating school;

To conduct in-service programs, including summer institutes, workshops, and demonstrations, to train teachers, administrators, and other school personnel in implementing the arts education programs;

To develop ways to infuse the arts into all aspects of the school curriculum as a means of enhancing and improving the quality and quantity of aesthetic education offered in the school and as a principle means for expanding the base for effective learning experiences in the total school program;

To enhance the quality of children's art experiences by drawing upon outstanding artists, performers and educators from outside the school system.

The very fact of its existence illustrates the change in attitude toward the arts in this country since the early years of the century. While there is admittedly much more to be done, the arts organizations mentioned, the school systems, and the U.S. Office of Education may together have a profound impact on education in the United States. A project of these dimensions is a far cry from the small and scattered experiments of the early 1920's.

CHILDREN'S THEATRE CONFERENCE

The 1969 AETA convention in Detroit celebrated the twenty-fifth anniversary of the founding of CTC. Symposia, panels, speakers, demonstrations, and productions enlivened a program in which such topics as funding, research, new concepts in curriculum, and scripts for today's children were discussed by the delegates. In their concern with providing drama for all children and learning of grants and funds to support far-reaching programs and their dissatisfaction with the mediocrity of much of what passes for children's theatre in this country, CTC members were voicing some of the same problems as the parent organization in other rooms at convention headquarters.

Though much remained to be done, much had already been accomplished during the quarter of a century of CTC's existence.

Among the accomplishments during these years were children's theatre and creative dramatics projects funded by local, state, and federal programs, improved communication on both national and local levels (newsletters and conferences), and co-ordination of activities with other community organizations. The unprecedented expansion during the fifties had resulted in *A Directory of Children's Theatres in the United States,* compiled and edited by Jed H. Davis and published by AETA in 1968. There were found to be 701 educational, community, and professional groups producing children's plays regularly. It is quite possible that the total number was two or three times larger, and a new edition of the *Directory* planned for 1973 may present quite a different picture. A count by states shows wide variation, though the activity was by no means confined to any one area: Alabama, 4; Alaska, 1; Arizona, 3; Arkansas, 5; California, 54; Colorado, 17; Connecticut, 9; D.C., 7; Delaware, 3; Florida, 19; Georgia, 9; Hawaii, 2; Idaho, 3; Illinois, 41; Indiana, 10; Iowa, 16; Kansas, 18; Kentucky, 9; Louisiana, 7; Maine, 2; Maryland, 6; Massachusetts, 12; Michigan, 24; Minnesota, 24; Mississippi, 4; Missouri, 16; Montana, 6; Nebraska, 8; Nevada, 1; New Hampshire, 8; New Jersey, 22; New Mexico, 3; New York, 88; North Carolina, 13; North Dakota, 3; Ohio, 26; Oklahoma, 8; Oregon, 7; Pennsylvania, 28; Rhode Island, 4; South Carolina, 7; South Dakota, 3; Tennessee, 10; Texas, 40; Utah, 4; Vermont, 1; Virginia, 12; Washington, 22; West Virginia, 8; Wisconsin, 23; and Wyoming, 1.

Twenty-two other groups reported production of plays for children but not on a regular basis. The remaining respondents were agents and national organizations. Fourteen publishers were listed as publishing plays for children's theatre. The majority continued to be published, however, by the Anchorage Press (formerly the Children's Theatre Press), Walter Baker in Boston, the Coach House Press in Chicago, and Samuel French in New York.

Although most children's plays were given in school auditoriums and community centers, Nashville and Wichita joined Palo Alto in building beautiful theatres exclusively for the production of children's plays. In 1969, Omaha announced a $1,000,000 building drive toward the same goal. More community theatres were hiring professional directors for children's plays in the sixties, thus upgrading standards. In Region 14, where the Showcase of professional theatre for children was a featured event, a significant change took place. The growing pains increased in direct proportion to the growth of the movement in this area. By the end of the sixties as many as fourteen plays were being selected from as many as eighty productions. There were also requests from sponsors to include puppet shows and films, though the original purpose of the showcase was to acquaint sponsors with living theatre of high quality.

By 1969 the Showcase had grown beyond the energies of its volunteer previewers, and it was recommended that it be dropped as a regional activity. The following year, however, the New York State Council on the Arts made funds available to continue the project in co-operation with the Region and the Saturday Theatre for Children. Professional critics were commissioned to evaluate productions; reviews were to be published by Region 14 and made available to members; and a one-day Showcase of outstanding work would be presented. This restructuring of the Showcase is another example of state funds enabling an organization to continue a project deemed worth-while but impossible to implement under the original procedures.

The need for new plays of literary quality has increased in proportion to the number of groups who are searching for scripts. Region 14 was acutely aware of this need and in 1967 took action by voting the sum of $1,500 to commission the writing of a new play by an author of demonstrated talent. In 1970, it was announced that Jonathan Levy was the playwright it had selected. This action marked a significant departure from the contests which had been the usual means of soliciting new scripts. The New Plays Committee was composed of Muriel Sharon, chairman, Mildred Dunnock, Beatrice Straight, Maria Cimino, and Ellen Gephart, all professionals in one or another area of theatre. This and the other projects, from script-writing to theatre-building, form a giant step toward a goal of quality.

An International Organization

In the opinion of many CTC members the most important happening of the decade was the creation of the International Association of Theatres for Children and Young People, known as ASSITEJ. This was the first organization to give critical attention to children's theatre on a world-wide scale. For many years Americans traveling abroad have returned with glowing accounts of work done for children in other countries. They have praised particularly the casting of the finest professional actors in children's plays and the respect accorded children's theatre by government and artists alike. With the formation of ASSITEJ in 1964 a new chapter in the history of the movement was about to be written.

The British Children's Theatre Association invited other nations to a meeting in May of that year. The thirty-three countries attending voted unanimously to form an international organization, and an executive committee from fifteen countries was set up. Sara Spencer was the United States representative at the October meeting in Venice. Annual meetings in Paris, Prague, and The Hague followed. Between each of the congresses a meeting of the Executive Committee was held at the same time as a festival of children's theatre. These have taken place in East Berlin; Nuremburg; Moscow; Sofia, Bulgaria; and Sibonek, Yugoslavia. Nat Eek became chairman of the United States Center and was elected vice-president of ASSITEJ at The Hague in 1968. Other members of the Executive Committee of the United States Center were Sara Spencer, Ann S. Hill, Orlin Corey, Muriel Sharon, Jed Davis, Moses Goldberg, George Latshaw, Patricia Snyder, and Paul Bruce Pettit (ex officio); the composition of this committee reflected a wide range of professional backgrounds and abilities.

The third General Assembly of ASSITEJ scheduled for October, 1970, in Venice, was of particular interest to the United

States since the Everyman Players under the direction of Orlin Corey were invited to perform. This was the first time that an American company was so honored. Of importance also was the scheduling of the 1972 Congress in America. By the end of the sixties plans were well under way to hold a mobile conference starting in Ottawa, moving to the State University in Albany, and ending with a two-day excursion in New York City. CTC members would be deeply involved as co-hosts, sharing and showing their work with fellow artists and teachers in a common search for excellence.

Educational Theatre

The educational theatre, which had expanded so vigorously during the forties and fifties, continued to grow, with change in scope rather than in policy. Government funding, discussed earlier, made possible the extension of many programs already in operation and helped to co-ordinate the work of the colleges and universities with the communities. This, perhaps, was the most significant development of the sixties in respect to the educational theatre.

COLLEGE AND UNIVERSITY PROGRAMS

A survey made by the CTC during this period revealed that 350 colleges and universities had programs in the field of children's drama, and about 250 others offered courses in children's theatre and creative dramatics or both. Workshops for teachers, summer courses, and units on children's dramatics in the curriculum were further manifestations of the extent to which the idea was spreading. Because of the number, no attempt will be made to describe individual programs. The few which are cited illustrate the directions in which educational theatre was moving.

Northwestern University and the Universities of Minnesota, Washington, Kansas, California at Los Angeles, Colorado, and Utah continued to lead in size and scope of offerings. At Kansas, for example, in 1964 children's plays were included among the major productions of the university theatre. This move to the main stage represented a shift in emphasis, which strengthened both programs and took drama to a reported 67,000 children each year.

The University of Minnesota, likewise, added new features such as the Peppermint Tent, in which a company of paid student actors perform children's classics during the summer. The Tufts Magic Circle, one of the first successful experimental summer programs, continued to serve as a community resource. Texas Women's University in Denton, whose archives revealed the first children's play of that city to have been produced in 1917, has played an active part from the first: plays for children by sophomores in the twenties, the addition of course work, original writing, and puppetry have all contributed to one of the longest histories in the movement. Among the newer programs which have attracted attention both for their offerings and for their administration are those at San Fernando Valley State College with Mary Jane Evans, director; New York University with Lowell and Nancy Swortzell, codirectors; and the University of Oklahoma with Nat Eek, director. Many small colleges throughout the country were also developing fine programs for their students, whose work in turn serves the community. Improvisation and theatre games were mentioned frequently as techniques and occasional plays were reported emerging from black theatre studios and experimental workshops.

AESTHETIC EDUCATION PROGRAM

In the public schools activity continued, with some innovations in curriculum and some programs made possible by government funds. One of the largest and most comprehensive plans was the Aesthetic Education Program located at the Central Midwestern Regional Educational Laboratory, Inc., in St. Louis. It is included here because of its size and the implications of its program for the arts in the future.

This long-range curriculum program, which included theatre for children, was launched by CEMREL in the late sixties, and planned for completion by 1973. National rather than regional in scope, it was funded by the U.S. Office of Education with the expectation that the completed materials and the philosophy on which they are based will have a profound effect on education throughout the country.

Brian Hansen, associate director of the program, viewed theatre as an important element, with creative dramatics, theatre games, children's plays, and professional productions all included in the plan. CEMREL is one of fifteen educational laboratories in the United States established under ESEA to improve education for all children; it is said to be the first to attempt a curriculum program in aesthetic education, which included all of the arts. Guidance by authorities from a variety of universities, money from the government, and co-operation from artists and museums illustrate the change in attitude toward the place of the arts in education by the sixth decade of the century.

MECA

A unique program, made possible by Title III, was developed in St. Louis by the Metropolitan Educational Center in the Arts (MECA). The stated purpose of the center is to supplement, enrich, and strengthen existing educational programs in the arts in the elementary and secondary schools. Federal fundings for a three-year period from 1967 to 1970 made possible a comprehensive program in the visual and performing arts for 700,000 pupils.

Two artists-in-residence at Washington University, Alan and Joanna Nichols, were invited to direct the theatre program. Improvisation was the technique chosen for the three companies, who went out to the schools. A basic belief of MECA is that the continued or repeated experience is far more valuable than a single exposure. To this end weekly museum trips, touring shows, and classes in dramatics for teachers distinguish this program from others.

HIGHER HORIZONS

This experimental program was introduced by the New York City Board of Education to aid the disadvantaged by alleviating inequities and enriching public education. Higher Horizons served fifty-two elementary schools, thirteen junior-high schools, and eleven high schools in the metropolitan area between the years 1959 and 1966. It was representative of many educational services offered throughout the country at this time and is mentioned here because of the rich inclusion of performing arts which was made possible by its geographic location.

The ultimate objectives of the program were no different from those of the school system in general; however, because they were dealing with hundreds of children from deprived neighborhoods, an intensive program of guidance and remedial services, field trips, incursions, and community education was organized. One of the most exciting facets was the experience in the arts. Co-operation of performing groups in the city made matinees available for tens of thousands of children, many of whom had never been outside their neighborhoods, and most of whom had never heard of such places as Carnegie Hall or Stratford, Connecticut.

Volunteers from the Junior League and students from colleges and universities in the area as well as Board of Education personnel contributed to the success of the program. Higher Horizons has served as a prototype for numerous other programs designed to improve education and develop the talents of the disadvantaged.[3]

Community Theatre for Children

The upsurge of theatrical activity in communities throughout the country precludes a listing of any but the best known, most innovative, or most extensive programs. The *Directory of Children's Theatres in the United States*, previously mentioned, provides statistics on all groups which responded to the request for information. A historical narrative such as this must, of necessity,

[3] Jacob Landers, *Higher Horizons Progress Report.*

be more selective. There were many other noteworthy groups; the omission of their names from this chapter is no reflection on their effectiveness. The section which follows will render a view of the principal patterns, with brief descriptions of the sponsoring and producing groups responsible for initiating activities.

Community children's theatres varied widely during the sixties, but the large-scale sponsoring program designed to serve hundreds, if not thousands, of children through the procuring of touring companies was a popular practice. The following represent some of the larger and more successful attempts of communities to acquaint boys and girls with the living theatre and its literature.

JUNIOR PROGRAMS OF CALIFORNIA, INC.

One of the largest of these sponsoring organizations is Junior Programs of California, Inc. Begun modestly in 1955 as a film series for children in the Los Angeles area, the idea attracted attention until in 1963 seven towns were involved. The result was a nonprofit organization reincorporated to become Junior Programs of California; under its aegis theatre, puppets, music, and dance were booked throughout the state in communities eager to obtain the best of the performing arts for their children. Soon more than 20,000 boys and girls each year enjoyed in their local auditoriums the finest programs which the organization could obtain. Performances are previewed by knowledgeable volunteer members of Junior Programs. Art exhibits and book displays were added later in an effort to broaden and deepen appreciation of the arts.

SEATTLE JUNIOR PROGRAMS, INC.

Also located in the West is the Seattle Junior Programs, Inc., mentioned in an earlier chapter. By the end of the sixties Seattle Junior Programs had been in operation for over thirty years and was annually bringing the best in theatre to the Greater Seattle area. More than 15,000 children and several thousand adults were reported to have attended each of the Junior Programs productions in a season. Many more thousands filled auditoriums on tours to neighboring communities. A board of thirty-five trustees serves as a sponsoring agent to handle business details and hire professional directors and stage personnel to produce the plays. Occasionally companies are imported to enrich the program. A typical season includes three plays (each presented twenty-one times), among which are a classic, a historical or modern play, and a musical. Performances are given at the Seattle Central Playhouse on Saturdays and Sundays.

When the Puget Sound Arts and Science Program was organized under Title III, Seattle Junior Programs was invited to assist in a liaison capacity. In 1968–69 its production of *The Red Shoes* toured the state of Washington, with more than 80,000 fourth-graders alone attending, many of whom had never before seen live theatre. The final tour was made under the Washington State Educational Enrichment Program, which replaced Title III. This is the type of co-ordination that came into being with government funds and community consciousness of the arts in the sixties. As an added activity, Seattle Junior Programs has for many years sponsored a biennial playwriting contest, with $800 offered in prizes. Scholarships are also awarded annually to outstanding students in drama who have indicated an interest in children's theatre.

MILLS THEATRE WORKSHOP IN NEW YORK CITY

Mills Theatre Workshop in New York City is an example of a small college with a program designed for neighborhood children and for college students specializing in early childhood education. Under the leadership of its founder, Nellie McCaslin, a semester of creative dramatics, a semester of play production, and two productions a year for the public constitute a combined curricular and cocurricular offering as well as a community service. One production is geared to older children; the other is a more informal, often improvisational program for children under eight. Two albums of records were made by the Workshop and distributed by a commercial recording company during the sixties, and a weekly radio program of songs and stories for children was presented by Mills students for a period of several years. The small size of the college, its single purpose, and its location in lower Manhattan have contributed to a unique focus on theatre as an exciting and rewarding experience for all.

NEW YORK UNIVERSITY

New York University, on the other hand, is an example of a large university in which children's theatre and creative dramatics are included as a specialized area of the Dramatic Arts Department. This program was added in the sixties and headed by Lowell and Nancy Swortzell, a husband-and-wife team whose earlier work at Rutgers was well known in the East. Their "Youtheatre" is a new venture with a promising future, housed in a splendid new auditorium, with a large group of drama majors from which to draw actors and technical staff.

FLORIDA STATE UNIVERSITY

Another educational institution was established in the sixties with several specific considerations in mind. One was the younger audience (five to eight); the second was improvisational drama; the third was training for college students through this new medium. According to Moses Goldberg, well-known children's theatre director previously associated with Minnesota's Peppermint Tent, the experimental techniques worked to everyone's satisfaction. Based on Brian Way's approach, productions encouraged these youngest of audiences to become involved through active participation. The audience had the opportunity to use their imagination, from the acceptance of an "invisible" prop man to the creation of dialogue and collaboration in building the plot. Moses Goldberg, in distinguishing between the interests and abilities of the younger and the older child, thus prepares for a later, more aesthetic theatre experience.

Florida State University was awarded a grant from the State Fine Arts Council for the year 1970-71, in support of this innovative program. This is another illustration of government assistance for children's theatre, as conceived and administered by an educational institution.

HONOLULU THEATRE FOR YOUTH

The Honolulu Theatre for Youth, established in 1955 as an adjunct of the city parks department, was by the end of the sixties Hawaii's largest theatre in terms of audience. Its touring program reached 72,248 children in the 1969–70 season; in spite of having no permanent home of its own, it has won national and state awards and is considered one of the finest cultural assets of the community. Plays are selected for more than entertainment value; as is stated in the brochure, "Each play contains something the child must reach toward to understand, something which challenges his intellect and causes him to grow."

Honolulu Theatre for Youth is made possible by the efforts of businessmen, university students, retired people, housewives, and professional actors: in short, it is a community effort which serves many children in a wide area. The Junior Theatre Workshop for boys and girls from seven to fifteen and printed material for classroom use augment the formal program. Plans are afoot to add drama by actors under the Artists in the Schools Program of the Department of Education. Financial support is state-wide and comes from local businesses, foundations, the state legislature, the Department of Parks, and the State Foundation on Culture and the Arts. This youngest state is providing today one of the most far-reaching programs of entertainment and education in the nation.

SATURDAY THEATRE FOR CHILDREN

Another type of community program was launched in 1960 in New York City by the All-Day Neighborhood Schools and the Bureau of Audio-Visual Education of the Board of Education. This was the Saturday Theatre for Children, established in an effort to bring some of the city's resources to the thousands of children for whom they would otherwise have been inaccessible. From the first season's successful tour of five schools, the program had reached over 450,000 children by the end of the decade. In an average year, 60,000 children made up the audience. Plays, opera, modern and ethnic dance troupes, puppets, and concerts were enjoyed for only thirty-five cents a seat.

DETROIT INSTITUTE OF THE ARTS

In the Middle West an ambitious program, which attracted national attention, was initiated at the Detroit Institute of the Arts. It has been highly successful in its efforts to reach the children of the Detroit community. The 1969–70 season included a four-part series totaling eighteen different programs. On the first Saturday of the month films are offered; on the second, music and dance; on the third, plays and musicals; on the fourth, puppets; and on the occasional fifth Saturday, "specials." Productions are given in a lavish, 1,200-seat theatre. The privilege of attending these programs in such a beautiful setting adds another dimension, that of making the theatre a place to go as well as a source of entertainment.

THE 92ND STREET YM–YWHA

By 1970 subscription series had become common practice throughout the country. In New York City, for example, the 92nd Street "Y," a pioneer in this practice, was presenting ten programs a season on Sunday afternoons at a special rate of ten dollars for ten tickets. Nearly twice as many additional entertainments for young people (nonsubscription events) were planned for selected dates throughout the season. Many performances were sold out; thus, the subscription policy was adopted to prevent disappointment and overcrowding.

In the sixties the "Y" added a summer program for the many children who must remain in the city. While there are touring companies which go to the playgrounds and parks, there is an advantage of attending the theatre in an air-conditioned auditorium without distraction or hazards of weather.

MIMES AND MASQUES THEATRE FOR YOUTH

Washington, D.C., saw the founding of a new sponsoring organization in 1965, which is included here as an example of the way communities were meeting the needs of their children. Within the first five years of its existence Mimes and Masques for Youth had hired twenty professional productions of high quality, which were attended by 140,000 students and 5,000 teachers. Ten to fifteen performances in school time reached children of all backgrounds, thus contributing to the educational services of the public schools of Washington.

THE GOODMAN THEATRE

Meanwhile, some of the leading community theatres described in earlier chapters were continuing production and in most cases expanding their programs. The Goodman Children's Theatre of Chicago, which qualifies both as community and educational theatre, was now under the direction of Bella Itkin. By the sixties, it had progressed beyond the tried-and-true titles to such plays as *A Midsummer Night's Dream*, *The Hare and the Tortoise*, and *Don Quixote of La Mancha* and had added a summer program for city children. The Goodman Theatre, one of Chicago's finest cultural resources, was thus continuing to contribute to the education of the children of the city during both winter and summer seasons.

KARAMU YOUTH THEATRE

The Karamu Youth Theatre in Cleveland is part of Karamu House, whose history dates back to 1915. In new quarters, it now offers the *Karamu Dozen*, a twelve-part program in which are included the creative arts, a performing-arts service, and a collaborative-arts program. "Now"-oriented plays for adults and young people are a new feature of the organization. Joanna Halpert Kraus's *Mean to Be Free* was produced in the 1969–70 season and is an example of a play for today based on the life of Harriet Tubman. Through its many services and extensive arts program, Karamu has lived up to its name, which in Swahili means "a place of joyful meeting for all."

CHILDREN'S THEATRES OF PALO ALTO AND NASHVILLE

Among the well-known children's theatres which continued to serve their communities in homes of their own are the Children's Theatres of Palo Alto and Nashville. The former has been in existence for over twenty-five years as a division of the recreation department and has the distinction of being the first children's theatre to be housed in a building designed for this purpose. Nashville's Children's Theatre was founded by the Junior League in the mid-thirties. Years of hard work and achievement paid off; the year 1960 saw the dedication of a $250,000 theatre for the exclusive use of the children of Nashville. Among those most instrumental in obtaining this facility was Ann S. Hill, one of children's theatre's most indefatigable workers and national director of CTC at the end of the sixties.

BOSTON CHILDREN'S THEATRE

Boston, long a leader in theatre for children, continued to support and initiate a variety of opportunities and experiences. The Boston Children's Theatre is comparable to the programs previously described in the numbers of children it reaches—100,000 a year. It is different in that it was established as a theatre *for* children and *by* children, a practice which today is less common. Under the direction of Adele Thane, the Boston Children's Theatre provides three services: creative dramatic classes, a series of productions at the New England Life Hall, and the Stagemobile, which takes to the road in the summer. Traveling within a fifty-mile radius of Boston, the Stagemobile presents two plays daily in parks and playgrounds. Boston Children's Theatre is sponsored by the recreation department, the Metropolitan District Commission, local P-TA's, and other civic groups.

THE TRIBAL PLAYERS OF BOSTON

Theatre Workshop, Boston, Inc., is one of the youngest groups in the country, unique in its aim and revolutionary in its approach. Deliberately eschewing the traditional titles and practices, this group involves the audience in environmental theatre pieces, which are designed to be experienced rather than observed. Its first play, *Tribe*, in 1968, explored the history of the American Indian in terms which children could understand. A new piece, *Creation*, opened the following year. Based on the theme of pollution, the urgency of the problem was communicated through words, mime, movement, sound, and improvisation with the audience a vital element. In the belief that both children and adults are necessary to the performance, joint tickets were sold, with extra tickets available for children.

The play *Creation* was co-sponsored by the Arlington Street Church and supported by a grant from the National Endowment on the Arts. That the experiment met with success was evidenced by critical acclaim, the length of the run, and an award from the Association for the Performing Arts. Barbara Linden, director, sees children's theatre in different terms from most leaders; to her it is total communication in total space, with no separation between performers and audience.

THE CHILDREN'S THEATRE OF RICHMOND, VIRGINIA

One of the oldest producing groups in the country, the Children's Theatre of Richmond, Inc., had by 1969 evolved from a small organization to a permanent, nonprofit corporation. The story of this evolution is as fascinating as it is illustrative of the changing times. The first plays in 1927 were sponsored by the P-TA. During World War II the Department of Recreation produced a series of plays in Miller and Rhoades Department store.

In 1946 the Junior League, seeing the need for a permanent organization, established the Children's Theatre of Richmond, working closely with the Department of Recreation as producer and Miller and Rhoades as patron.

The year 1962 brought two major changes: an independent Board assumed full responsibility for production, and the Junior League discontinued the bonus puppet shows it had previously offered. Four years later a director for the entire season was employed; under his leadership the theatre expanded its program and added trouping throughout the state. In 1969 the Richmond, Fredericksburg and Potomac Railroad offered the use of an old repair shop for a theatre workshop. Thus a wide variety of community groups contributed to the support of an organization for over a period of forty years. Its flexibility has been a factor in maintaining stability and, thereby, continuous service to the children of the community.

ADVENTURE THEATRE

Adventure Theatre of Chevy Chase, Maryland, added a new educational program at the close of the sixties. This was the "In-School Players," a special troupe formed to bring live theatre not only into the schools but into the classrooms, cafeterias, or even outdoors on the grass. Folk tales were chosen as material, with music especially composed for the plays. The reaction to this program was so enthusiastic that portions were filmed by the U.S. Information Agency, translated into eighteen languages, and shown on television in approximately sixty countries of the world.

PIXIE THEATRE FOR YOUNG PEOPLE

Greensboro, North Carolina, offers an excellent example of the growing town-and-gown collaboration. When the Junior League and the Women's College of the University of North Carolina, both of whom produced plays for children, merged their organizations in 1962, the result was the Pixie Playhouse. The addition of a full-time director ensured a full season of plays.

Pixie is governed by two boards, representing the University, the League, the community, and the Playhouse staff.

DISTRICT OF COLUMBIA RECREATION DEPARTMENT

Dramatic activities have been popular with recreation departments throughout the country, but few have conducted as long and lively a program as the District of Columbia Recreation Department. Its Children's Theatre of Washington, organized in 1946, has grown into a producing, sponsoring, and teaching organization with the Junior League, the Congress of Parents and Teachers, and the Archdiocese of Washington as affiliates. The Children's Theatre gives eight productions a year: two self-produced, two professionally produced, two semiprofessional, and two puppet shows.

HONOLULU THEATRE FOR YOUTH

The Honolulu Theatre for Youth received an award from the National Recreation and Park Association in the spring of 1966 for its outstanding contribution to the recreation and park movement. It has since received legislative grants to cover the costs of transporting sets and casts to the various islands. Honolulu Theatre for Youth today reaches an annual audience of 70,000 and is the only theatre operating state-wide with assistance from the Department of Parks.

TEEN-CHILDREN'S THEATRE OF THE DALLAS THEATRE CENTER

Another group which was begun in the fifties has become one of the largest and most active in the country. This is the Teen-Children's Theatre of Dallas, Texas, a producing and teaching organization. Since its founding in 1959 it has become allied with the Graduate School of Trinity University as well as with the Dallas Theatre Center, a community organization. Thirteen productions a year, including a Christmas spectacular, are given with two to fifteen performances of each, either in the Center or on tour. Classics, historical plays, fantasies, modern and musical plays, as well as original class plays, are included. Casts are made up of experienced teen-agers and Center resident company members. It is mentioned here because of its growth, which took place in the sixties.

HARWICH JUNIOR THEATRE

The Harwich Junior Theatre, Cape Cod, begun in the early fifties, deserves further mention as an experiment which has proved its worth to the community and to the children who live in it. The famous Exchange Hall in Harwich Center served for many years as playhouse and workshop for the summer drama program. In an aura of Victorian elegance youngsters constructed and painted scenery as they prepared the four productions offered during the summer months. Today they work in a new building of their own in West Harwich. Qualified professional adults have always guided the children. Well-known designers and illustrators have given their services to this theatre, which has always striven for the most exacting professional results. Guest directors are invited to direct the plays, in accord with Betty Bobp's strong belief that the theatre benefits from a variety of viewpoints and techniques. Among the guest directors over the past eighteen years have been George Latshaw, Aurand Harris, and Helen Avery.

Creative dramatics, dance, and music classes are conducted by trained leaders, assisted by college students. Recently the summer experiment was expanded to include a winter program. The installation of heat in the theatre made possible a Christmas show for the first time in 1969. Winter classes were added, thus making the Harwich Junior Theatre the only summer theatre for children on the Eastern seaboard and a year-round center for the creative arts. Funds have come from a variety of sources, but an annual grant from a private foundation has helped maintain the program in an attractive and suitable setting.

Among the other children's theatres which have attracted attention for their extensive community service are the Davenport, Iowa, Junior Theatre; the Tulsa Children's Theatre; the Louisville Children's Theatre; the Birmingham Children's Theatre; the Children's Theatre of Winston-Salem; the Community Children's Theatre of Kansas City; the Mummers' Theatre of Oklahoma City; and the Children's Theatre Company of the Minneapolis Institute of Arts. It is apparent that the communities of America have continued their support of children's theatre both as sponsors and producers. It is also apparent that the majority have met the challenge of rising population and rising costs by co-ordinating their efforts with those of other organizations, with mutually satisfying results.

Professional Theatre for Children

Professional children's theatre companies mushroomed in the fifties, but by the end of the following decade certain significant changes had taken place. Some companies were disbanding; some were merging; others, strengthened by community patronage and government support, were finding themselves in a stronger position than before. The last years of the sixties saw fewer professional companies in operation, but those which had weathered the problems of booking, casting, touring, and competition with television and films were commanding public attention. Federal and state funds did not guarantee the future, but they did make it possible for a company of high quality to perform and thus become known to many communities. A number of groups which had begun operation in the fifties, therefore, continued; others with innovative ideas and techniques sprang up—some to meet with success.

Earning a living in children's theatre has been a problem from the beginning, making it necessary for many actors to hold outside jobs. This condition has affected rehearsal time, with the result that plays for children too frequently lack the hours of preparation and attention to detail given plays for adults. Many actors have left children's theatre for some other area of the entertainment field or for different professions. Low salaries, difficult working conditions, and frustration with the artistic results have militated against the development of stable, professional companies in America.

One of the important developments of the sixties was, therefore, the drawing up of the first Equity contract for professional children's theatre (PACT) with Actors' Equity (AEA); the new contract called for the following improvements: a three-year agreement between producer and actor; salaried rehearsals; regulation of the length of the working day; safe and sanitary conditions in all auditoriums; eligibility for health, pension, and welfare benefits; reasonable notice of termination of services by actors and producers; and standardization of salaries.

These conditions, though admittedly hard for many producers to meet, were negotiated in the interest of making a precarious and part-time job into a full-time and sound profession. It is too early to tell whether the contract will prove a success, but Max Traktman (Maximilian Productions) stated his point of view in a Region 14 *Newsletter*: "We of the Producers' Association of Children's Theatre have high hopes that our new agreement will pave the way and provide the means of bringing the finest in children's theatre to young audiences everywhere."[4]

PACT

When Actors' Equity moved to establish a union contract for employment in children's theatre, a group of thirteen New York producers formed an association known as PACT to bargain collectively with the union. Max Traktman, chairman, explained that a showcase of all work was vital to their survival. Whereas many of these companies had depended on being selected for the Region 14 Showcase as a means of acquainting sponsors with their work, they were now in the position of having to hold a showcase of their own to ensure an appearance. They held the first one in the spring of 1969 at the 92nd Street "Y" in New York. This showcase took place in the same auditorium and week in May as

---

[4] (October, 1968).

the Region 14 Showcase. Many sponsors attended both, but questions were raised as to the objectives of the two groups. The PACT Showcase was clearly a commercial enterprise, open to all members of the organization, whereas the Region 14 Showcase was a public service dedicated to showing only the best professional work done in the area according to CTC standards.

Companies which appeared on the first PACT Showcase were the Traveling Playhouse, the Performing Arts Repertory Theatre (PART Productions), the Gingerbread Players and Jack, the Pixie Judy Troupe, the Prince Street Players, the National Theatre Company, Periwinkle Productions, Maximilian Productions, Denis Tyrrell Productions, Silver Buttons Productions, and Janmar Productions.

The success of the PACT Showcase led to a re-evaluation of the Region 14 Showcase, already a problem in terms of magnitude and the volunteer manpower needed to handle it. The regional Showcase continued to support professional theatre for children, but in a somewhat different way. The number of productions involved and the fact that New York City is America's theatre center made it possible for both showcases to exist and to serve the needs of the public.

THE TRAVELING PLAYHOUSE

The Traveling Playhouse of New York is one of the longest-lived companies in operation. By May, 1969, it had completed its twentieth season and had given more than 4,250 performances before a combined audience of over 3,000,000 children. Home base continued to be the 92nd Street "Y," but the group has journeyed through the entire United States, including five coast-to-coast tours. Its *Robin Hood* has been produced twice on national television, and commercial recordings have been made of three of its most popular productions. Kay and Ken Rockefeller, producers, have headed the company since the beginning, a fact which may in part account for its longevity.

THE MERRY-GO-ROUNDERS

Following the example of many other organizations during the sixties, the Merry-Go-Rounders entered into a merger in 1968. Dance Adventures, Inc., producers of the Merry-Go-Rounders, merged with the Foundation for Modern Dance Education, a nonprofit educational organization in New Jersey. The merger was an attempt to strengthen this unusual company, whose high standards and superior productions have been acclaimed since its beginning.

STORY TIME DANCE THEATRE

By the end of the sixties Story Time Dance Theatre was well established as a touring company in the mid-Atlantic states. Sheila Hellman of New Jersey, director, held to her original concept of children's theatre: the integration of dance, drama, music, and audience participation. Ten actor-dancers with complete scenery and costumes offer a program which is advertised as possible for presentation anywhere. Fables, classical stories, and original dance-dramas comprise the repertory, which has been seen in schools, community centers, camps, and on local television.

PERCIVAL BORDE AND COMPANY

Programs celebrating ethnic and racial customs burst on the scene in the sixties. One of the more powerful of these was Percival Borde's *Drums of the Caribbean*, which found enthusiastic audiences on all levels. To the beat of drums Borde's company expressed in language that even the youngest children could understand the work, the religion, the carnival, and the spirit of the Island people, whose African culture bears Spanish, French, English, and Dutch influences. Borde's distinguished background on the professional stage and in America's finest universities brought new life to children's theatre, further closing the gap between theatre and education in a performance relevant to the times and superb in showmanship.

THE PAPER BAG PLAYERS

The enthusiasm which the Paper Bag Players engendered in the first years of their existence has grown with each succeeding season. Dedication to creative work, skillfully presented in a highly original style, has set the "Bags" apart from all other performing groups. Their program, consisting of short sketches, dances, and songs, in which choreography, mime, and dialogue are combined, represents in the opinion of many the most imaginative work being done in children's theatre today.

Titles of their different productions suggest their humor and originality: *Scraps, Cut-ups, Group Soup, Baked Alaska, Dandelion,* and *Hot Feet.* Performing with the minimum in the way of costumes and props (paper bags and cardboard cartons, for the most part), they succeed in inventing a wide variety of ideas and characters.

Recognition has come their way in the form of both funds and citations. A Rockefeller Foundation grant made possible the creation of *Dandelion.* The New York State Council on the Arts has given support, and the National Foundation on the Arts awarded them a grant in 1968, the first ever given to a children's theatre company. Further recognition came in 1965, when they were given an "Obie" for raising the level of children's theatre through intelligence, imagination, and respect for its audiences. In 1967 the AETA Award was given to them for "their delight, imaginative freshness and artistry; which has set a standard in professional children's theatre which will be very difficult to emulate."

Perhaps their most enthusiastic audiences were in London, where they performed in the Royal Court Theatre and were seen on television. Judith Martin has been their producer from the beginning, though members of the company have changed from time to time.

THE BLUE PEACOCK PLAYERS

The Blue Peacock Players, a New York company of two, has been in existence since 1963. Ednamati and Evana are the coproducers and dancers, who offer children their rich background of Eastern folklore and art. Dance-dramas with narration and beautiful costumes set the Blue Peacock Players apart from other performing groups; schools find them particularly suitable for assembly programs and have welcomed their exotic presentation of unusual and worth-while material. Their five different programs make it possible for them to appear from season to season, and their ability to vary the length of a show recognizes the practical needs of community program chairmen who want to include the Orient in a season's offerings.

CHILDREN'S THEATRE INTERNATIONAL, INC.

Vera Stilling's long association with children's theatre, first as a sponsor and later as a producer, culminated in 1961 with the formation of Children's Theatre International. In partnership with William Schill, her company has won particular praise for visual beauty in scenery and costume. Plays are generally based on classics, although the first and still popular production, *Petey and the Pogo Stick*, was an original script. Polished and inventive, Children's Theatre International has introduced new titles each year, all suggesting the countries of their origin: *Big, Little, and In-Between* (three Irish folk tales); *Babu* (East Indian); *A Box of Tears* (Japanese); and *Hans Brinker* (Dutch).

A recent addition to the repertory has been Hourglass Productions for young folks. This recognition of the high-school audience came as a result of the acknowledged dearth of drama for boys and girls of this age; it has, however, in no way diminished the original effort to bring the world's classics to children. By the end of the sixties Children's Theatre International was not only entertaining audiences in different parts of the country but working directly with such school systems as the Westchester Regional Educational Center in the development of an arts-humanities program for elementary and secondary students.

MAXIMILIAN PRODUCTIONS

Another professional company which began with an individual

style of production was Maximilian Productions. Founded in 1962 in New York City by Max Traktman and Peggy Simon, it has had the advantage of stability and a point of view. Productions are designed as musicals and the style is lively and modern—sometimes described as "camp"—but the technical excellence and original approach represent professional achievement.

Titles of past and current plays are suggestive of the originality of this company: *Gabriel Ghost, The Blue Planet, Fiesta Mexicana! Are There Alligators in the Sewers of the City of New York?*, and *This Was America*. Maximilian Productions belongs to the present and bears little resemblance to the children's theatre of the past.

THE PEPPERMINT PLAYERS OF NEW YORK

A company which was established in 1960 and which was well received by audiences until 1965 deserves special mention here for two reasons. Unlike the majority of professional groups, the Peppermint Players did not tour but were members of a resident company, with the Martinique off-Broadway theatre in Manhattan as home base. The five musicals in the repertory were *Jack and the Beanstalk, Pinocchio, Sleeping Beauty, Ali Baba,* and *The Emperor's New Clothes*. Original-cast scores were still being distributed at the end of the sixties, at a rate of more than 80,000 a year. The repertory without the music was filmed and is currently in distribution in the United States, Canada, and Europe by McGraw Hill.

Coproducers, Carole Schwartz Hyatt and Paul Libin, deliberately disbanded the company after five years despite its commercial success because they believed that new forms of technology and more relevant titling were mandatory for growth. They had enjoyed the experience of producing musical adaptations for children but felt at the same time that change was essential to growth and that basic changes were not possible at that time. This point of view was to be stated again and frequently by the close of the decade by other producers, some of whom have effected changes reflecting the changing times.

PERFORMING ARTS REPERTORY THEATRE FOUNDATION, INC.

In 1969 the Performing Arts Repertory Theatre Foundation, known as PART, received the Jennie Heiden Award for "excellence in professional children's theatre" at the AETA convention in Detroit. Presently under the leadership of Robert Adams and Jay Harnick, this company launched the first of its "Preludes to Greatness" series in 1962 with the musical *Young Abe Lincoln*. The reaction to this production, while mixed, gave recognition to a new concept of children's entertainment. Subsequent enthusiasm on the part of sponsors attending the Region 14 Showcase indicated that the company had an idea they would buy—and they did. The series was based on two premises: first, that children need heroes on whom to pattern their lives; and second, that theatre, in order to instruct, must first of all entertain. Other musicals in the series which followed were *Young Tom Edison, Young Jefferson, Young Mozart, Young Mark Twain,* and *Martin Luther King, Jr.* In 1967, when PART was incorporated, it was playing to children from Connecticut to Illinois and Virginia and in art centers from Michigan to the Carolinas. By the end of the 1967–68 school year, over 100,000 children had attended performances.

PART has been endorsed by the New York State Department of Education as curriculum oriented and by thirty-eight school systems for in-school-time performances. The company mails study guides to schools well in advance of performance dates to aid in preparation and discussion. *Young Abe Lincoln* had the distinction of playing at Ford's Theatre in Washington for three weeks under the sponsorship of the U.S. Department of the Interior, and every fifth- and sixth-grade pupil in metropolitan Washington was said to have been in attendance.

The most recent development in the growth of this company has been the establishment of the National Theatre Center for the Young. In co-operation with New York University and Town Hall, plans are under way to create a permanent home for children's theatre in this country. Productions are all musical and make use of eight to ten Equity actors.

THE POCKET PLAYERS

The Pocket Players of New York City, under the direction of Muriel Sharon, was established in the sixties. Miss Sharon, who is chairman of the Children's Drama Department of the 92nd Street "Y," has an enviable background, which includes work in the professional theatre as well as a degree in childhood education. Her aim, high artistic standards, has been achieved through the use of scripts of fine quality, an emphasis on style appropriate to the play, and an insistence upon perfection of detail.

Among the plays which have been performed by the Pocket Players are *Master of All Masters*, *The Tale of the Donkey*, *The Glass Slipper*, and *Emil and the Detective*; all are children's classics, yet none has enjoyed wide production in this country. Miss Sharon has made a practice of employing the best professional assistance available in the staging of her plays. For example, Marcia Brown, illustrator and author of children's books, designed sets and costumes for *The Glass Slipper*, while Allan Baker, a dancer formerly with Sadler's Wells and the Royal Ballet, was choreographer. The emphasis on the artistic quality has been reflected in the limited number of offerings by this group: four plays in a period of seven years.

A nonprofit organization, the Pocket Players pays Equity salaries, even though the group does not limit itself to small casts or other common money-saving measures. The uniqueness of this company lies in its uncompromising stand for quality in a period of competition and quick results.

THE PHOENIX THEATRE

One of the well-known companies which has participated in theatre for the schools of New York City is the Phoenix. Between 1960 and 1962 the Phoenix sent a company with excerpts from classical plays to 242 schools in the metropolitan area. By special arrangement with the Bureau of Audio-Visual Instruction, the

Phoenix *Hamlet* played to more than 100,000 high-school students in its own theatre, and for three years the Phoenix and the Board of Education offered a teacher-training program in theatre appreciation. In 1963 it leased a 1,600-seat theatre in downtown Manhattan, priced tickets at $1.50, and presented two full productions at a series of special performances for school children. Despite the enthusiastic response to this enterprise, lack of funds forced suspension of activities.

In 1969 a small unit called the "Portable Phoenix," an educational project of Theatre Incorporated, the Phoenix Theatre, appeared on the Region 14 Showcase. The company offered two productions, *Falstaff and Hal,* adapted from Shakespeare, and *New York and Who To Blame It On* for junior- and senior-high school pupils. In addition, the company announced three types of workshops for students: Theatre Games, Prepared Readings, and Vocational Seminars. By spending up to six hours in a school, the company hoped to do more than present entertainment. Though not children's theatre in the strictest sense, the Phoenix was proving its interest in young audiences in co-operation with the public schools.

THE LITTLE THEATRE OF THE DEAF

In December, 1968, the Little Theatre of the Deaf made its New York debut in the Forum Theatre of Lincoln Center. Part of the highly praised National Theatre of the Deaf, this group presented a new concept in children's theatre: a program of poems and stories combining mime and narration. This is the only company of professional deaf actors playing for both hearing and non-hearing audiences.

A special holiday program featured Dylan Thomas' *A Child's Christmas in Wales* and works by Ogden Nash, e. e. cummings, and James Thurber. With a company of five—four actors and a narrator—they toured schools both preceding and following this engagement. The group was scheduled to appear on the Region 14 Showcase in 1969, but a European engagement at that time prevented it. A nonprofit, federally funded organization, the The-

atre of the Deaf is a distinctive project of the Eugene O'Neill
Memorial Theatre Foundation.

THE PRINCE STREET PLAYERS

Audiences at the PACT Previews in New York in the spring
of 1969 were startled by the appearance of a new group known
as the Prince Street Players. *Mother Goose Go-Go*, performed
in mini-skirts, was a twentieth-century children's musical with a
hard-rock beat. Though many in the audience questioned its interpretation of traditional material, none denied its vitality and
sense of fun.

This company specializes in musical adaptations of familiar
stories for the "now generation"; what effect it will have on children's theatre remains to be seen. The Prince Street Players do
have a special point of view and professional competence in
projecting it.

THE ROBERT F. KENNEDY THEATRE
FOR CHILDREN

The Robert F. Kennedy Theatre for Children, formerly known
as the American Children's Theatre, leaped into the spotlight
with its *première* of *Toby Tyler* in 1967. From the Lincoln Center Library in New York City, where it was first seen, *Toby Tyler*
went on to Broadway, where it is said to have had the longest run
of any children's play, and to a subsequent summer season in the
parks of the metropolitan area. In December of the same year the
Robert F. Kennedy Theatre presented Dickens' *Christmas Carol*
with a cast of Broadway actors. The following Christmas, Orson
Bean starred as Scrooge and James Earl Jones narrated.

Producer Martin Gregg believes that children's theatre should
attract the finest professional talent, and he has held firmly to this
conviction. In the spring of 1969 the Robert F. Kennedy Theatre offered *Peter and the Wolf*, narrated by Cyril Ritchard and
danced by members of the New York City Ballet. Costumes and
scenery by Raoul Pène du Bois and choreography by Jacques

d'Amboise made this an event of significance, despite mixed reviews and reactions. It is Gregg's dream that financial support may be obtained to make possible a diversified program of dance, drama, and music, performed by the finest Broadway casts for all children, regardless of their economic status. Single brilliant productions rather than repertory distinguish Gregg's approach to children's theatre from that of his fellow producers.

TONY MONTANARO

The enjoyment of mime theatre was extended to children on the Eastern seaboard during the sixties with the arrival of Tony Montanaro. "Talent" and "discipline" were the words most frequently used to describe his performance, which included a group of sketches arranged according to the particular audience and the length of time allotted to the presentation. His was one of the few programs which literally knew no age level: elementary, high-school, and college students responded with delight to his art and admired his technical skill. A background in dance and study with Marcel Marceau in addition to a degree from Columbia University had prepared Montanaro admirably for the work in which he was engaged.

Requests for workshops as well as for performances on college campuses far from metropolitan New York have cut down his time for engagements in children's theatre. His enthusiastic supporters can only hope that he will again bring his unique one-man performances back to the elementary-school audience, where they proved to be so appropriate and effective.

PERIWINKLE PRODUCTIONS

Periwinkle Productions of Monticello, New York, must be cited for its innovative use of poetry on the stage. *Poetry in 3-D* for younger children and *Poetry Now* for the seventh grade and up were designed for the purpose of stimulating appreciation for this form of literature through lively reading, movement, and costume. In 1962, Sunna Rasch, whose educational background matched her theatre experience, first tried out her ideas in upstate New York. By 1970 she was touring the country with an enthusiastic following. This unusual presentation found favor as an assembly program.

Because of the concentration of performing groups in New York, a large number from this area have been discussed here. There was professional work going on elsewhere in the sixties, however. Some of the better known, older, or more unusual are described next.

NATIONAL CHILDREN'S THEATRE ASSOCIATION

The National Children's Theatre Association had begun operation in Dallas in 1958–59. A decade later it reported playing to more than 200,000 children each season. A self-sustaining educational organization, it is endorsed by educators and sponsored by local organizations throughout the South and Midwest. It has offered three productions a year, all dramatizations of children's classics; during the twelve years of its existence all plays have been directed by Edwin Child, a factor which may account for the stability and steady growth of this professional company.

THE MAGIC BASKET

An imaginative concept of theatre for children was developed during the sixties in Los Angeles. This was the Magic Basket, founded in 1960 by Laura Olsher. First performances were given at the Stage Society Theatre in Hollywood; touring dates followed. In 1966, under Title I, the Magic Basket took literature to children in the schools as an aid to reading and cultural enrichment.

Laura Olsher acts as narrator and storyteller, with two other actors completing the cast of each play. They portray various characters in dance and pantomime, with original music used to enhance the mood. The producer's rich background in children's theatre, radio, film, and television, as well as her teaching experience in Northwestern University and in the University of California at Los Angeles, bring unusual qualifications to a program which places its emphasis on introducing fine literature to children through simple and direct means.

THE EVERYMAN PLAYERS

A group which claimed wide attention in the sixties is the Everyman Players under the direction of Orlin and Irene Corey of Shreveport, Louisiana. In contrast to the other groups mentioned, the Everyman Players base their art on the philosophy of good theatre, which may be enjoyed and understood by children, rather than on the presentation of standard juvenile literature. To this end they have offered such plays as *The Book of Job*, *The Pilgrim's Progress*, *Reynard the Fox*, *Don Quixote of La Mancha*, and *The Great Cross Country Race (The Tortoise and the Hare)*.

The Coreys have toured their plays in this country and abroad, frequently stopping in one place for a run of several weeks. *The Book of Job* has been seen on three continents, including performances at two world's fairs, two off-Broadway seasons, two United States tours, and four international tours. In 1964–65, *Reynard the Fox* toured South Africa as well as the United States, with one nine-week engagement at the Kentucky Lake Amphitheatre. One unique feature of the work of this husband-and-wife team is its visual beauty. Irene Corey, a gifted designer, creates costumes and settings for the productions which her husband directs. In addition to their work as producers, the Coreys enjoy an international reputation as lecturers and teachers. Though frequently identified as leaders in religious drama, they are more accurately described as theatre artists committed to values for man, with children as an important concern. Their belief in the unlimited grasp of the imagination in response to art includes audiences of children or children in audiences. Proof of the viability of their point of view is the success which their productions have enjoyed. Everyman Players appeared on television in London twice in 1970; they performed *The Tortoise and the Hare* in

Venice and at the Third ASSITEJ General Assembly; and they undertook a national tour of a new production of *The Pilgrim's Progress* in 1971.

THE SAN FRANCISCO PLAYERS GUILD

Though established in 1949, the San Francisco Players Guild deserves particular mention in the sixties because of the growth and scope of its program. After twenty seasons and 4,136 performances, the Guild today sponsors a touring company of six professional actors skilled in the techniques of performing for a wide range of age levels and a variety of ethnic backgrounds. Educational booklets are sent to schools in advance of performances in the belief that live theatre stimulates learning and self-expression. Positive response to the program is attested by the increase in performances. From thirty-seven performances of *Circus Day* in 1949 the number increased to three hundred performances of *Katya, the Wonder Girl*, in the 1968–69 season. The Guild states that it is the most extensive children's theatre project in the country today.

Modest admission charges make it possible for all children to attend. Productions are supported by the Guild Auxiliary, private donations, and foundations, and are produced under the guidance of Mrs. Theodore Lyman Eliot.

THE STUDIO ARENA THEATRE OF BUFFALO

Buffalo's Studio Arena Theatre, established in 1927, has recently added a new dimension to an already ambitious program. "Project Curtain Call" is a service made possible by Title I funds and designed to bring professional theatre to school children in the economically depressed areas of Buffalo. In the 1966–67 season three productions were mounted for travel to fifty-three schools, to be shown to 10,000 fourth-, fifth-, and sixth-graders. Two productions are seen in school auditoriums, with the third enjoyed as a theatre experience at the Studio Arena. "Project Curtain Call" is sponsored by the Board of Education and administered by the Arena Theatre with a Project Director, an Associate Director, a Technical Director, and a Program Supervisor.

Casts of plays are made up of actors in the resident company, supplemented by some local supporting actors. *The Canterville Ghost, Androcles, The Wind in the Willows, Alice in Wonderland,* and *The Indian Captive* are among the titles offered under Title I during the years 1966–70. In 1939 national recognition came to Studio Arena in the form of a Rockefeller Foundation grant. Today it has a fully professional company with a staff of thirty-five and a company of twenty-two. Well-known actors appear regularly in Arena Theatre plays for adult audiences, thus enriching a fine community offering. A school which includes classes in creative dramatics for children as well as classes for adults rounds out one of the most comprehensive theatre programs in the country.

THE PLAYERS' THEATRE OF NEW HAMPSHIRE

One of the newest companies in the United States, the Players' Theatre of New Hampshire, has already attracted serious attention for its unusual treatment of seldom-performed classics. The group was organized in 1967 and in the three remaining years of the decade it produced *The Devil and Daniel Webster, The Pranks of Scapin, A Christmas Carol, The Story of a Soldier, The Headless Horseman,* and its own dramatization of Plato's Law Dialogue, *The Crito.* The Players' Theatre, under the direction of Harvey Grossman, has toured the Eastern states, performing in schools, colleges, and community centers; it has been associated with the New Hampshire Commission on the Arts and with two Title III programs. An Achievement Award from the New England Theatre Conference for pioneer work recognized the artistic terms in which the Players' work was presented: mime, mask-playing, dialogue, song, and dance.

The varied repertory enables the company to play for all levels from elementary school to college. This group is a vivid illustration of what was happening in children's theatre by the end of the decade: imaginative work was getting support from government funds through new agencies, which in turn served existing organizations.

THE BARTER THEATRE OF ABINGDON, VIRGINIA

Abingdon, Virginia, has the distinction of possessing the first and only state-subsidized theatre in the United States. Founded in 1932 by Robert Porterfield, who is still its director, the Barter Theatre was literally what its name implies: a theatre where seats could be purchased with produce from local farms. A jar of beans, a smoked ham, a bunch of flowers could and still can purchase tickets, although the majority of patrons today pay the box-office price. This imaginative device of bringing theatre to a region far from Broadway proved to be a sound business venture in the depression years. Today the Barter Theatre has the largest professional company in continuous operation outside New York City, a training school for young actors, and, in addition to an extensive season, an annual tour of hundreds of towns in the rural South. The Barter repertory includes both classics and contemporary plays, in an effort to offer a cross section of the world's best drama to the community in which it is located.

In keeping with its program of expansion, the Barter Theatre introduced children's plays to its schedule in 1961. Thereafter five or six productions have been given annually, with five performances a week during the summer season. Equity actors, following the principle of the adult theatre, offer a varied program of fantasy, historical, and modern plays to hundreds of children who would otherwise have no opportunity of seeing them. The Barter Theatre is a unique example of a professional company with community support and state subsidy, serving the boys and girls who will become the adult audience of tomorrow.

THE LONG WHARF THEATRE OF NEW HAVEN, CONNECTICUT

The Long Wharf Theatre Extension Program for children,

located in New Haven, Connecticut, has aroused public interest in the scope of its activities and the depth of its involvement with the inner city. This program is an example of a professional regional theatre which has taken children's theatre seriously as a part of its total program. The director, Arvin Brown, is a young man whose interest in children's theatre was aroused while studying in England. Subsequent work on a doctorate at Yale in the early sixties brought him into contact with Harlan Kleiman, executive director of the Long Wharf Theatre.

Children's theatre activities opened officially in 1965 and were intended for ages four to eleven. The range was soon extended to fourteen as the needs of the community became known. The Long Wharf Theatre, as it has developed, is a clear example of the ways in which professional theatre can work with the community to provide a variety of services. Phases of the work include the bringing of elementary-school children to the theatre to see plays, both classics and new scripts, selected for their enjoyment and learning. High-school students are brought from poverty areas to participate in the regular adult theatre program. A touring group is sent into the ghettos, and selected work-study students from the OEO program are placed with the theatre for apprenticeship training. In other words, the organization was established to act as entertainer, educator, and skill-trainer, demonstrating the viability of theatre as an instrument to raise the motivation of inner-city youth.

Begun on a small experimental basis, the Long Wharf has grown and expanded its services to include more school districts, working in close co-operation with teachers and curriculum. By 1967, the Long Wharf had touched the lives of thousands of children from inner-city schools. Developed and sponsored by the Ford Foundation, Community Progress, Inc., the New Haven Board of Education, and the Long Wharf Theatre, the Extension Program is a shining example of what can be accomplished when professional theatre and community services work together toward common goals. One of the ways in which this program differs from many others is in its extensive preparatory and fol-

low-up activities, initiated through the United Curriculum Services of the Board of Education.

Despite the short period of its existence, the Long Wharf Theatre has been hailed by educators as one of the most valuable educational, social, and psychological forces in the lives of all area
children, particularly the disadvantaged.

THE PICK-A-PACK PLAYERS OF MILWAUKEE

The Pick-A-Pack Players began operation in 1960 under the
auspices of the Milwaukee Repertory Theatre. Its purpose was to
bring live theatre to an area which lacked professionally produced plays for children and which offered only television and
motion pictures to the young. It continues to be committed to
this aim and to this end offers its work to all children in the Milwaukee area. Its repertory now includes fourteen plays, all classics.

The adult acting company carries major responsibility, but children from the creative dramatics classes are frequently cast in
children's roles. Director Edith Mahler estimates that by the end
of the sixties more than 120,000 persons had seen Pick-A-Pack
productions at the "Rep" or in one of a score of communities in
Wisconsin and northern Illinois. A rigorous touring schedule,
with good dramatizations of children's classics, has acquainted
hundreds of audiences with living drama and has provided some
children with the opportunity to act in the plays.

LOOKING GLASS THEATRE

One of the newest producing groups, which uses improvisation
as a technique, is the Looking Glass Theatre in Providence, Rhode
Island. Frankly experimental, Looking Glass Theatre is now incorporated as a nonprofit organization dedicated to educational
theatre. It is a member of the Rhode Island Fine Arts Council, the
AETA, and the Educational Drama Association of Birmingham,
England. From the beginning actors working in the round have
improvised *with* their audiences rather than *for* them. A story
may undergo unexpected change as the audience enters into and

suggests or participates in the action. Looking Glass Theatre is reported to be the first adult company, performing exclusively for children, to participate in Title III. Members of the company have also led classes at the University of Rhode Island, thus further closing the gap between community and educational theatre.

LIVING STAGE

Living Stage is a project of Arena Stage in Washington, D.C. Established in 1966, it has grown in depth and scope of program until today it includes a threefold educational program and a touring schedule reaching from Washington to Hawaii. Under the direction of Robert Alexander, Living Stage has moved into the forefront of children's theatre with improvisation as its medium. Its three activities are the Teacher-Training Program, Improvisational Workshops for three different age groups, and the Theatre for Children and Youth. The last is presented by an improvisational touring company which goes into schools, recreation centers, churches, and inner-city neighborhoods. Performances involve the audience in participatory drama, a technique which is aimed at reaching today's children in a vital and meaningful way. Success is measured in large part by the degree to which the audience helps create the play. Often members of the audience join the actors in playing in the stories which they have helped to create. In addition to improvisational drama, Living Stage also presents musicals both at Arena Stage and on tour; these likewise deal with the concerns of children in today's world.

Funded by the National Endowment on the Arts, the D.C. Commission on the Arts, and private foundations, Living Stage has demonstrated its ability to reach and teach children in a new way.

PUBLICATION FOR CHILDREN'S THEATRE

A number of new titles were added to the catalogues of plays for children during the sixties, and several new books on children's theatre and creative dramatics appeared. Growing dissatisfaction with the traditional content spurred some efforts in the direction of new scripts and good plays not generally produced for the elementary-school age. The 1969 catalogue of the Anchorage Press reflected this trend. Play contests continued throughout the country, but the fine new literature dreamed of for the past two decades had still to be written. Interest in improvisation provided variety in performance but did not replace scripts in most quarters. Research was encouraged, and a number of topics on both master's and doctoral levels were printed each year in the *Educational Theatre Journal.*

Two doctoral studies made in the field during this period hold particular interest. "Education through Theatre for Children" by Robert Milton Leech proved the thesis that the life of a child is enriched by placing him in an audience. Children's theatre should, therefore, possess sincerity, simplicity, excitement, and imagination in addition to skill in the creation of the script and technical aspects of the production.[5] The second dealt with "Differences in Contemporary Views of Theatre for Children." Research revealed that theatrical and literary values were held to be of equal importance but that respondents thought scripts for children's theatre inferior to those written for adults. The objectives held by the majority who answered were basically the same as those held in the past: to provide the audience with a true theatre experience; to entertain and bring joy; to provide a learning experience; to enhance appreciation of life's values and awareness of other cultures; and to develop a discriminating audience for the future.

The majority of respondents thought good theatre training to be the best preparation for work in the children's field. Half expressed the view that children's theatre is slowly becoming recognized as important. A list of the sixteen most frequently produced plays was heartening; in spite of the plea for better scripts, figures showed *Androcles and the Lion* (Harris), *Land of the Dragon* (Madge Miller), and *The Wizard of Oz* (many different

[5] Robert Milton Leech, "Education through Theatre for Children."

adaptations) to lead in popularity. *Tom Sawyer* and *The Emperor's New Clothes* followed in that order.[6]

The most important development in the sixties was unquestionably government funding. This money made possible large-scale programs, enabling thousands of children to experience live theatre. It also stimulated the trend toward co-operative planning by producers and sponsors. Improved transportation and communication helped neighboring towns and communities work together in scheduling performances by the same companies. The Equity contract at the close of the decade may or may not have been an advantage; what it does prove is that children's theatre is no longer the province of the amateur. In the development of an art conceived and nurtured largely through the efforts of educators, social workers, and dedicated nonprofessionals, this act may one day prove to have been the turning point.

[6] Wesley Van Tassel, "Differences in Contemporary Views of Theatre for Children."

IX

Time for Assessment

I n 1956, Robert Kase declared that children's theatre had come of age. By 1970, however, though more firmly entrenched and widespread, children's theatre cannot yet claim to have achieved full stature. A number of problems have yet to be solved before children's theatre in America can take its place as a full-fledged member of the family of the performing arts. The nearly seventy years since its birth have been witness to a variety of changes, expansion of activities, and some experimentation. Most important, however, has been the growing acceptance of the values of theatre among educators and laymen throughout the land. Some of the same problems which have hampered its growth from the beginning still exist; the solution of these problems will inevitably affect the direction which children's theatre takes in the future.

Objectives Guiding Children's Theatre

From the first the children's theatre movement has been guided by certain specific objectives, two of which have been stated repeatedly. These are to provide worth-while and appropriate entertainment for young audiences, and to promote individual and social growth through experience in the dramatic arts. Of the groups described in this book some have stressed one of these objectives more than the other, depending upon whether the activities were set up primarily for the audience or for the participants. No group, however, has failed to include one of these basic tenets in explaining its *raison d'être*. These purposes have not changed in essence over the years, but a greater emphasis is being placed upon the entertainment and educational values of the performance in the present period than at any time heretofore.

This emphasis may be the result of the clear distinction now made between children's theatre and creative dramatics. Whereas the latter is participant centered and holds as its primary objective the emotional, social, and intellectual development of the individual child, the former, being audience centered, is free to emphasize the artistic and educational aspects of the performance. Acting in children's theatre plays is valuable training for the participants, but the greatest value of children's theatre is the vicarious experience which it offers to young audiences. Good literature, well produced, with high artistic standards, is the major concern. There is no conflict in ideology between children's theatre and creative dramatics since they serve different purposes and supplement each other.

A Review of the Major Developments

In reviewing the activities of the past seventy years, we find that the children's theatre movement in the United States has been characterized by phenomenal, if erratic, growth. From the time of the earliest dramatic activities recorded by the settlement houses to the present day, there has been an increase in all types of productions and producing groups. Systematic surveys were not conducted until recently, yet there is sufficient evidence to reveal an extraordinary and continued development.

NATIONAL ORGANIZATIONS

Six national organizations have played an important part in the development of children's theatre since 1910. The Drama League of America, founded in that year and dedicated to the promotion of better theatre on both professional and nonprofessional levels, was the first of such organizations to initiate activities, publish suitable plays and materials, and help struggling groups to maintain their existence. For twenty-one years the Drama League was a potent force in America; a number of little theatre groups, some of which are still in operation, owe their existence to the interest and support extended them by this national organization. The Drama League placed an emphasis on quality as well as on the promotion of new activities.

To the Association of Junior Leagues of America must be given the credit for having made the longest continuous contribution to children's theatre of any organization in the United States. In all parts of the country, in urban and rural areas, as individual Leagues and in conjunction with other civic organizations, through classes and through production, the Junior League has made children's theatre a cause to which thousands of young women have been dedicated. They have contributed time, energy, and money to countless projects. Their productions have ranged in quality from the frankly amateur to the most highly professional, but all have shared the concern of those responsible for them.

The all-women touring shows are less numerous today than in the past, and many Junior Leagues are now devoting their efforts to sponsorship rather than to production. Without the work of the Junior League over the years it is doubtful that children's theatre in America would have been stimulated and sustained.

With the establishment of the Federal Theatre in the mid-thirties a new and imaginative approach to children's entertainment was taken. Though primarily a relief measure, the Federal Theatre for Children made a distinct contribution by introducing plays in many communities throughout the United States which had previously known only movies, by employing original techniques and scripts, and by taking a scientific approach to juvenile audience reaction. Though this program was in effect for only three years, the fact that it was administered on a nationwide scale made it an important chapter in the history of the children's theatre movement.

A national organization which came into being during the thirties but which did not begin its program for another ten years is the American National Theatre and Academy. A service organization, dedicated to the extension of the living theatre, both professional and nonprofessional, it has taken an interest in recent developments in the children's field. ANTA surveys to determine types of activity, publications, and theatre services have been most helpful to children's theatre groups. While ANTA is oriented to all theatre, and more involved on the adult level, it is nevertheless a national organization to which children's theatre leaders may apply for help.

The two remaining organizations, the American Educational Theatre Association and the Children's Theatre Conference, emanated from the educational field. While the first of these is primarily concerned with the college and university, it has not only made provision for children's work to be discussed at its meetings and in its journal but, in approving the Children's Theatre Conference as a division of the association, has recognized the importance of work on this level.

With the founding of the Children's Theatre Conference in 1944, the most significant national organization was established. Through its regional structure a concerted effort has been made to promote more and better entertainment for children in all types of theatre. This national organization is the only one founded for the sole purpose of promoting children's dramatic activities through an expanding program of publications, research, workshops, and meetings. Identified with this conference are the majority of well-organized community, educational, and professional groups.

GROWTH AND CHANGE

When the Children's Educational Theatre was founded in 1903, it was hailed as a unique experiment. Subsequent ventures multiplied rapidly until by 1944, 80 groups were represented with delegates at the first meeting of the Children's Theatre Conference. Within a decade this number was close to 500. By the mid-sixties the membership numbered 1,000; today it is approximately 1,500. Furthermore, this figure does not constitute a complete count since not every leader and director in children's theatre is a member of this organization, and many plays are produced sporadically each year as individual entertainments. According to the 1968 survey conducted by the Children's Theatre Conference, there were 701 known organizations in the 50 states producing plays for children on a regular basis. Granting the probability of additional groups who failed to respond to the survey, it is an impressive record of growth.

Although many experiments have been short lived, some have been highly successful. A number of ventures on educational, community, and professional levels have endured the passage of time; and a stable organization, the Children's Theatre Conference, is now firmly established. Within the singular structure of this body, children's theatres in all parts of the country have been united. This unification has resulted in the identification of common problems and the clarification of common aims. There is general concurrence among the members today that when a children's theatre is a part of a local or national organization it is a stronger and more effective force than when it exists as a separate entity.

Through improved channels of communication such as the national regional newsletters, journals, and publicity releases, new ideas are shared, successful ventures are described, and the work of various producing groups in all areas is publicized. The result is a co-operative effort on a national scale. Although the educational theatre through the Children's Theatre Conference continues to exert the most influential guidance, it remains a democratic form of leadership operating within the framework of the organization.

Indeed, in comparing children's theatre today with that of earlier periods, co-operation through organization is the most

Aurand Harris' *Rags to Riches* was given its première performance at the Harwich Junior Theatre in the 1960's. Photograph by Richard Graber.

The Everyman Players of Shreveport, Louisiana, under the direction of Orlin and Irene Corey, produced *Reynard the Fox*. Courtesy Orlin and Irene Corey.

Percival Borde in *Drums of the Caribbean*, 1968. Courtesy Briggs Management.

The Blue Planet by Peggy Simon, offered in the 1960's by Maximilian Productions in New York City. Courtesy Maximilian Productions.

Dan'l confronts the Devil in *The Devil and Daniel Webster* at the Players Theatre of Manchester, New Hampshire, in the 1960's. Courtesy Briggs Management.

Out of the Frying Pan, by C. E. Webber, a 1969–70 production of Theatre 65 of Evanston, Illinois. Courtesy Theatre 65.

Children from East River Day Care Center meet the cast after a Mills College of Education performance of *The Gingerbread Boy* in 1964. Photograph by J. Jaffe. Courtesy Mills College of Education.

An audience at a Mills production. The faces tell their own story. Photograph by J. Jaffe. Courtesy Mills College of Education.

Nat Eek, chairman of the United States Center for ASSITEJ.

Aurand Harris, playwright for children's theatre.

Orlin and Irene Corey, co-producers of the Everyman Players, Shreveport, Louisiana.

striking point of difference. Whereas the majority of the early enterprises sprang up independently, there has been a growing tendency in recent years toward co-ordination of activities. On the community level it has been evident in the number of children's theatres established under the sponsorship of recreational centers and civic playhouses; on the educational level it has been apparent in the university–public school relationship; and on the professional level it is evident through community sponsorship of touring companies. In a number of instances cited in the last two chapters, all three types of theatres have joined together in co-ordinated community programs. This practice seems to have had a stabilizing effect, since, through the combining of resources, more ambitious programs are being launched and wider audiences are being reached.

One problem persists in regard to sponsorship. The average sponsor is a civic-minded mother, recruited when her own children are young. As her children move on to high school, unless her interest is exceptionally strong, she tends to leave the field at the point when she has become most valuable to it. Hence we have the phenomenon of the changing sponsor. With this function in the hands of large organizations or community boards, however, the problem may be overcome. A sizable nucleus of knowledgeable persons can be cultivated so that when some members leave, an ongoing force is ensured.

It has been in the community and educational theatres that the most extensive work so far has been accomplished. This has been in part a response to the lack of appropriate entertainment for boys and girls of elementary-school age. The movies have come up with an occasional screenplay for children, but in general the film industry has ignored this audience. Television programming for children has also been a source of disappointment from the beginning. It is not the purpose of this book to discuss these media; however, children are exposed to them for many hours each week and have therefore come to expect showmanship and technical expertise in entertainment.

The educational theatre has been aware of this need and has

worked on the training of leaders as well as establishing programs of plays for children. A number of master's and doctor's degrees have been granted to candidates who wished to do specialized study in this field. The results of the college and university efforts are now being felt on all levels. Creative dramatics leaders, teachers sympathetic to the performing arts, and administrators willing to book assembly programs and support field trips to the theatre are growing in number. While the patterns vary widely from one school system to another, the picture has changed fundamentally within the past decade. The living theatre is at last being accepted as having educational value.

With the inclusion of children's theatre in the White House Conference of 1950, the United States government recognized the significance of this phase of the arts as a contribution to the development of healthy personality and aesthetic appreciation. In the sixties federal funds were provided, with the result that programs now exist on a scale unheard of in any previous decade. While the need is still being expressed for permanent funding and better plays, the emphasis in the educational theatre today is on evaluation and more imaginative planning for the future.

PROFESSIONAL THEATRE FOR CHILDREN

In the professional field progress until recently has been somewhat slower. Ever since Franklin Sargent's first attempt to establish young people's plays in New York, there have been numerous professional efforts to launch some kind of children's entertainment. To Clare Tree Major belongs the credit for establishing the first nationally known company of professional actors touring the United States with children's plays. Junior Programs, Inc., launched the first large-scale productions of drama, music, and dance and secured, in the interest of the best quality of entertainment, the services of some of America's finest artists. With the founding of the Children's World Theatre in the late forties, a third important company began operation.

The fifties and sixties saw the establishment of new and different groups; the Paper Bag Players, Maximilian Productions, the Traveling Playhouse, the Merry-Go-Rounders, PART Productions, and Children's Theatre International are but a few which have withstood the competition of other media, the loss of actors to jobs in the adult professional theatre, and the soaring costs of production. The special problems of a hazardous profession are visited upon those producers who believe in the potential of children's theatre and have sacrificed money and years of their professional lives in an effort to further it. Low income, hard touring conditions, and the difficulties of keeping a group together have been, and continue to be, the major obstacles to building strong and stable repertory companies.

Although some children's theatre actors belong to Actors' Equity, most do not. Many actors are young and inexperienced and have looked to children's theatre as a means of employment rather than as an artistic end in itself. The amateur status which children's theatre has generally held has not attracted America's finest professional artists. This situation appears to be changing. The recent negotiation of the Equity Children's Theatre contract in New York City gave formal recognition to this branch of the entertainment field. Salaried rehearsals, controlled length of the working day, improved working conditions and benefits were designed to attract and hold talented performers. Although there is understandable concern over the ability of many companies to meet the terms, the Equity contract is regarded by some producers as one of the most promising steps toward stabilizing companies and raising the standards of theatre for children.

Professional companies which have remained in operation for several seasons have proved that there is an audience for children's plays if a well-publicized touring program and moderate prices make them available. Just as communities have found sponsorship to be the most satisfactory means of obtaining a varied program, so have the professional companies found sponsorship a more efficient way of operating. The past fifteen years have seen a noticeable trend away from the centralized playhouse with a resident company to community sponsorship of the touring performance. Where neighboring communities have worked together to secure

275

the finest artists and plays, all involved have profited. Co-operation of this kind means more engagements for the company and lower fees for the individual sponsors.

Professional theatre for children is important for its contribution to the maintenance of aesthetic standards. While it is true that professional theatre has not always been superior to the non-professional, the fact that the former can be more selective in casting and may demand a greater technical skill of its production staff should make for a higher level of work. In not subscribing to the same social and educational objectives of the college and community theatres, the professional producer has the freedom to concentrate on the artistry of the performance.

Past experience, however, has shown the precariousness of these ventures. The freedom of the professional producer carries with it a financial responsibility unknown to the director of university and community plays, whose work is subsidized. Where there has been steady and co-ordinated sponsorship by Parent-Teacher groups, schools, and local organizations, professional companies have managed to survive. By public support of the best, this branch of the theatre may be kept alive and boys and girls of the future provided with entertainment above the level of that originating in the average local community. In view of the rising costs of production in a high-risk profession, however, it is quite possible that even widespread public support will not be sufficient. Additional monies are essential if first-rate companies are to be encouraged and maintained.

In the opinion of many, financial aid in the form of government subsidy is the only means by which this can be done. Without a permanent program of funding it is quite possible that professional theatre in this country may never realize its potential; or it may revert to an earlier phase of entertainment for the privileged minority instead of a rich experience for all, regardless of ability to pay. Theatre is a communal art, created by artists and strongest when enjoyed by a large and heterogeneous audience. Research shows that the most brilliant periods in theatre history were those in which the playwright, the producer, and the audience, composed of all classes, were in collaboration. Children's theatre is no exception.

PUBLICATION FOR CHILDREN'S THEATRE

In the field of publication there has been noteworthy, if more limited, progress. From an almost total dearth of drama for children at the turn of the century, a school of authors has been developed. Fourteen publishing houses now handle children's plays, and four of them are devoted exclusively to this specialized field of publication. It has been recognized that writing for the child audience demands a special skill and knowledge. Leading playwrights have not been attracted to the field, and few writers of children's plays have written fine and lasting dramas. It is frequently said that the visual aspects of many productions today are superior to the scripts; this emphasis suggests a significant weakness. A theatre needs literature on which to build.

The fairy tale continues to be the most popular choice among playwrights, who generally prefer adaptations to the writing of original plots. Comparatively few original scripts have appeared in the past seventy years, although there is a widespread request for modern plays with themes relevant to the lives of today's children. Plays with black subject matter for black children and stories reflecting the life of the urban child have been demanded but few have been written. Many recent works are entertaining and meet the criteria set up by the Children's Theatre Conference in regard to character, theme, and plot. It is generally agreed, however, that few of them possess the universal and lasting literary quality of the average play written for the adult audience.

Recently there have been requests for plays appealing to different age levels. A complaint frequently voiced is that programs are offered to children without respect to age and that some are even advertised as appropriate for children from four to twelve. It is obvious that a play, like a book, rarely appeals to so wide a range. Some sponsoring organizations have attempted to solve the problem by refusing to admit preschool-age children. Others have gone a step further and offered two separate play series: one for children under eight and the other for those from eight to twelve. This latter practice makes for greater satisfaction on the part of both audience and actors than the production which does not take age into consideration. The difference in interests and tastes, not to mention the attention spans of children of varying age levels, are thereby recognized and respected. One of the real concerns to both sponsor and producer today is the loss of the older child from the audience. Bored with plays geared to a four-year-old's interests, the twelve-year-old outgrows children's theatre before he is ready for adult fare. Television and the movies fill his need for entertainment, and the habit of theatregoing is not instilled.

There are deeper implications involved here, however, for the boys and girls of today will be the adult audience of tomorrow. The living theatre is dependent upon an eager and knowledgeable audience for its existence. By not challenging the interests of the child over ten, we are failing both him and the living theatre of the future.

A further and related plea has been voiced more recently. In addition to the need for plays on contemporary themes, it is also asked why we so rarely reflect the racial and ethnic diversity of our country in the casting of plays.[1] Integrated companies performing with skill could offer boys and girls from the beginning of their theatre experience an exciting picture of American society as it can be, if the gifts of all people are accepted with respect and appreciation.

There remains, therefore, a pressing need for more plays of good literary quality, geared to different age levels, or of such universal human interest that people of all ages can respond to them. If our best professional dramatists or authors of children's books could be persuaded to write for the child audience, a repertory of new and superior plays might be the result. While it is readily admitted that the writing of juvenile literature makes special and exacting demands, the fact that a number of our

[1] Joanna Kraus, "Taking Children's Theatre to the Moon," *Players Magazine*, Vol. XLV (April–May, 1970), 186–87.

leading dramatists have been successful in their movie and television attempts suggests their ability to adapt their skill to other media. Can they not also write for the child? Financial inducement has been wanting in the past, but grants to playwrights under the new funding programs might spur an effort in this direction. It seems worth trying.

According to Sara Spencer of the Anchorage Press, half of the producers whom this publishing house serves choose the tried-and-true classic titles. The more discriminating ask for more adventurous material. The three leading titles of the 1969–70 season were *Aesop's Fables*, *Androcles and the Lion*, and *The Great Cross Country Race*. Perhaps these choices point to a change in taste in script selection.

Trends and New Directions

A study of the sixties reveals several definite trends and possibly new directions for the children's theatre of the future. One trend which has been evident since the thirties is revealed in the educational preparation of the children's theatre practitioner. It is agreed that he needs all of the basic training in production techniques that the worker in the adult theatre is expected to acquire; in addition, it is important for him to receive specialized education in child psychology and in the techniques peculiar to this branch of theatre. Neither professional schooling nor academic background alone is adequate preparation for work in high-quality children's theatre.

Geraldine Brain Siks, one of the country's leading authorities in this field, commented in 1967 on the American attitude as compared with that of several European countries she had recently visited. Her observation was that where theatre education was systematically organized, it was promoting in European children an intelligent appreciation of the art. This country, she observed, had not yet achieved this goal to the same degree.[2]

2 "A View of Current European Theatre for Children and a Look Ahead in the United States," *Educational Theatre Journal*, Vol. XIX (May, 1967), 191–97.

Traditionally Americans have not supported the theatre as an art, nor has there been a national philosophy providing drama education for children. Until these two points of view have changed, children's theatre will remain on the edge rather than on the main stage of American theatre.

Since 1967, however, some significant developments have taken place. The broad Title I and Title III projects throughout the country have brought theatre to children and children to the theatre in areas where it had not before existed. The 1970 spring conference of the Associated Councils of the Arts dealt with the subject of community school commitment. The theme of "Youth, Education, and the Arts" brought together community leaders, teachers, school administrators, businessmen, journalists, government and union officials, philanthropists, parents, artists, and students—truly the broadest assembly of concerned persons ever gathered to consider and plan for a richer art education for children from preschool to high-school level. Among the speakers who were invited to address the conference were Nancy Hanks, chairman of the National Council on the Arts; James Allen, United States commissioner of education; and Samuel Gould, then chancellor of the State University of New York. The fact that federal funds are now available to support education and experience in the arts points to a new direction for children's theatre.

A new plan in the educational theatre is to present plays for children's audiences in the Kennedy Center for the Performing Arts in Washington, scheduled for completion in 1971. The Kennedy Center has already expressed an interest in AETA divisional festivals, and a committee is at work with plans for a showcase of American children's theatre. This move reaffirms the position that children's theatre deserves a place among the offerings chosen for this prestigious center.

As for recognition on the international level, ASSITEJ will meet on this continent in 1972. The Children's Theatre Conference, the United States Center for ASSITEJ, and Canada will act as hosts for a mobile conference moving from Ottawa to Albany. For the first time American educational institutions and American professional children's theatre will be viewed by experts from abroad. This kind of sharing may be the beginning of a larger relationship which will enrich and strengthen theatre for children in America.

In searching for trends, one reliable source of information is the theatrical agent. Records of performances, a knowledge of audience tastes, and an awareness of changing styles give the agent a privileged view of the movement. According to Frances Schram of Briggs Management, one of the most experienced agents dealing exclusively with children's entertainment, the greatest difference between children's theatre today and that of fifteen years ago is America's attitude toward it. Large towns, small towns, rich towns, poor towns—all want and are actively seeking the performing arts for their children. In her opinion, however, the change is still more quantitative than qualitative. An artist has to grow, and if he cannot grow in his field, he may grow out of it. The mere spread of activities does not necessarily mean a superior result. Until children's theatre can attract the serious artist and offer him room for growth, it will be left with the beginner or the merely competent. A start has been made, it is true, but the need remains to persuade the serious artist to enter and remain in the field.

Trends in form and style parallel in some respects those of the adult theatre. The favored entertainment of the sixties was the musical, with the straight play in short shrift. This was as true of the children's theatre as it was of Broadway. Among the professional offerings of the past few seasons there were few without music and dance; most were regular musical comedies, with a format similar to that seen on Broadway. Evolving also during this period was the musical "spoof" of the classical tale. Current references and parody characterized this form. By the end of the sixties the "spoof" in New York had become more than an amusing experiment; it was a clearly developed style, albeit a controversial one.

Also developing during the latter part of the decade was the episodic or semi-documentary program with educational content.

Drawing on the folk and cultural heritage of the people who make up America, this experiment in presenting material may eventually result in a new dramatic form. Content is expressed in scenes without the structure of plot to distract or advance a story. Voices, Inc., a group of singers in New York City, is a case in point. Song, narrative, dance, and movement are used to tell the story of the black man in America. By dispensing with the conventional story line, this group has succeeded in making history come alive as well as proving the relevancy of the material to today's world.

A third trend in form has resulted from the surge of interest in improvisation. Since no scripts are used, it is difficult to judge how widespread this practice is. Two well-known producers who use this technique are Shirley Trusty in New Orleans and Robert Alexander in Washington. The Looking Glass Theatre in Providence has already been mentioned as a company dedicated to this technique. Publicity releases indicate that a number of other groups in different parts of the country are also experimenting with improvisation and that it is popular with young audiences.

DRAMATIC CRITICISM

During the last two months of the year 1969, there were in New York City unprecedented numbers of listings of children's entertainment in the *New York Times*. The first Annual Celebration of the Arts for Children was presented at the City Center from November 15 to 30; while it included film, music, and dance as well as drama, it represented a massive effort to bring the performing arts of high quality to the children of the New York metropolitan area. During the Christmas holidays the *New York Times* listed twenty-two professional productions for children, four of which were appearing on Broadway. The *Times* further printed reviews of several of these programs in the Theatre Section, in which the performances were criticized with the respect accorded adult drama.

If recognition by the critics is any criterion, professional children's theatre may at last be moving into the main arena. From the beginning professional criticism, like financial support, has been conspicuously lacking. If, as some of the recent developments suggest, monies are being supplied in sufficient quantity to support superior and serious efforts, the critics may be willing to concern themselves with the products. This is not to imply that the future of children's theatre lies in the hands of the critics, but until children's theatre is taken seriously and evaluated according to the highest standards of the adult theatre as well as those of juvenile literature, it cannot take its place as a legitimate art form.

Much has been said about the mediocrity of children's theatre in this country; much of the criticism is valid. What is rarely mentioned, however, is the dedication over the years of those men and women who have harbored a dream and worked to make it come true. "Idealistic" and "indefatigable" are the words which most accurately describe the worker in children's theatre throughout its history. Money has never been a motive nor has the dream of fame. The actor, producer, writer, and sponsor all knowingly enter a field in which the risks are great, the profits slim, and the future unpredictable. Only a few names are remembered, or indeed have even been known, of the hundreds of men and women who have given their best efforts to the cause of live theatre for children.

Faith in an idea and a commitment to keeping it alive for each generation of boys and girls are the common denominators of both professional and amateur; discouragement and failure have not destroyed their enthusiasm. The fact that so much of the work has been on a low level has been a matter of concern but not a reason for giving up the dream that someday their cause will be recognized as an important area of the living theatre in America.

A permanent program of financial aid, more and better scripts, fine actors, the benefit of professional criticism, encouragement of experimentation, an opportunity for regular and well-publicized performances, public demand—all these are required if children's theatre in this country is to achieve full stature. It has been said that today's children are more sophisticated and more knowledgeable than those of any preceding generation; they have known television from birth and they take its technical expertise for granted. The living theatre, however, offers another dimension. This is the special relationship created by actor and audience together in the act of performance, and it can no more be duplicated by technological means than it can be repeated precisely in any other time or place. The magic of theatre lies in its temporal quality, which transcends space and is therefore alive and elusive. May the living theatre be for today's children, as it has always been at its best, an exciting adventure with content relevant to their interests and needs and form which offers aesthetic satisfaction. When this happens, children's theatre will be more than a place to go on a Saturday afternoon. It will indeed be a place of enchantment.

Bibliography

1. Documents, Directories, Catalogues, and Pamphlets

American National Theatre and Academy. *The ANTA Story.* New York, American National Theatre and Academy, 1956. [Unpaged pamphlet.]

Arberg, Harold. *Support for the Arts and the Humanities.* Washington, D.C., Government Printing Office, 1968.

Briggs, Elizabeth D. (comp.). *Subject Index to Children's Plays.* Chicago, American Library Association, 1940.

Children's Theatre Conference. *Pamphlets for New Members.* Washington, D.C., a publication of the American Educational Theatre Association, n.d.

Children's Theatre Conference Newsletters. [Newsletters from the Children's Theatre Conference (1950–70).]

Children's Theatre Conference Regional Newsletters. [Newsletters for individual regions, from time publication was begun to 1970.]

Children's Theatre in the U.S.A. [Pamphlet prepared by the United States Center for ASSITEJ, 1965.]

Davis, Jed H. (comp). *A Directory of Children's Theatres in the United States.* Washington, D.C., a publication of the American Educational Theatre Association, 1968.

Gault, Judith (comp.). *Federal Funds and Services for the Arts.* Washington, D.C., United States Department of Health, Education, and Welfare, 1967.

Hill, Ann S. *European Children's Theatre and the Second Congress of the International Children's Theatre Association.* Washington,

D.C., a publication of the American Educational Theatre Association, 1968.

Landers, Jacob. *Higher Horizons Progress Report.* New York, Board of Education of the City of New York, January, 1963.

Pacesetters in Innovation. Washington, D.C., United States Government Printing Office, 1966, 1967, 1968.

2. *Miscellaneous Unpublished Material*

Adventure Theatre. Scrapbook Collection of Mimeographed Materials and Pictures.

Association of Junior Leagues of America. "Children's Theatre and Puppetry Statistics." Compiled in typewritten form for the author.

Brochures from all professional companies cited.

Children's World Theatre. History prepared for the author.

Comer, Virginia Lee. "Highlights of the American Educational Theatre Association Children's Theatre Conference in Seattle, Washington, August 1–5, 1946." Mimeographed Report. New York, Children's Theatre Conference, 1946.

Drake, Mrs. Reah Stanley, and Others. "Promoting Good Theatre for Children in Binghamton." Mimeographed record of activities. Binghamton, New York, Children's Theatre Council, 1939.

Equity Library Theatre. "Equity Library Theatre for Children." Mimeographed information distributed by Equity Library Theatre, 1956.

Junior Programs, Inc. "Records and Press Releases." Mimeographed material from the files of Dorothy McFadden.

Junior Programs, Inc. "Scrapbook of Programs and Press Notices." New York, Theatre Collection of The New York Public Library.

Living Arts Project, Dayton, Ohio, 1970. Scrapbook.

Major, Clare Tree. "Scrapbooks of Programs, Press Notices, Photographs and Mimeographed Materials." New York, Theatre Collection of The New York Public Library.

Saturday Theatre for Children. Mimeographed reports. New York, New York City Board of Education.

Seattle Junior Programs. Report. Seattle, Junior Programs typewritten report in 1970.

Shohet, Max. "Scrapbook of WPA Children's Theatre." Miscellaneous collection of clippings, letters, press releases, mimeographed questionnaires, and research files. New York, Theatre Collection of The New York Public Library.

Stanistreet, Grace. "What Is Adelphi's Children's Theatre?" Mimeographed material from Adelphi College. Garden City, Adelphi College, n.d.

State Arts Councils. Reports prepared for the author in response to requests for information.

Tribal Players. "Scrapbook Collection," Boston, Tribal Players, 1970.

3. *Theses and Dissertations*

Graham, Kenneth. "An Introductory Study of the Evaluation of Plays for Children's Theatre in the United States." Salt Lake City, University of Utah, 1947.

Jones, Charles. "An Evaluation of the Educational Significance of the Children's Theatre of Evanston." Evanston, Northwestern University, 1953.

Leech, Robert Milton. "Education through Theatre for Children." Austin, University of Texas, 1962.

Meek, Beryl. "The Establishment of a Children's Theatre in a Teacher Training Institute." New York, New York University, 1942.

Van Tassel, Wesley. "Differences in Contemporary Views of Theatre for Children." Denver, University of Denver, 1968.

Willert, Oriel. "Fifty Years of Children's Theatre in America." Seattle, University of Washington, 1953.

4. *Books*

Addams, Jane. *The Second Twenty Years at Hull House.* New York, The Macmillan Company, 1930.

———. *The Spirit of Youth and the City Streets.* New York, The Macmillan Company, 1909.

———. *Twenty Years at Hull House.* New York, The Macmillan Company, 1910.

Adix, Vern. *Theatre Scenecraft.* Anchorage, Kentucky, Children's Theatre Press, 1956.

Brockett, Oscar. *The Theatre, An Introduction.* New York, Rinehart and Winston, 1966.

Chilver, Peter. *Staging a School Play.* New York, Harper and Row, 1967.

Chorpenning, Charlotte. *Twenty-One Years with Children's Theatre*. Anchorage, Kentucky, The Anchorage Press, 1955.

Ciaccio, Mary Eleanor. *Prologue to Production*. New York, Association of Junior Leagues of America, 1951.

Clapp, Henry A. *Reminiscences of a Dramatic Critic*. Boston, Houghton-Mifflin Company, 1902.

Clay, James, and Daniel Krempel. *The Theatrical Image*. New York, The McGraw Hill Book Company, 1969.

Corey, Irene. *The Mask of Reality*. Anchorage, Kentucky, The Anchorage Press, 1968.

Davis, Jed, and Mary Jane Watkins. *Theatre for Children*. New York, Harper and Row, 1961.

Dean, Alexander. *Little Theatre Organization and Management*. New York, D. Appleton, Century Company, 1926.

Eastman, Fred, and Louis Wilson. *Drama in the Church*. New York, Samuel French Company, 1934.

Fisher, Caroline, and Hazel Robertson. *Children and the Theatre*. Rev. ed. Stanford, Stanford University Press, 1950.

Flanagan, Hallie. *Arena*. New York, Duell, Sloan and Pearce Company, 1940.

Heniger, Alice Herts. *The Kingdom of the Child*. New York, E. P. Dutton and Company, 1918.

Herts, Alice Minnie. *The Children's Educational Theatre*. New York, Harper and Brothers, 1911.

Houghton, Norris. *Advance from Broadway*. New York, Harcourt Brace Company, 1941.

Hughes, Glenn. *A History of the American Theatre*. New York, Samuel French Company, 1951.

Jagendorf, Moritz (ed.). *Nine Short Plays for Children*. New York, The Macmillan Company, 1928.

Kase, Robert. *Children's Theatre Comes of Age*. New York, Samuel French Company, 1956.

McCleery, Albert, and Carl Glick. *Curtains Going Up*. New York, Pitman Publishing Company, 1939.

Macgowan, Kenneth. *Footlights Across America*. New York, Harcourt Brace Company, 1929.

Mackay, Constance D'Arcy. *Children's Theatre and Plays*. New York, D. Appleton Century Company, 1927.

————. *How to Produce Children's Plays.* New York, Henry Holt and Company, 1915.

————. *The Little Theatre in the United States.* New York, Henry Holt and Company, 1917.

Mackaye, Percy. *The Civic Theatre.* New York, The Kennerley Publishing Company, 1912.

————. *Community Drama.* Boston, The Houghton Mifflin Company, 1917.

Mauer, Muriel, and Others for Seattle Junior Programs, Inc. *Children's Theatre Manual.* Anchorage, Kentucky, Children's Theatre Press, 1951.

Mayhew, Katherine Camp, and Anna Camp Edwards. *The Dewey School.* New York, Appleton Century, 1936.

Miller, Madge. *Miniature Plays.* Anchorage, Kentucky, Children's Theatre Press, 1954.

Moses, Montrose J. *Another Treasury of Plays for Children.* Boston, Little, Brown, & Company, 1926.

————. *A Treasury of Plays for Children.* Boston, Little, Brown, & Company, 1921.

————. *Concerning Children's Plays.* New York, Samuel French, Inc., 1931.

Parkhurst, Helen. *Education on the Dalton Plan.* New York, E. P. Dutton, 1922.

The Performing Arts, Problems and Prospects: The Rockefeller Panel Report on the Future of Theatre, Dance and Music in America. New York, The McGraw Hill Book Company, 1965.

Seattle Junior Programs, Inc. *Children's Theatre Manual.* Anchorage, Kentucky, Children's Theatre Press, 1951.

Siks, Geraldine Brain, and Hazel Brain Dunnington. *Children's Theatre and Creative Dramatics: Principles and Practices.* Seattle, University of Washington Press, 1961.

Wald, Lillian. *The House on Henry Street.* New York, Henry Holt and Company, 1915.

————. *Windows on Henry Street.* Boston, Little Brown & Company, 1934.

Ward, Winifred. *Playmaking with Children.* New York, Appleton, Century, Crofts, Inc., 1947.

————. *Stories to Dramatize.* Anchorage, Kentucky, Children's Theatre Press, 1952.

———. *Theatre for Children*. New York, D. Appleton, Century Company, 1939. Third revised edition, Anchorage, Kentucky, Children's Theatre Press, 1958.

Whiting, Frank. *An Introduction to the Theatre*. New York, Harper and Brothers, 1954.

Whitman, Willson. *Bread and Circuses*. New York, Oxford University Press, 1937.

5. *Articles*

Adamoska, Helenka. "Junior League Children's Theatre," *Drama*, Vol. XXI (April, 1931), 37.

Alexander, Selma. "Need for a Children's Theatre," *Drama*, Vol. XXI (May, 1931), 16.

Andrews, Hazel M. "Vocational and Moral Guidance through Dramatics," *Education*, Vol. XLI (September, 1921), 130.

Anonymous. "Accent on Youth," *Theatre Arts Monthly*, Vol. XXXII (June, 1948), 59.

———. "Adventure in Drama," *The Playground*, Vol. XXIII (November, 1929), 510–11.

———. "American Children's Theatre," *Literary Digest*, Vol. CXVII (June, 1934), 32.

———. "At Burlingame's Play Centers," *Recreation*, Vol. XXXVII (May, 1943), 69.

———. "Boys and the Theatre," *Atlantic Monthly*, Vol. CVII (March, 1911), 350–54.

———. "Century of the Child in the Playhouse," *Current Opinion*, Vol. LIV (February, 1913), 121–23.

———. "Chart of Recreational Activities Reported in 1941," *Recreation*, Vol. XXXVI (June, 1942), 136.

———. "The Child and the Imaginative Life," *Atlantic Monthly*, Vol. C (October, 1907), 480–88.

———. "Child Drama in Park and Playground," *The Playground*, Vol. XXII (December, 1928), 517–19.

———. "Child Labor on the Stage," *Survey*, Vol. XXIV (July 23, 1910), 635–36.

———. "Children's Civic Theatre of Chicago," *Drama*, Vol. XVII (October, 1926), 30.

———. "Children's Educational Theatre," *Atlantic Monthly*, Vol. C (December, 1907), 798–806.

———. "A Children's Folk Theatre," *Recreation*, Vol. XXVI (April, 1932), 4–5.

———. "Children's Players of New York City," *Drama*, Vol. XXI (April, 1931), 28.

———. "Children's Theatre," *Charities and the Commons*, Vol. XVIII (April 6, 1907), 23–24.

———. "Children's Theatre," *Drama*, Vol. XVI (October, 1925), 32–33.

———. "Children's Theatre," *Drama*, Vol. XXI (December, 1930), 30.

———. "Children's Theatre," *Drama*, Vol. XXI (February, 1931), 29.

———. "Children's Theatre at the University of Tulsa," *The Playground*, Vol. XXII (March, 1928), 697–98.

———. "Children's Theatre Cooperates with Book Stores," *Publishers' Weekly*, Vol. CXXXIV (August 27, 1938), 579.

———. "A Children's Theatre for Children," *Drama*, Vol. XX (November, 1929), 53.

———. "Children's Theatre in Nine States," *American Magazine of Art*, Vol. XXVI (January, 1933), 42.

———. "Children's Theatre—1945," *Recreation*, Vol. XL (October, 1946), 388.

———. "Children's Theatre of Chicago," *Drama*, Vol. XVII (October, 1926), 12.

———. "Children's Theatre Planned," *Literary Digest*, Vol. CXVII (June, 1934), 32.

———. "Children Unhappy When Unions Hold up Pocahontas," *Newsweek*, Vol. V (January 5, 1935), 25–26.

———. "A Class Full of Creators," *Life*, Vol. XL (March 5, 1956), 105–16.

———. "Cleveland Theatre for Youth," *Design*, Vol. XL (March, 1939), 1–2.

———. "Community Children's Theatre," *Recreation*, Vol. XXVIII (September, 1934), 269.

———. "Decade of Children's Theatre," *Theatre Arts Monthly*, Vol. XXXVIII (November, 1954), 84.

———. "Disciplined: King Coit Children's Theatre," *New Yorker*, Vol. XXX (May 22, 1954), 24.

———. "Drama Comes to the Playground," *Recreation*, Vol. XXVI (July, 1932), 202–203.

———. "The Drama Tourney," *The Playground*, Vol. XXII (March, 1929), 699–703.

———. "A Fairy Tale Interpreted in the Light of the Present," *School and Society*, Vol. LIII (January 18, 1941), 77.

———. "How Much Children Attend the Theatre, The Quality of the Entertainment They Choose, and Its Effect on Them," *The Pedagogical Seminary*, Vol. XVI (September, 1909), 367–71.

———. "Junior Drama League," *Drama*, Vol. XX (October, 1929), 28.

———. "Junior League Theatre Conference," *Drama*, Vol. XX (February, 1930), 139.

———. "Junior Repertory Theatre of Minneapolis," *Drama*, Vol. XXI (April, 1931), 29.

———. "Karamu House," *Life*, Vol. XXX (June 18, 1951), 67.

———. "Los Angeles Children's Theatre Guild," *Drama*, Vol. XXI (April, 1931), 30.

———. "Make Believe Land," *Recreation*, Vol. XXXIX (December, 1945), 459.

———. "Moral from a Toy Theatre," *Scribners*, Vol. LVIII (October, 1915), 405–12.

———."National Drama Week," *The Playground*, Vol. XIX (February, 1926), 625.

———. "Our Thespians in Dead Earnest," *Literary Digest*, Vol. LXXXV (May 16, 1925), 26–27.

———. "Playground Activities in Oakland," *The Playground*, Vol. XXI (January, 1928), 529.

———. "Playground Drama through the Institute," *Recreation*, Vol. XXVI (August, 1932), 246–48.

———. "The Play of Imagination in the Tiniest Theatre in the World," *Survey*, Vol. XXXIV (September 18, 1915), 551.

———. "Racketty-Packetty House," *Outlook*, Vol. CIII (January 11, 1913), 58.

———. "Report of the Seventeenth Annual Convention of the Drama League of America," *The Playground*, Vol. XX (July, 1926), 237–41.

———. "Richmond's Children's Theatre—Second Edition," *Recreation*, Vol. XXXVII (November, 1943), 434–74.

———. "Schools and the Drama," *Review of Reviews*, Vol. XLV (March, 1912), 367–68.

———. "Snow White," *New York Dramatic Mirror*, Vol. LXVII (November 13, 1912), 6.

———. "Tall Stories for Small Audiences," *Dance Magazine*, Vol. XXVIII (February, 1954), 57.

———. "Ten Cent Drama for San Francisco Children," *Survey*, Vol. XXXIV (April 24, 1915), 80.

———. "Theatre and Education," *Outlook*, Vol. CXV (March 7, 1917), 411–13.

———. "The Theatre as an Educative Agent," *Current Literature*, Vol. XLV (October, 1908), 441–44.

———. "A Theatre for All Children," *Literary Digest*, Vol. XLVII (January 11, 1913), 74–75.

———. "The Theatre of Youth Players," *The Playground*, Vol. XXII (February, 1929), 629–30.

———. "A Theatre Workshop for Children," *Recreation*, Vol. XXVIII (October, 1934), 327.

———. "Three Years of the Drama League," *The Nation*, Vol. XCVIII (March 26, 1914), 322–23.

———. "To Reorganize Children's Theatre," *Charities and the Commons*, Vol. XX (June 6, 1908), 307–308.

———. "Toward a Community Theatre," *Recreation*, Vol. XXXIX (August, 1945), 235–36.

———. "Training the Imagination," *Outlook*, Vol. LXIV (February 24, 1900), 459–61.

———. "Unique Children's Theatre," *Recreation*, Vol. XLV (November, 1951), 319.

———. "Unlocking the World of the Wonderful through the Children's Theatre," *The American City*, Vol. XL (January, 1929), 106–107.

———. "Where Children Play at Giving Plays," *Literary Digest*, Vol. LXXXVI (August 1, 1925), 25–26.

Arnold, Frank R. "Play Service in Utah," *Education*, Vol. XXXIX (December, 1918), 244–48.

Bailey, E. V. "How to Organize and Operate a Children's Theatre," *Emerson Quarterly*, Vol. VI (January, 1927), 10–14.

Baker, George P. "What the Theatre Can Do for the School," *Ladies' Home Journal*, Vol. XXX (January, 1913), 26.

Barclay, Dorothy. "Children's Theatre Progress," *New York Times Magazine Section* (September 10, 1950), 47.

Barty, Margaret. "Children and the Post-War Theatre," *Theatre World*, Vol. XXXIX (August, 1943), 7–8.

Behner, Elsie. "For and By," *Players Magazine*, Vol. XXXII (November, 1955), 41.

Bell, Campton. "Conference and Progress," *Theatre Arts Monthly*, Vol. XXXIII (September, 1949), 53.

Benet, Rosemary. "Children's World Theatre," *Saturday Review*, Vol. XXXIII (January 21, 1950), 47.

Best, Mrs. A. Starr. "The Drama League at 21," *Drama*, Vol. XXI (May, 1931), 35–39.

Black, Donald, and Rose Kennedy. "Footlights for Small Fry," *Colliers*, Vol. CXXI (February 7, 1948), 54.

Bloyom, Marian. "Yakima Children's Theatre Gets Its Start," *Players Magazine*, Vol. XXVII (April, 1951), 156–57.

Braden, George. "Municipal and School Outdoor Theatres in California," *American City*, Vol. XXXVIII (March, 1920), 98–100.

Brinkerhoff, Mary. "Talent Unlimited," *Recreation*, Vol. XLIII (February, 1950), 534.

Brush, Martha. "The Eighth Annual Children's Theatre Meeting," *Educational Theatre Journal*, Vol. IV (December, 1952), 342–49.

———. "The Seventh Annual Children's Theatre Meeting," *Educational Theatre Journal*, Vol. III (December, 1951), 192–97.

Buchanan, Roberta. "Point of View," *Players Magazine*, Vol. XXXII (December, 1955), 63–64.

Butterworth, Bette. "Theatre in the Round We Go," *Recreation*, Vol. XLVII (June, 1954), 342–43.

Cabell, Elvira D. "The Children's Educational Theatre," *English Journal*, Vol. I (April, 1912), 251–55.

Carmer, Carl. "Children's Theatre," *Theatre Arts Monthly*, Vol. XV (May, 1931), 410–20.

Carville, Virginia. "The Key to Karamu House," *Extension*, Vol. L (March, 1956), 20–21, 42, 45–46.

Casey, M. "Drama and the Teen-Age Boy," *Players Magazine*, Vol. XXX (October, 1952), 6–7.

Caswell, Margaret. "Boston Revives the Medieval Pageant Wagon," *Recreation*, Vol. XXVII (July, 1934), 204–205.

Caulkins, E. Dana. "Recreation in Westchester County," *Recreation*, Vol. XXVII (August, 1933), 221.

Champlin, W. D. "An Experiment in Drama," *Recreation*, Vol. XXV (February, 1932), 617, 640.

Chancerel, Leon. "Youth and the Theatre," *World Theatre*, Vol. II (December, 1952), 3.

Chipman, Sands. "Story Books Come to Life in a Children's Theatre," *Drama*, Vol. XXI (April, 1931), 27–31.

Chorpenning, Charlotte. "Adults in Plays for Children," *Educational Theatre Journal*, Vol. III (May, 1951), 115–19.

———. "Putting on a Community Play," *The Quarterly Journal of Speech*, Vol. V (January, 1919), 31–44.

———. "The Special Audience," *Theatre Arts Monthly*, Vol. XXXIII (September, 1949), 51–52.

Ciaccio, Mary Eleanor. "Ninth Annual Children's Theatre Meeting," *Educational Theatre Journal*, Vol. V (December, 1953), 355–63.

Clarke, T. "I've Got the Best Job on Earth," *National Parent-Teacher Magazine*, Vol. XLIX (November, 1954), 16–19.

Cohen, Helen Louise. "Education in the Theatre Arts," *Theatre Arts Monthly*, Vol. VIII (October, 1924), 392.

Collins, Lillian Foster. "The Little Theatre in School," *Drama*, Vol. XX (November, 1929), 52.

Comer, Virginia Lee. "A Children's Theatre Takes to the Road," *Recreation*, Vol. XXXIV (September, 1940), 363–65, 402.

———. "Organizational Problems in Children's Theatre," *Dramatics*, Vol. XLVIII (November, 1948), 13.

———. "The White House Conference and Educational Theatre," *Educational Theatre Journal*, Vol. III (October, 1951), 218–23.

Daggy, Maynard Lee. "The Story of the Theatre of Youth," *Players Magazine*, Vol. XIII (March–April, 1937), 5.

Dann, Neva F. "Dramatics in Amsterdam," *Drama*, Vol. XXI (April, 1931), 28.

De Publio, John. "The Sponsor's Role," *Players Magazine*, Vol. XXXI (May, 1955), 186.

Drennan, Bertha. "Plays for Children," *Commonweal*, Vol. XIV (June 24, 1931), 205–206.

Dunham, Myra. "A Children's Theatre in a Great Store," *Emerson Quarterly*, Vol. X (November, 1929), 9–10.

Elicker, Virginia Wilk. "City-Wide Dramatic Program at Lakewood, Ohio," *Players Magazine*, Vol. XXI (May, 1945), 24.

Eustis, Morton. "Wonderland—Broadway in Review," *Theatre Arts Monthly*, Vol. XVII (February, 1933), 101–103.

Finley, John H. "A Modern Perspective on the Public Recreation Movement," *The Playground*, Vol. XXIV (December, 1930), 509–10.

Fisher, Caroline, and Theltgen, M.S. "How Two Children's Theatres are Functioning in Wartime," *The American City*, Vol. LVIII (June, 1943), 97–98.

Fitzgerald, Burdette. "Children's Theatre Conference," *Players Magazine*, Vol. XXIV (December, 1947), 64.

———. "Oaks from Acorns," *Players Magazine*, Vol. XXIV (March, 1948), 135.

Freitag, Beverly. "How One Children's Theatre Became Successful," *School and Society*, Vol. XXXIX (April 7, 1934), 427–30.

Gerstenberg, Alice. "The Chicago Junior League," *Drama*, Vol. XVIII (January, 1928), 118.

Gilbertson, Alice. "Curtain Going Up," *Recreation*, Vol. XXXVII (November, 1943), 432–34.

Golden, Ben. "A Children's Theatre on Tour," *New Theatre*, Vol. X (October, 1935), 8–9.

Goodall, Grace M. "Drama in the Parks," *Recreation*, Vol. XLV (March, 1952), 545–47.

Goodreds, Vincent S. "Education in Dramatics or Drama in Education," *Education*, Vol. LIV (May, 1934), 564.

Gordon, Dorothy. "Creating Audiences for the Future," *Drama*, Vol. XXI (June, 1931), 12.

Gordon, F. E. "Best for a Dime," *Parents' Magazine*, Vol. XIV (March, 1939), 20, 32, 34.

Gots, Judith. "More than Make Believe," *Recreation*, Vol. XLVII (September, 1954), 433–34.

Griffin, Alice. "Theatre U.S.A.," *Theatre Arts Monthly*, Vol. XXXIII (September, 1949), 50–60.

———. "Theatre U.S.A.," *Theatre Arts Monthly*, Vol. XXXVII (October, 1953), 81–85.

———. "Theatre U.S.A.," *Theatre Arts Monthly*, Vol. XXXVIII (May, 1954), 82–86.

———. "Theatre U.S.A.," *Theatre Arts Monthly*, Vol. XXXIX (August, 1955), 74.

———. "Theatre U.S.A.," *Theatre Arts Monthly*, Vol. XL (November, 1956), 95.

———. "Theatre U.S.A.," *Theatre Arts Monthly*, Vol. XLI (February, 1957), 67.

Haaga, Agnes. "A Directory of American Colleges and Universities Offering Training in Children's Theatre and Creative Dramatics," *Educational Theatre Journal*, Vol. X (May, 1958), 150–63.

———. "Twelfth Annual Children's Theatre Meeting," *Educational Theatre Journal*, Vol. VIII (December, 1956), 321.

Harrington, Mildred. "Mrs. Major's Stock Company Plays to Children Only," *American Magazine*, Vol. CV (February, 1928), 60.

Harrison, Gloria. "Recreation Goes Dramatic," *Recreation*, Vol. XXXVII (May, 1943), 66.

Hayes, R. "King Coit Children's Theatre," *Commonweal*, Vol. LX (May 21, 1954), 175.

Heiderstadt, D. "Curtain Going Up," *Wilson Library Bulletin*, Vol. XVIII (May, 1944), 642–43.

Heniger, Alice Herts. "The Drama's Value for Children," *Good Housekeeping*, Vol. LVII (November, 1913), 636–43.

Herendeen, Anne. "Adults Not Admitted," *Theatre Guild Magazine*, Vol. VIII (December, 1930), 31–32.

Herts, Alice Minnie. "The Children's Educational Theatre," *The Atlantic Monthly*, Vol. C (December, 1907), 798–806.

———. "Making Believe," *Good Housekeeping*, Vol. LXIV (March, 1917), 22–23.

Hines, A. B. "Boys' Club Dramatics," *The Playground*, Vol. XXII (April, 1920), 38–41.

Hjelte, George. "In the National Emergency," *Recreation*, Vol. XXXV (November, 1941), 493.

Hobbs, Mabel Foote. "The Children's Playground Theatre," *The Playground*, Vol. XXI (March, 1928), 662–70.

———. "The Place of Drama in Recreation," *Recreation*, Vol. XXIX (July, 1935), 211.

Horton, Louise. "It's Fun," *Dramatics*, Vol. XXIII (April, 1952), 12.

Hoyt, Raymond E. "The Problems We Face," *Recreation*, Vol. XXXV (July, 1941), 228.

Hughes, Carol. "Cleveland's Cradle of Talent," *Coronet*, Vol. XX (July, 1946), 51–54.

Humphrey, Edith. "Children's Theatre Comes Home," *High School Thespian*, Vol. XV (March, 1944), 4–5.

Israels, Belle L. "Another Aspect of the Children's Theatre," *Charities and the Commons*, Vol. XIX (January, 1908), 1,310.

Johnson, J. L. "Summer Theatre for Children," *The American Home*, Vol. XXIII (May, 1940), 62.

Johnson, Raymond. "Report from the South," *Theatre Arts Monthly*, Vol. XXXIII (September, 1949), 56.

Jones, Beatrice A. "A Community Children's Theatre," *Recreation*, Vol. XXVIII (September, 1934), 269.

Jones, Wyatt. "The Junior League Story," *Town and Country*, Vol. CX (August, 1956), 52–53, 88.

Kennedy, H. S. "Children Need Recreation in Wartime," *The American City*, Vol. LVII (July, 1942), 64.

Keusink, Polly. "Theatre for Pint-Sized Hamlets," *The American Home*, Vol. XLIX (February, 1953), 24–26.

Kogen, Dean. "Playing in the Streets," *Players Magazine*, Vol. XLV (June–July, 1970), 219–22.

Kraus, Joanna. "Taking Children's Theatre to the Moon," *Players Magazine*, Vol. XLV (April–May, 1970), 186–87.

Kupper, Herbert. "Fantasy and the Theatre Arts," *Educational Theatre Journal*, Vol. IV (March, 1952), 33–38.

Laflin, Lewis. "The Goodman Children's Theatre," *Drama*, Vol. XIX (October, 1928), 12–13, 32.

Law, Mouzon. "A Directory of American Colleges and Universities Offering Curricular Programs in Children's Theatre," *Educational Theatre Journal*, Vol. VI (March, 1954), 40–46.

Layman, Pauline. "A Unique Children's Theatre," *Emerson Quarterly*, Vol. VI (May, 1928), 3–6.

Lewis, George. "Children's Theatre and Teacher Training," *Players Magazine*, Vol. XXVII (October, 1950), 11.

Lippman, L. B. "Children's Theatre," *Saint Nicholas*, Vol. LI (February, 1924), 427.

Lobdell, Robert. "Planning a Show Wagon," *Recreation*, Vol. XLVIII (January, 1955), 32–33.

Loney, Glenn. "The Long Wharf Theatre," *Players Magazine*, Vol. XLV (June–July, 1970), 223–28.

McCabe, Lida R. "Making All the Fairy Tales Come True," *Arts and Decorations*, Vol. XVIII (October, 1922), 14–15.

McCaslin, Nellie. "Children's Theatre in Indianapolis," *Players Magazine*, Vol. XXII (January, 1945), 24.

McFadden, Dorothy. "Europe Challenges American Parents," *National Parent-Teacher Magazine*, Vol. XXI (June, 1937), 10–11.

——. "The Future of Professional Children's Theatre," *Players Magazine*, Vol. XX (February, 1944), 9.

Mackay, Constance D'Arcy. "Children's Theatre in America," *Woman's Home Companion*, Vol. LIV (June, 1927), 22.

——. "Drama in Which Young People Can Participate," *Drama*, Vol. XVI (October, 1925), 32–33.

——. "The Most Beautiful Children's Theatre in the World," *Drama*, Vol. XIV (February, 1924), 167.

——. "The School Theatres of New York City," *Players Magazine*, Vol. XXI (May, 1945), 26.

Mackenzie, Catherine. "Children's Own Theatre," *The New York Times Magazine Section* (January 19, 1947), 30.

McSweeney, Maxine. "Matinees for Children," *Recreation*, Vol. XXXV (May, 1941), 91–93.

Major, Clare Tree. "Children's Theatre," *New York State Education*, Vol. XXII (October, 1934), 45–47.

——. "A Children's Theatre at Columbia," *Columbia University Institute of Arts and Sciences Institute Magazine*, Vol. II (October, 1929), 10.

——. "Children's Theatre in Nine States," *The American Magazine of Art*, Vol. XXVI (January, 1933), 42.

——. "Child's Play," *Theatre Arts Monthly*, Vol. XXXV (October, 1952), 32.

——. "Playing Theatre," *Columbia University Institute of Arts and Sciences Institute Magazine*, Vol. III (February, 1931), 9.

——. "A Saturday Morning Children's Theatre," *Columbia University Institute of Arts and Sciences Institute Magazine*, Vol. I (May, 1929), 9.

Marks, Paul. "Taking Children's Theatre Plays on the Road," *Players Magazine*, Vol. XVII (October, 1940), 6, 10, 28.

Martin, Margaret. "On the Playgrounds," *Recreation*, Vol. XXXIX (August, 1945), 232.

Meader, Dorothy. "Duluth Children's Theatre," *School Arts*, Vol. XXXVIII (November, 1938), 85–87.

Meadowcraft, Clara. "At the Children's Matinee," *Saint Nicholas,* Vol. XLI (February, 1914), 351–57.

Meuden, Emma. "Dramatics in Progressive Schools," *The Playground,* Vol. XXIII (April, 1929), 17–18.

Mohn, Margaret E. "Children's Theatre—Minnesota Plan," *Players Magazine,* Vol. XXVI (May, 1950), 194–95.

Morrison, Adrienne. "Drama for the Youngest Set," *Theatre,* Vol. LII (September, 1930), 40, 62.

Morse, William W. "Educational Theatre," *Outlook,* Vol. LXXXIX (June 11, 1908), 572–77.

Moses, J. Garfield. "The Children's Theatre," *Charities and the Commons,* Vol. XVIII (April 6, 1907), 23–34.

Moses, Montrose J. "Children's Plays," *Theatre Arts Monthly,* Vol. VIII (December, 1924), 831–35.

Moyne, Sheila. "The Never-Never Land to Iran," *Arts and Decoration,* Vol. XXIV (December, 1925), 36.

Murray, Myrtle. "She'll Be Riding Six White Horses When She Comes," *Recreation,* Vol. XXVII (September, 1933), 290.

Nancrede, Edith D. "Dramatic Work at Hull House," *The Playground,* Vol. XXII (August, 1928), 276–78.

Newmayer, Sara. "For Children It Is Not Make-Believe," *New York Times Magazine Section* (December 5, 1948), 24–26.

Newton, Peter. "The Toy Theatre, a Children's Playhouse Where Children's Fairy Tales Come True," *The Craftsman,* Vol. XXVIII (April, 1915), 36–41.

Oberle, Marcella. "Children's Theatre Conference at Michigan City," *Educational Theatre Journal,* Vol. XI (December, 1959), 296–303.

Oberreich, Robert. "Unique Children's Theatre," *Recreation,* Vol. XLV (November, 1951), 319.

Ogden, Jean. "A Theatre for Children," *Recreation,* Vol. XXXVIII (February, 1944), 623.

Palmer, Winthrop. "Make Believe for Children," *Drama,* Vol. XVIII (March, 1928), 173–74.

Partridge, Pauline. "The House of Fairies," *Sunset,* Vol. LVI (April, 1926), 38–39.

Patten, Cora Mel. "The Children's Theatre Movement," *Drama,* Vol. XVIII (November, 1927), 51.

Patten, Hazel R. "A Program Carries On," *Recreation,* Vol. XXXIX (January, 1946), 513–15.

Plotkin, Charlie. "Putting the Fine Arts into Education through Junior Programs," *Progressive Education*, Vol. XVII (April, 1940), 251–54.

Pollette, John. "Tryout Plays for Children's Theatre," *Players Magazine*, Vol. XXVII (October, 1951), 8.

Powell, Anne. "Federal Children's Theatre in New York City," *Recreation*, Vol. XXX (October, 1936), 344–45.

Powell, Jessie. "The Children's Players," *Emerson Quarterly*, Vol. XI (November, 1930), 17–18.

Price, Grace. "Helping the Beginning Playwright," *Players Magazine*, Vol. XXVIII (November, 1951), 38.

Pyle, M. T. "Theatre School for Children," *Recreation*, Vol. XXXIX (August, 1945), 230–31.

Resnick, Jack. "Children's Theatre—New York," *Federal Theatre Magazine*, Vol. II (December, 1936), 3.

Richards, Stanley. "450,000 Miles of Children's Theatre," *Players Magazine*, Vol. XXXI (December, 1954), 66–67.

Robertson, Hazel. "It Belongs to Them," *Recreation*, Vol. XXXV (December, 1941), 545–46.

Rockefeller, Kay. "Live Drama for Children," *Child Study*, Vol. XXX (Spring, 1953), 18–20.

Rogers, James Edward. "The Psychology of the Drama," *The Playground*, Vol. XIX (February, 1926), 625.

Rounds, Charles. "A Theatre for Children," *Education*, Vol. LIV (September, 1933), 57–59.

Royal, Patricia. "Children's Theatre Goes Traveling," *Recreation*, Vol. XXXIX (January, 1946), 535–36, 550–51.

Sands, Mary K. "Dramatics for the Few or the Many?" *Players Magazine*, Vol. VIII (November–December, 1931), 2.

Savage, Mrs. George. "Audiences for Tomorrow," *Players Magazine*, Vol. XXII (September–October, 1945), 14, 20–21.

———. "The Business Side of It," *Theatre Arts Monthly*, Vol. XXXIII (September, 1949), 54.

Schoell, Edwin. "College and University Productions, 1953–54," *Educational Theatre Journal*, Vol. VII (May, 1955), 149.

Schott, V. W. "Peter Pan Players of Wichita, Kansas," *The American Library Association Bulletin*, Vol. XXVI (October, 1932), 768–72.

Shade, Edwin. "Children's Theatre, A Community Project," *Players Magazine*, Vol. XXVIII (December, 1951), 66.

Shell, Alyce. "A Community Children's Theatre Grows," *Recreation*, Vol. XXX (February, 1937), 555–56.

Sherwood, Robert. "A Message from Robert Sherwood," *Recreation*, Vol. XLIV (January, 1951), 40.

Siks, Geraldine Brain. "Out of Your Cage," *Players Magazine*, Vol. XXXI (January, 1955), 89–90.

———. "A View of Current European Theatre for Children and a Look Ahead in the United States," *Educational Theatre Journal*, Vol. XIX (May, 1967), 191–97.

Smith, C. C. "Child Actors in the King Coit Productions," *Theatre Arts Monthly*, Vol. II (September, 1927), 720–23.

Smith, Milton. "The Place of Drama in Leisure Time," *Recreation*, Vol. XXVII (January, 1934), 462.

Spencer, Sara. "A Decade of Children's Theatre," *Theatre Arts Monthly*, Vol. XXXVIII (November, 1954), 84.

Spottiswoode, Raymond. "Children in Wonderland," *Saturday Review of Literature*, Vol. XXXI (November 13, 1948), 60.

Stamey, Nancy. "A Children's Theatre Is Born," *Players Magazine*, Vol. XXXII (October, 1955), 17.

———. "Footlights Up!" *Recreation*, Vol. XLIV (December, 1950), 388–89.

Stephens, Louise. "A Purpose and a Plan," *Players Magazine*, Vol. XXVII (March, 1951), 134.

Strauss, Ivard N. "Dramatics as a Dynamic Force in Education," *Education*, Vol. LVI (October, 1935), 75–81.

Strawbridge, Edwin. "Do Your Play for, Not to, the Children," *Recreation*, Vol. XLVII (October, 1954), 484–86.

Thomas, Cate. "Report from the New England States," *Theatre Arts Monthly*, Vol. XXXIII (September, 1949), 55.

Van Hercke, Ethel. "A Different Kind of Little Theatre," *Recreation*, Vol. XXXIII (January, 1940), 549–50.

Waldron, Webb. "Children's Delight," *Readers Digest*, Vol. XXXIV (January, 1939), 33–36.

Wallace, Richard. "One Hundred Thousand Children Can't Be Wrong," *Cue*, Vol. IV (August 8, 1936), 8–9, 14–15.

Ward, Winifred. "A Passport to the Never-Never Land," *Drama*, Vol. XXI (April, 1931), 25–26.

———. "The Sixth Annual Children's Theatre Conference," *Educational Theatre Journal*, Vol. II (October, 1950), 199–207.

Watkins, Mary Jane. "The Tenth Annual Children's Theatre Conference," *Educational Theatre Journal*, Vol. VI (December, 1954), 348–54.

Weed, Helen. "Theatre by Children in Tacoma," *Players Magazine*, Vol. XXVI (January, 1950), 89.

Weller, Charles. "A Children's Playhouse," *Survey*, Vol. XXXV (February 19, 1916), 615.

Welty, Susan. "Children's Theatre Notes," *Players Magazine*, Vol. XVII (October, 1940), 19.

———. "In the Children's Theatres," *Players Magazine*, Vol. XVII (November, 1940), 19.

Wernaer, Robert. "Work of the Drama League in Boston," *The Nation*, Vol. XCIX (September 10, 1914), 310–11.

Wilson, Margery. "Children's Theatre in the Round," *Educational Theatre Journal*, Vol. II (May, 1950), 104–107.

Winthrop, Palmer. "Make-Believe for Children," *Drama*, Vol. XVIII (March, 1928), 173.

Wright, L. "The Forgotten Audience," *Dramatics*, Vol. XXIV (October, 1952), 26–27.

Wyatt, E. V. "Adventures of Marco Polo," *Catholic World*, Vol. CLIV (November, 1941), 216.

———. "Children's Audiences," *Catholic World*, Vol. CXLV (February, 1937), 669–70.

———. "The Rose and the Ring at the Cosmopolitan Club," *Catholic World*, Vol. CLV (April, 1942), 87–88.

Young, Betty, and Virginia Ray. "Henry Street Playhouse Presents Fine Saturday Children's Programs," *Parents' Magazine*, Vol. XXXI (March, 1956), 22–b, 22–d.

Young, Margaret. "The Child in the Theatre," *Players Magazine*, Vol. VIII (June, 1932), 3–4, 21.

Young, Stark. "Nala and Damayanti," *The New Republic*, Vol. LXXXIV (May 8, 1935), 370.

Index